GAME DEVELOPMENT ESSENTIALS

GAME AUDIO DEVELOPMENT

Aaron Marks

Jeannie Novak

DELMAR
CENGAGE Learning™

Australia • Brazil • Japan • Korea • Mexico • Singapore • Spain • United Kingdom • United States

Game Development Essentials:
Game Audio Development
Aaron Marks & Jeannie Novak

Vice President, Editorial: David Garza

Director of Learning Solutions: Sandy Clark

Senior Acquisitions Editor: James Gish

Managing Editor: Larry Main

Senior Product Manager: Sharon Chambliss

Editorial Assistant: Sarah Timm

Vice President, Marketing: Jennifer McAvey

Executive Marketing Manager: Deborah S. Yarnell

Marketing Manager: Erin Brennan

Marketing Specialist: Jonathan Sheehan

Production Director: Wendy Troeger

Production Manager: Stacy Masucci

Senior Content Project Manager:
    Kathryn B. Kucharek

Senior Art Director: Joy Kocsis

Technology Project Manager:
    Christopher Catalina

Production Technology Analyst: Thomas Stover

Cover Image: *Guitar Hero II* courtesy of
    RedOctane

For product information and technology assistance, contact us at
Professional & Career Group Customer Support, 1-800-648-7450

For permission to use material from this text or product,
submit all requests online at **cengage.com/permissions.**
Further permissions questions can be emailed to
permissionrequest@cengage.com

Library of Congress Control Number: 2008926710

In-Publication Data has been applied for.

ISBN-13: 978-1-4283-1806-9

ISBN-10: 1-4283-1806-2

Delmar
5 Maxwell Drive
Clifton Park, NY 12065-2919
USA

Cengage Learning is a leading provider of customized learning solutions with office locations around the globe, including Singapore, the United Kingdom, Australia, Mexico, Brazil, and Japan. Locate your local office at:

international.cengage.com/region

Cengage Learning products are represented in Canada by Nelson - Education, Ltd.

For your lifelong learning solutions, visit **delmar.cengage.com**

Visit our corporate website at **cengage.com**

Notice to the Reader

Publisher does not warrant or guarantee any of the products described herein or perform any independent analysis in connection with any of the product information contained herein. Publisher does not assume, and expressly disclaims, any obligation to obtain and include information other than that provided to it by the manufacturer. The reader is expressly warned to consider and adopt all safety precautions that might be indicated by the activities described herein and to avoid all potential hazards. By following the instructions contained herein, the reader willingly assumes all risks in connection with such instructions. The publisher makes no representations or warranties of any kind, including but not limited to, the warranties of fitness for particular purpose or merchantability, nor are any such representations implied with respect to the material set forth herein, and the publisher takes no responsibility with respect to such material. The publisher shall not be liable for any special, consequential, or exemplary damages resulting, in whole or part, from the readers' use of, or reliance upon, this material.

Printed in Canada
1 2 3 4 5 12 11 10 09 08

CONTENTS

Chapter 2 Game Audio Basics: tools, equipment & skills 37

Chapter 5 Function of Game Music: building the atmosphere. 129

Chapter 6   Creating Game Music: the melding of art & technology 157

Chapter 7 Game Voiceovers: adjusting personality to the characters 195

Introduction

Game Audio Development:
the interactive soundscape

In recent years, game audio has experienced unsurpassed growth and diversification associated with career paths, tools, and techniques. Audio makes up one third of the overall game experience, and its importance cannot be understated. Game audio is a complex subject because of how it is created, programmed, and implemented in order to produce an entertaining and truly interactive experience. Film composers interested in migrating to the game industry often have a rude awakening after realizing that every game experience is unique and involves a form of "co-authorship" shared with the audience (players). This gameplay combines with technology factors—and as better hardware, software, and implementation methods are discovered, a game's audio assets must also improve in order to take advantage of these enhancements. With these elements contributing to an already difficult creation process, it is essential to have a reliable guide at your disposal to make sense of it all.

This book is an all-encompassing resource designed to walk you through the creation and implementation process associated with all aspects of game audio development—including sound effects, music, and voiceovers. This book goes into great detail on each game audio discipline. While some content creators focus on a single specialty, the majority of game audio professionals are expected to "do it all"—whether you're an in-house employee, third-party contractor, or freelance audio professional. Game companies hiring outside help especially prefer to work with a single individual or company who can meet all of their needs. This book will familiarize you with the methods that will complement established studios and workflow. Included are contributions from a wealth of top game composers, sound designers, voice directors, and voice talent who share their secrets to success. By pointing out typical stumbling blocks and offering dozens of solutions from working experts, this book will help you formulate a plan to streamline your approach and let your talents shine!

Although game development and audio programs at colleges and universities have traditionally neglected game audio, there has recently been a tremendous push by students and faculty alike to incorporate game audio into curricula. With its unique combination of pedagogical and industry approaches, this book can be used as an asset when addressing the needs of the education market—and it will aid in establishing much needed game audio tracks and degree programs.

Aaron Marks
Fallbrook, CA

Jeannie Novak
Santa Monica, CA

About the *Game Development Essentials* Series

The *Game Development Essentials* series was created to fulfill a need: to provide students and creative professionals alike with a complete education in all aspects of the game industry. As more creative professionals migrate to the game industry, and as more game degree and certificate programs are launched, the books in this series will become even more essential to game education and career development.

Not limited to the education market, this series is also appropriate for the trade market and for those who have a general interest in the game industry. Books in the series contain several unique features. All are in full-color and contain hundreds of images—including original illustrations, diagrams, game screenshots, and photos of industry professionals. They also contain a great deal of profiles, tips, and case studies from professionals in the industry who are actively developing games. Starting with an overview of all aspects of the industry—*Game Development Essentials: An Introduction*—this series focuses on topics as varied as story & character development, interface design, artificial intelligence, gameplay mechanics, level design, online game development, simulation development, and audio.

Jeannie Novak
Lead Author & Series Editor

About *Game Development Essentials: Game Audio Development*

This book provides an overview of game audio development—complete with historical background, techniques, strategies, and future predictions.

This book contains the following unique features:

- Key chapter questions that are clearly stated at the beginning of each chapter
- Coverage that surveys the topics of game audio development concepts, process, and techniques
- Thought-provoking review and study exercises at the end of each chapter suitable for students and professionals alike that help promote critical thinking and problem-solving skills
- Case studies, quotations from leading professionals, and profiles of game audio developers that feature concise tips and techniques to help readers focus on issues specific to game audio development
- An abundance of full-color images throughout that help illustrate the concepts and practical applications discussed in the book

There are several general themes that are emphasized throughout this book, including:

- Defining the role of the game audio developer and how it fits into the game development team
- Exploring design and technology considerations associated with game audio development
- Illustrating creation, recording, capturing, editing, mastering, and testing techniques associated with game audio
- Investigating game audio development issues associated with sound effects, music, and voiceovers
- Evaluating existing games and how they've been brought to life through game audio development

Who Should Read This Book?

This book is not limited to the education market. If you found this book on a shelf at the bookstore and picked it up out of curiosity, this book is for you too! The audience for this book includes students, industry professionals, and the general interest consumer market. The style is informal and accessible with a concentration on theory and practice—geared toward both students and professionals.

Students that might benefit from this book include:

- College students in game development, interactive design, entertainment studies, communication, and emerging technologies programs
- Sound design, music, voice acting, art, design, programming, and production students who are taking game development courses
- Professional students in college-level programs who are taking game development courses
- Game development students at universities who are taking game audio courses

The audience of industry professionals for this book include:

- Sound designers, composers, voice actors, managers, directors, and producers who are interested in becoming game audio professionals
- Game art, design, programming, and production professionals who are interested in becoming game audio developers
- Professionals such as producers, artists, designers, writers and composers in other arts and entertainment media—including film, television, and music—who are interested in transferring their skills to the game development industry

How Is This Book Organized?

This book consists of three parts—focusing on foundation, construction, and refinement.

Part I   Foundation—Focuses on providing a historical and conceptual context to game audio development. Chapters in this section include:

- **Chapter 1   History of Game Audio Development: how did we get here?**—discusses functions, platforms, technology, roles, and the history of game audio development

- **Chapter 2   Game Audio Basics: tools, equipment & skills**—explores computers, interfaces, software, development systems, instruments, hardware, and skills necessary to be a successful game audio professional

Part II   Function & Process—Focuses on the process of creating and implementing game audio sound effects, music, and voiceovers. Chapters in this section include:

- **Chapter 3   Function of Game Sound Effects: bringing the game to life**—reviews the purpose, placement, disciplines, methods, and production cycle associated with game sound effects

- **Chapter 4   Creating Game Sound Effects: the art of sound design**—explores the pre-production, recording, editing, scripting, formatting, conversion, and beta testing process associated with game sound effects

- **Chapter 5   Function of Game Music: building the atmosphere**—discusses the purpose, placement, disciplines, methods, and production cycle associated with game music—with emphasis on adaptive and interactive music

- **Chapter 6   Creating Game Music: the melding of art & technology**—focuses on the pre-production, composition, recording, editing, and beta testing process associated with game music

- **Chapter 7   Game Voiceovers: adding personality to the characters**—explores placement, categories, recording, editing, and beta testing associated with game voiceovers—with emphasis on choosing voice actors and directing voiceover sessions

Part III   Finishing Touches—Focuses on post-production techniques, along with thoughts on the future of game audio development. Chapters in this section include:

- **Chapter 8   Creating the Total Soundscape: the successful blend of audio elements**—explores production, asset assembly/prioritization, mastering, implementation, and final beta/playtesting associated with game audio

- **Chapter 9   Future of Game Audio Development: the best is yet to come**—highlights trends, career paths, resources, and future predictions related to game audio development

The book also contains a **Resources** section—which includes a list of game development news sources, guides, directories, conferences, articles, and books related to topics discussed in this text.

How to Use This Text

The sections that follow describe text elements found throughout the book and how they are intended to be used.

key chapter questions

Key chapter questions are learning objectives in the form of overview questions that start off each chapter. Readers should be able to answer the questions upon understanding the chapter material.

tips

Tips provide advice and inspiration from industry professionals and educators, as well as practical techniques and tips of the trade.

quotes

Quotes contain short, insightful thoughts from industry professionals, observers, players, and students.

case studies

Case studies contain anecdotes from industry professionals (accompanied by game screenshots) on their experiences developing specific game titles.

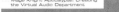

sidebars

Sidebars offer in-depth information from the authors on specific topics— accompanied by associated images.

notes

Notes contain thought-provoking ideas provided by the authors that are intended to help the readers think critically about the book's topics.

profiles

Profiles provide bios, photos, and in-depth commentary from industry professionals and educators.

chapter review

Chapter review exercises at the end of each chapter allow readers to apply what they've learned. Annotations and guidelines are included in the instructor's guide, available separately (see next page).

About the Companion DVD

The companion DVD contains the following media:

- Game audio software: ACID Music Studio, ACID Pro, ACID Xpress, Sound Forge, Sound Forge Audio Studio, Vegas Pro, and Super Dooper Music Looper Xpress (Sony Creative Software); Wwise (Audiokinetic); and FMOD Ex Programmers API and FMOD Designer (Firelight Technologies).

- Audio demos: Keith Arem, Mike Brassell, Adam DiTroia, Eric Doggett, Rodney Gates, Tom Graczkowski, Richard Jacques, Jon Jones, Jamie Lendino, Ben Long, Nathan Madsen, Lennie Moore, Christos Panayides, Matt Piersall, Chris Rickwood, Tim Rideout, George (The Fat Man) Sanger, Mark Scholl, Jed Smith, and Watson Wu.

- Audio asset lists and contract templates: sound effects asset list, contracts (simple, standard, and complex), dialogue asset list, dialogue game demo, music license contract, script, and talent release

- Game engines: Torque (Windows and Mac versions 1.5.1) and Game Maker (version 7)

- Modeling and animation software: Autodesk 3ds Max (version 9) and Autodesk Maya (version 8.5 PLE)

- Articles and documentation: Gas Powered Games (Chris Taylor GDD template), Torn Space (Michael Black *Sub Hunter* GDD), Wizards of the Coast (*Uncivilized: The Goblin Game* [code name: *Salmon*] call for game design/submission), NCsoft (*City of Heroes / City of Villains / Dungeon Runners / Tabula Rasa: Caves of Donn* developer diaries, *Guild Wars: Eye of the North* dungeons & quests), CCP Games (*EVE Online*), Dragon's Eye Productions (*Furcadia*), Harvey Smith/ Witchboy's Cauldron (game design articles), and Barrie Ellis/One-Switch Games (game design articles)

- Game demos/trial versions: Emergent (*Zorsis: The Forbidden Terror on Station Z*); Take Two Interactive Software (*Prey*), Blizzard (*Diablo II*), Firaxis (*Civilization IV, Sid Meier's Railroads!*), Stardock (*Galactic Civilizations II: Gold Edition*), THQ (*Company of Heroes*), Enemy Technology (*I of the Enemy: Ril'Cerat*), Star Mountain Studios (*Bergman, Weird Helmet, Frozen, Findolla*), GarageGames (*Marble Blast: Gold, Think Tanks, Zap!*), Max Gaming Technologies (*Dark Horizons: Lore Invasion*), Chronic Logic (*Gish*), Large Animal Games (*Rocket Bowl Plus*), 21-6 Productions (*Tube Twist, Orbz*), CDV (*City Life, Glory of the Roman Empire, War Front: Turning Point*), Last Day of Work (*Virtual Villagers, Fish Tycoon*), Hanako Games (*Cute Knight Deluxe*), Microsoft (*Zoo Tycoon 2: Marine Mania*), U.S. Army (*America's Army*), Cyan Worlds, Inc. (*Myst Online*), CCP Games (*EVE Online*), and Wizards of the Coast (*Magic: The Gathering Online*)

About the Instructor's Guide

The instructor's guide (e-resource, available separately on DVD) was developed to assist instructors in planning and implementing their instructional programs. It includes sample syllabi, test questions, assignments, projects, PowerPoint files, and other valuable instructional resources.

Order Number: 1-4283-1807-0

About the Authors

Music has always been a part of Aaron Marks' life—but it wasn't until 1995, when his overgrown hobby became On Your Mark Music Productions, that he began selling it to the world. Aaron started with the Southern California radio and tele-

vision scene composing jingles and scoring public service announcements. Although he set his sights on Hollywood, he fell headfirst into the game industry instead; his sound design and voiceover talents exploded—leading him to music, sound design, and voiceover credits on over 100 game titles for the Xbox and Xbox 360, PlayStation 2 and 3, Wii, Dreamcast, CD/DVD-ROM, touch screen arcade games, Class II video slot machines, Class III mechanical and video slot machines, coin op/arcade, online and terminal based video casino games, and numerous multimedia proj-

ects. Aaron also authored The Complete Guide to Game Audio and has written for Game Developer Magazine, Gamasutra.com, Music4Games.net, and the Society of Composers and Lyrists. He wrote an accredited college course on game audio for the Art Institute Online, is a member of the AES Technical Committee for Games, was on the launch committee for the Game Audio Network Guild (G.A.N.G.), and is the owner of On Your Mark Music Productions—where he continues his pursuit of the ultimate soundscape, creating music and sound for a multitude of projects.

Jeannie Novak is the founder of Indiespace—one of the first companies to promote and distribute interactive entertainment online—where she consults with creative professionals in the music, film, and television industries to help them migrate to the game industry. In addition to being lead author and series editor of the *Game Development Essentials* series, Jeannie is the co-author of *Play the Game: The Parent's Guide to Video Games* and three pioneering books on the interactive entertainment industry—including *Creating Internet Entertainment.* Jeannie is the Online Program Director for the Game Art & Design and Media Arts & Animation programs at the Art Institute of Pittsburgh – Online Division, where she is also Producer & Lead Designer on a educational business simulation game

Photo credit: Luis Levy

that is being built within the *Second Life* environment. She has also been a game instructor and curriculum development expert at UCLA Extension, Art Center College of Design, Academy of Entertainment and Technology at Santa Monica College, DeVry University, Westwood College, and ITT Technical Institute—and she has consulted for the UC Berkeley Center for New Media. Jeannie has developed or participated in game workshops and panels in association with the British Academy of Television Arts & Sciences (BAFTA), Macworld, Digital Hollywood, and iHollywood Forum. She is a member of the International Game Developers Association (IGDA) and has served on selection committees for the Academy of Interactive Arts & Sciences (AIAS) DICE Awards. Jeannie was chosen as one of the 100 most influential people in high-technology by *MicroTimes* magazine—and she has been profiled by CNN, *Billboard Magazine,* Sundance Channel, *Daily Variety,* and the *Los Angeles Times.* She received an M.A. in Communication Management from the University of Southern California (USC), where she focused on using massively multiplayer online games (MMOGs) as online distance learning applications. She received a B.A. in Mass Communication from the University of California, Los Angeles (UCLA)—graduating summa cum laude and Phi Beta Kappa. When she isn't writing and teaching, Jeannie spends most of her time recording, performing, and composing music. More information can be found at *www.jeannie.com* and *www.indiespace.com.*

Acknowledgements

The authors would like to thank the following people for their hard work and dedication to this project:

Jim Gish (Acquisitions Editor, Delmar/ Cengage Learning), for making this series happen.

Sharon Chambliss (Senior Product Manager, Delmar/Cengage Learning), for her reliability, professionalism, and management throughout the series.

Kathryn Kucharek (Senior Content Project Manager, Delmar/Cengage Learning), for her terrific help during the production phase.

Sarah Timm (Editorial Assistant, Delmar/ Cengage Learning), for her ongoing assistance throughout the series.

David Ladyman (Media Research & Permissions Specialist), for his superhuman efforts in clearing the media for this book.

IMGS, Inc., for the diligent work and prompt response during the layout and compositing phase.

Per Olin, for his organized and aesthetically pleasing diagrams.

Ian Robert Vasquez, for his clever and inspired illustrations.

David Koontz (Publisher, Chilton), for starting it all by introducing Jeannie Novak to Jim Gish.

A big thanks also goes out to the people who provided inspiration or contributed their thoughts, ideas, and original works to this book:

Adam DiTroia (DiTroia Audio Creations)

Alexander Brandon (Obsidian Entertainment)

Barrie Ellis (One-Switch)

Ben Long (Noise Buffet)

Bill Louden (University of Phoenix; Austin Community College)

Billy Martin (Lunch With Picasso Music)

Bob Rice (Four Bars Intertainment)

Brian Tuey (Treyarch)

Chad W. Mossholder (Sony Online Entertainment)

Charlie Cleveland (Unknown Worlds Entertainment)

Chris Rickwood (Rickwood Music for Media)

Chris Taylor (Gas Powered Games)

Christos Panayides

Clint Bajakian (Sony Computer Entertainment America)

Dan Wood

David Javelosa (Santa Monica College)

Don Daglow (Stormfront Studios)

Eric Doggett (MoonDog Media, LLC)

Fernando Arce (damselflymusic)

George ("The Fat Man") Sanger

Greg O'Conner-Read (Music4Games.net)

Harvey Smith (Witchboy's Cauldron)

Henning Nugel (Nugel Bros. Music)

Hope Levy

Jamie Lendino (Sound For Games Interactive)

Jed Smith (betafish music)

Jeff Tymoschuk (GreenWire Music & Audio)

John Hight (Sony Computer Entertainment)

Jon St. John (Jon St. John Productions)

Jonathan D. Jones (Jam Design; On Your Mark Music)

Keith Arem (PCB Productions)

Kemal Amarasingham (dSonic Inc.)

Kristopher Larson (Tension Studios)

Lani Minella (AudioGodz)

Larry G. Goldman (Lake Balboa Studios)

Lennie Moore (3l33t Music)

Mark A. Temple (Enemy Technology)

Mark Scholl (Screaming Tigers Music, Inc.; International Game Technology)

Matt Piersall (Okratron5000)
Matt Sayre (The Game Composer)
Michael Black (Torn Space)
Michael McCann (Behavior Music Inc.)
Mike Brassell (Brassell Entertainment, Inc.)
Nathan Madsen (NetDevil)
Paul Lackey (Electronic Arts)
Richard Jacques (Richard Jacques Studios)
Robert Burns (High Moon Studios)
Roddy Toomim (Cryptic Allusion, LLC)
Rodney Gates (High Moon Studios)
Ron Jones (Ron Jones Productions)
Russell Burt (Art Institute of California
    - Los Angeles)

Simon Amarasingham (dSonic Inc)
Simon Pressey (BioWare)
Spencer Nilsen (Ex'pression College for
    Digital Arts)
Steve Johnson (Sony Computer
    Entertainment America)
Tim Larkin (Soundminds/Cyan Worlds/)
Tim Rideout (Tim Rideout dot com)
Todd M. Fay (Aethem)
Tom Graczkowski (TDimension Studios)
Tom Salta (Persist Music)
Watson Wu (WOOTONES, LLC)
Will Davis (Codemasters)

: :

Thanks to the following people and companies for their tremendous help with referrals and in securing permissions, images, and demos:

Adobe
Adrian Wright (Max Gaming Technologies)
Ai Hasegawa, Hideki Yoshimoto & Janna
    Smith (Namco Bandai)
Alexandra Miseta (Stardock)
Andrea Silva
Angus Baigent (Steinberg Media
    Technologies)
Annie Belanger (Autodesk)
Ashima Dayal (Davis & Gilbert LLP)
Boffy b (Wikipedia Commons)
Brett Paterson (Firelight Technologies)
Brian Hupp (Electronic Arts)
Brian Nimens (Sound Ideas)
Brianna Messina (Blizzard Entertainment)
Briar Lee Mitchell (Star Mountain Studios)
Bruce McIntyre (E-MU Systems)
Bryan Lam (RedOctane)
Carla Humphrey (Last Day of Work)
Codemasters
Daniel Weizmann (Waves Audio Ltd.)
David Swofford (NCsoft)
Dennis Shirk (Firaxis)
Don McGowan & Genevieve Waldman
    (Microsoft Corporation)
Dr. Cat & Emerald Flame (Dragon's Eye
    Productions)
Edward Spiegel (U&I Software)

Eric Fritz (GarageGames)
Factor 5, Inc.
Florian Grote (Native Instruments)
Frank Gilson (Wizards of the Coast)
Gale Andrews (Audacity Team)
Garth Chouteau & Nicole LeMaster
    (PopCap)
Gary Kerzner (IK Multimedia)
Gena Feist (Take-Two Games)
Gene Semel (Electronic Arts)
Georgina Okerson (Hanako Games)
Grace Wong (NetDevil)
Henrik Markarian (NovaLogic)
Inon Zur
Intellivision Productions, Inc.
Interactive Audio Special Interest Group
    (IAsig)
Jana Rubenstein, Kristin Parcell, Makiko
    Nakamura & Eijirou Yoshida (Sega of
    America)
Jocelyn Portacio & Rivka Dahan (Ubisoft)
John Austin (Emergent Technologies)
Josiah Pisciotta (Chronic Logic)
Jrod2 (Wikipedia Commons)
Karine Légcron & Genevieve Laberge
    (Audiokinetic)
Kate Ross (Wizards of the Coast)
Kathryn Butters (Atari Interactive)

Kelly Conway & Esther Choe (Sony Online Entertainment)

Ken Ellison (FluidGUI)

Kristen Keller (Atari)

Kyle Ritland (Avid/Digidesign)

Linda Law (Project Bar-B-Q)

Lori Mezoff (U.S. Army)

Mario Kroll (CDV Software)

Mark Overmars, Sandy Duncan & Sophie Russell (YoYo Games)

Mark Rein & Sheri Christie (Epic Games)

MIDIplugins

Mitchell Soule (RAD Game Tools)

Miyako Yoshida & K. Kodama (Taito Corporation)

Monolith

Nintendo

Paul Lipson (Game Audio Network Guild)

Pete Hines (Bethesda Softworks)

Robert Taylor (Activision)

Roland/Cakewalk

Ryan & Justin Mette (21-6 Productions)

Sonic Reality

Sound Blaster

Steve Clarke (Minnetonka Audio Software, Inc.)

Steve Foldvari (Sony Creative Software)

Steve Martz & Bill McQuaide (Audio Engineering Society)

Steve Nix (id Software)

Ted Brockwood (Calico Media)

Tim Conrardy (Camel Audio)

Tony Fryman (Cyan)

Udo Hoppenworth & Paul Hughes (SAE Institute)

Valerie Massey (CCP Games)

Vikki Vega (Sony Computer Entertainment America)

Wade Tinney (Large Animal Games)

Wendy Zaas (Rogers & Cowan)

Questions & Feedback

We welcome your questions and feedback. If you have suggestions that you think others would benefit from, please let us know and we will try to include them in the next edition.

To send us your questions and/or feedback, you can contact the publisher at:

Delmar Learning
Executive Woods
5 Maxwell Drive
Clifton Park, NY 12065
Attn: Graphic Arts Team
(800) 998-7498

Or the series editor at:

Jeannie Novak
Founder & CEO
INDIESPACE
P.O. Box 5458
Santa Monica, CA 90409
jeannie@indiespace.com

DEDICATION

To the two most wonderful people in my life--my wife Cynthia and my daughter Kristina. Without their love and support, this book would not have been possible. During the course of writing this book, the game audio world lost two incredibly talented and selfless artists. I also dedicate this effort to the memories of Ingo Nugel and Simon Castles, both true friends and beloved colleagues who are truly missed.

—Aaron

To Luis, who inspires me to make my own kind of music.

—Jeannie

Part I:
Foundation

CHAPTER

History of Game Audio Development

how did we get here?

Key Chapter Questions

■ What are the primary *functions* of audio in games?

■ What significant *technological advancements* have had the most impact on the improvements of game audio?

■ What was the importance of the *Musical Instrument Digital Interface (MIDI)* standard on early game music?

■ What are the key *format* features of today's game music and sound effects?

■ What are the advantages and disadvantages of in-house audio *team members* and their independent contractor counterparts?

Video games have become incredibly popular entertainment media—so much, in fact, that the multi-billion dollar a year game industry has entirely eclipsed the revenues of the film, television and music industries combined. This medium allows players to enter make-believe worlds and live experiences never before possible. Imagine storming the beaches of Normandy on D-Day, driving at speeds of over 200 miles per hour through city streets, or piloting a spacecraft through the outer reaches of space! The visual, gameplay, and audio elements in a game engages three of the player's five senses (sight, touch, and hearing)—which combine together to form an entertaining, cognitive encounter. Compared to today's standards, games consisted of basic graphics, uncomplicated gameplay, and minimal audio. Let's take a look at how game audio has evolved into a viable industry segment in its own right.

Functions of Game Audio

Taking sound as our focus, there are three basic functions of audio in games which have been in place since day one. Sound gives the player feedback to what is happening onscreen, immerses players in the experience, and provides entertainment. Let's consider each function.

Feedback

It is not enough to see something like an onscreen button being depressed; the player also needs to hear it to believe it. By engaging another sense in the process, a certain realism is introduced that unconsciously makes it more genuine. In simple terms, this illustrates the need for the player to have audio provide *feedback* and reinforce what is visually displayed.

Reprinted with permission from Microsoft Corporation

The audio in a good first-person shooter (*Halo: Combat Evolved,* shown) always lets you know exactly where you are.

Can you imagine a first-person shooter (FPS) played in silence? How would players know they are being injured or if their health status was low? How would they hear commands from the game interface or from other players? How would they know the time bomb they planted was just about to go off and that they should run away from it? What about the bad guy sneaking up behind them? In today's complex game experiences, the player really needs audio to provide feedback to be successful in the game and to enjoy the experience. Without it, or with poorly constructed audio, the game ultimately suffers.

Immersion

A good game has the ability to mentally connect with players and transport them from their spot on the couch into the game. In order to accomplish this successfully, distractions from the outside world should be dealt with. Ambient and environmental sound effects are among the audio elements that provide *immersion* by bringing the game setting to life. The scenery comes alive (birds chirp, cars drive by, an airplane flies overhead, a police siren can be heard in the distance); sounds that are expected in a particular setting make it believable and, more importantly, mask the sounds that are present in the real world. Nothing breaks the spell faster than a sound from outside of the game interrupting the experience.

Audio helps provide the best games with a rich, immersive environment (*The Elder Scrolls IV: Oblivion*, shown).

Another approach to audio immersion is through the use of music. Since we are already pre-conditioned by movies, it is a natural progression that games would follow suit. From the instant a game is loaded, players are enveloped in both music and sound that are designed to draw them in and conceal the outside world. Ambient sounds aren't always appropriate, but suitable music can work wonders.

Entertainment

The singular reason games exist is to provide *entertainment*. Every bit of the graphics, gameplay, and sounds are created with that specific purpose in mind—and it's important during the development of a project to always be mindful of this fact. This is not to say that inconsequential sounds such as a cricket or falling shell casing have to be fun, but primary sounds like gunshots or explosions better be.

Used with permission of Sony Online Entertainment

Gunshots wouldn't be nearly as much fun without audio
(*PlanetSide: Core Combat*, shown).

All sounds are created to fit the theme of the game, but some sounds are purposefully selected based solely on their entertainment value. Have you ever enjoyed pulling the trigger repeatedly on a weapon because the sound was just so cool? This single sound has incredible impact and can contribute to the fun; ultimately, this is what games are all about, isn't it? Keep these basic functions in mind when creating and adapting audio for a game project to ensure a more successful presentation and entertaining experience.

The History of Game Audio

Game audio began as simple, monotone beeps that were coded by programmers. In the early days, there were no game composers, sound designers, graphic artists, level designers, or producers; it was primarily a one-person development team. Due to the technologies available at the time and to the overwhelming amount of work facing the lone programmer, sound was an afterthought and was simple by design. After playing today's games, it's almost inconceivable to imagine a game without surround sound, a full orchestral score, Hollywood style sound effects, or celebrity voiceovers—but the early years of game audio were indeed quite humble.

Arcade & Console Systems

In 1971, *Computer Space* became the first manufactured arcade video game available to the public, but it wasn't until the introduction of Atari's *Pong* a year later that this new form of entertainment became a sensation. The sounds comprised single-tone, electronically generated beeps—highly simplistic by today's standards but still serving a purpose. It wasn't until 1977 that sound showed a slight improvement with the appearance of the Atari 2600 home *console system*.

Courtesy of Atari Interactive, Inc.

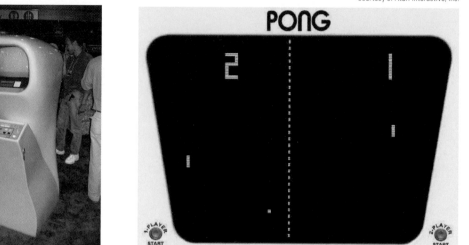

Computer Space (left) and *Pong* (right) were the vanguard of arcade video games.

Arcade and home units began their own separate journeys as the evolution of games progressed. Arcade cabinets were customized for each game and sound was developed specifically for the needs of the game. Popular arcade games such as Atari's *Asteroids*, Nintendo's *Donkey Kong* and Namco's *Pac-Man* all offered game-specific player controls and sound playback systems. Unfortunately, improvements in sound reproduction were hardly noticeable. However, since home consoles systems are improved upon less frequently, they typically show the most gains as each manufacturer battles for market position.

Courtesy of NAMCO BANDAI Games America Inc.

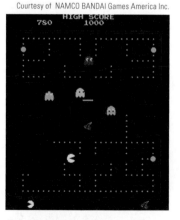

Pac-Man had a game-specific sound playback system.

Mattel premiered the Intellivision system in 1979 with a sound generator capable of three-part harmony. Atari raised the bar with its 5200 system in 1982, introducing the first use of a dedicated audio processor that allocated four channels to instrumentation and individual sound playback. This chip also controlled pitch, volume, and distortion values of each channel—which, at the time, was a massive improvement in sound. From there on out, sound continued to improve by leaps and bounds with each new console.

© Intellivision Productions, Inc.

Courtesy of Atari Inc.

Mattel Intellivision (left) and Atari 5200 (right)

The original Nintendo Entertainment System (NES), introduced in 1985, utilized five monophonic sound channels—and a year later, the Sega game system showed what they could do with three individual sound processors capable of a four-octave range. In 1989, consoles that were capable of stereo output were introduced. Both the NEC Turbo Grafx (with six voice channels) and Sega Genesis (with ten) set new standards and also gave it a kick in the pants by later delivering an add-on with the ability to play back CD-quality audio.

Nintendo

© Sega. All Rights Reserved.

Nintendo Entertainment System [NES] (left) and Sega Genesis (right)

Audio processor capabilities marched forward as processing power, memory and miniaturization technologies expanded. The never-quite-satisfied video game aficionados continued their push for bigger and better, and the console manufacturers and game developers did not disappoint. With enhanced graphics and more complex gameplay, increased sound quality followed closely in trail. The next generation of game systems were always highly anticipated as dramatic improvements became available. Take note of the growing list of sonic improvements for each console as game audio blossomed into a complex and very specialized discipline.

In 1991, the Super Nintendo Entertainment System (SNES) was unveiled. This was the first console capable of applied acoustics and Dolby ProLogic surround sound. (Although surround sound wasn't touted as a feature of the system, games that embedded surround encoding into the stereo signal could take advantage of it.) The system utilized an 8-bit sound controller chip with eight channels, built-in sound processing, and polyphony of eight notes per voice. It also had its own dedicated sound effects chip that freed resources from the main sound processor.

Nintendo

© Sega. All Rights Reserved.

Super Nintendo Entertainment System [SNES] (left) and Sega Saturn (right)

The Sega Saturn, revealed in 1995, used a multi-function game sound generator manufactured by Yamaha called the Saturn Custom Sound Processor. This gem consisted of a Pulse Code Modulation (PCM) sound generator and its own digital-to-analog converter that allowed for sampled instrument sounds stored on the chip to be converted and played back. It contained a 32-slot sound generator, a 16-channel digital mixer, and eight dedicated channels for FM synthesis modulation. Additionally, the sound processor was MIDI (Musical Instrument Digital Interface) and could create special effects such as reverberation and variable room acoustics. The original Sony PlayStation, also introduced that year, could handle sources up to 24 channels at a 44.1 kHz sampling rate.

PlayStation (left) and Nintendo 64 (right)

Home console systems progressed on often parallel paths. The Nintendo 64 had an incredible 100-channel capability, a maximum 48 kHz sampling rate, and could even make use of the new MP3 format. It was also MIDI compliant and offered 16-bit stereo output. However, with this particular system, the developer had to carefully plan their use—each audio channel consumed 1% of the CPU resources. A typical game used 16-24 channels.

Continuing through the lineage of home consoles, the Sega Dreamcast in late 1999 offered a dedicated Yamaha sound processor, 64 audio channels, and 2 MB of sound RAM. Unfortunately, what was to be the platform that saved Sega's console division was overshadowed by the PlayStation 2 only a few months later in 2000. Sony's console provided the capability to play DVDs and audio CDs back in either stereo, DTS, Dolby Digital 5.1, or ProLogic II encoding embedded in the analog signal. It could also provide 48 audio channels, selectable 44.1 or 48 kHz sampling, and dedicated 2 MB of audio RAM storage. Sega could not quite acquire significant market share before buzz for the PS2 gained momentum and eventually took control.

Sega Dreamcast (left) and PlayStation 2 (right)

Nintendo

Reprinted with permission from Microsoft Corporation

GameCube (left) and Xbox (right)

The other two dominating console manufacturers, Nintendo and the first entry by Microsoft, also established a solid footing in 2001. Considerable improvements were made in the graphics and processor speed of both consoles—and, thankfully, audio was not forgotten. The Nintendo GameCube used a dedicated audio processor, simultaneous 64 playback channels, 48 kHz sample rate, 16-bit resolution, and Dolby Digital surround sound capable through a digital out and Dolby ProLogic II through analog outputs. The Microsoft Xbox also used its own dedicated audio processor, 64 playback channels capable of up to 256 stereo voices, and a new 3D audio enhancement feature; it was also MIDI compliant and offered Dolby Digital surround sound. Both were solid machines that offered a lot of bang for the buck.

Personal Computers

The *personal computer* wasn't initially developed with video games in mind, but its importance in the history of games and game audio is indisputable. Interest grew for these new home machines around the late 1970s and early 1980s, and the ability to play games on them quickly became the catalyst that fed the frenzy. Computer games were highly simplistic, often plain text-based adventure games without graphics or sound. The first big improvement came when graphics were introduced—first in monochrome then in the four primary colors. The first sound eventually heard was a simple, square wave beep from the computer's internal speaker—typically only a single note—and with this, audio began its uphill climb in this new frontier.

Courtesy of Boffy b (Wikipedia Commons)

Personal computers and video games quickly found each other.

As with game consoles, home computers were highly dependent on the accessible technologies of the time. Considering that the mouse didn't become readily available until the mid 1980s, you can imagine the initial sluggishness of other computer capabilities we take for granted. It wasn't until 1988, with the initial involvement of video game companies such as Sierra, that the sound card was unveiled with a focus on games.

The first *sound cards* were developed by AdLib and Creative Labs—both with their own built in, internal sound processors. The AdLib card provided nine monophonic sound channels, while Creative Labs' Creative Music System card had 12 stereo channels available. On paper, the Creative Labs card looked like the better of the two—but, unfortunately, it sounded quite horrible.

Courtesy of Creative Technology Ltd.

Sound Blaster X-Fi XtremeGamer Fatal1ty

The most significant change in sound quality came when Creative Labs introduced the Sound Blaster card in late 1989. The company effectively cloned the AdLib card and added a sound coprocessor to play and record digital audio. This opened the door to games finally using sampled audio instead of only their onboard FM synthesis capabilities. By today's standards, the initial quality wasn't that impressive. Recordings could be made at slightly better than telephone quality at 12 kHz, and playback was accomplished at 23 kHz—comparable to AM quality sound.

Improvements in sound cards came primarily during the early 1990s. In 1991, the Creative Labs Sound Blaster Pro could record at 22 kHz sample rate and playback up to 45 kHz in mono or 22 kHz stereo. A year later, their Sound Blaster 16 enabled 16-bit resolution and sample-based synthesis—and it was MIDI compliant. Creative Labs continued its line-up with almost yearly improvements: AWE32, AWE64, Sound Blaster Live—and new Audigy cards offering 48 kHz sample rate, 16-bit resolution, stereo and 5.1 channel output, and digital effects processing. Other companies and their cards—such as Gravis Ultrasound and Ultrasound MAX, AdLib Gold 1000 and 2000, Mediavision Pro Audio Spectrum, and the Roland SCC1—were all worthy sound cards that offered various improvements while fighting for their share of the market.

The computer sound card played an enormous role in the types of games that were developed and, ultimately, what players enjoyed. Some very forward-looking game companies saw a captive audience and knew something had to be done to make PC gaming a viable option. They wisely worked closely with computer and peripheral manufacturers to make it happen. While this may have served their interests, it undoubtedly catapulted the quality of the game experience and audio which we enjoy today.

Musical Instrument Digital Interface & Downloadable Sounds

The *Musical Instrument Digital Interface (MIDI)* standard was created in 1983 as a way to regulate the communications protocol that allows electronic instruments, computers, and other equipment to synchronize and control one another. Before this, musical instruments such as synthesizers, samplers and sequencing devices had various issues that made connecting equipment from different manufacturers almost impossible. After the industry-wide adoption of MIDI, this problem practically disappeared and a new era in music creation was born.

Diagram by Per Olin

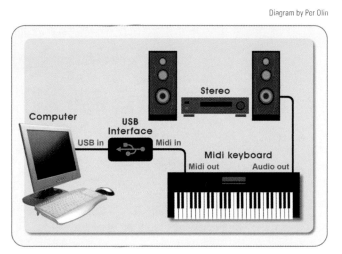

A musical instrument digital interface (MIDI) setup incorporates several different devices that work together to create sound.

MIDI has often been equated to the electronic version of the paper roll on a player piano. The digital file doesn't actually contain sound but provides the information that triggers the sound device. The file tells the instrument what note to play, when to turn it on and off, and the intensity at which to play it. It can also control parameters like volume, pitch, vibrato, panning, and tempo, allowing for very complex musical performances.

For games, the MIDI standard held incredible potential. Since MIDI files are small and can control many parameters needed in professional musical production, game developers were quick to adopt this space-saving standard as a way to improve the overall game experience. Sound card manufacturers utilized dedicated sound processors, with an internal sound bank of 128 sounds and the ability to playback 16 of these simultaneously. They were also MIDI compliant, which enabled game composers to compose music much more engaging than the previous electronic beeps using the sound card's internally stored sounds. While players weren't actually hearing the playback of digitized recordings, it was a welcome improvement.

The one major downside to using MIDI files in games is that playback of the music could be unpredictable. While the composer would create music based on the standard general MIDI sound bank, the quality of the sound card would actually determine the condition of the music. Budget sound cards use lower quality instrument samples that degrade the production and results in cheesy sounding music. The only way to ensure that the player hears what the developer intends is to allow playback of the actual recording or for the developer to utilize specifically designed sounds known as sound fonts.

Courtesy of Sonic Reality

The esoundz website (www.esoundz.com) is one of many online sources of downloadable sound (DLS) files.

The *downloadable sound (DLS)* file was introduced in the early 1990s as a way to maintain higher quality control over playback of MIDI sequenced music. Instead of being at the mercy of sound card manufacturers and the irregularity of their instrument samples, sound fonts are created to load directly into a sound card's memory, and playback is triggered the same as standard general MIDI sounds. This gives the developer and game composer the ability to control the quality and finally ensure the music is heard as it is intended, no matter what system or sound card the player has. An added advantage to this new format is that an almost infinite palette of instruments can be loaded—even new samples for each game level—as a way to keep the player immersed and entertained.

Game Composers & Sound Designers

Much of the advancement in game audio over the years can be attributed to obvious improvements in technology, development of more powerful game consoles, and the creativity of game developers. However, in the late 1970s and early 1980s, the first *game composers* emerged to play their own role in creating music within the narrow technological confines available at the time. As sound advanced in complexity, developers realized that more than overloaded programmers were needed to charm the player—and a new career was born.

In addition to their knowledge and skill in music, early game composers were also technically savvy. They not only understood the internal workings of the game platform but had the ability to coerce the sounds that made the music. Often, composers would work with programmers to develop specific tools and methods to physically plug into a game console and allow the composer to create sound using the internal sound bank. This forged a pivotal relationship between the technical and creative forces—and composers became an indispensable part of the development team.

Illustration by Ian Robert Vasquez

Game composers must understand the technology of game audio and the art of creating music.

As the use of digitized audio became widespread in the mid to late 1980s, sound effects also moved away from electronic beeps and synthesized sounds—turning toward recorded, sampled sound. This allowed the creativity of sound effects to literally explode—and with it, an addition to the development team emerged: the *sound designer*.

Early *game sound designers* took cues from the film industry for their sound effects creation methods, but were faced with challenges not seen in film production. Due to space and memory constraints of early game platforms, low sample rates and resolutions degraded the sound quality and forced new techniques to overcome these limitations. Sound designers were not only responsible for recording and creating sound effects, but they had to devise methods to ensure that their audio actually sounded good on playback as well. As this particular career progressed, sound designers also began to work closely with programmers to discover innovative ways to implement their sounds. The sound designer has played a critical role in the advancement of sound with a continuous enhancement of game sound effects and their presentation.

Illustration by Ian Robert Vasquez

Sound designers are faced with challenges not seen in film production.

The talents of the game composer and sound designer have played central roles in the history of game audio. Technological advancements are always praised but ultimately they are nothing without those who understand the inner workings of game hardware and can fully exploit their capabilities. As each new console generation is introduced, new resources and techniques will appear to carry on the tradition.

Tool Advancements

An often overlooked element in the evolution of game audio involves the *tools* used to create and implement sound. It's not enough to have highly skilled individuals creating evocative musical scores and colossal sound effects, or painstakingly writing thousands of lines of code to trigger them; the tools at their disposal play a massive role as well. In the beginning, the only tool available was the persistence of the programmers and their knowledge of the computer language. However, as time progressed, shortcuts were developed to decrease the complexity and the time involved in the development cycle.

It started with industrious game programmers creating mini-programs that could simply be positioned inside of the game code. They could use this code in any game utilizing the same platform by simply copying and adapting it to the new game. Obviously, not having to rewrite this code saved considerable time and began somewhat of a standardization of game audio development. For sounds, these smaller programs are referred to as audio engines—and they helped propel the increased quality of game audio.

As the necessity for these audio engines became evident, third-party programmers and companies concentrated their efforts on this specialized need. The advantage to this approach was that there was a dedicated team creating the engines, and often more brainpower resulted in increased features. As certain challenges were overcome successfully, this led the way to more complex and interesting audio playback possibilities.

Another tool that played a significant role in game production was the development system. These machines were introduced by console manufacturers for use by developers to give them a better idea of how their game would look, sound and act on a specific game platform. This solution is effective because artwork and coding is done on other computer systems, and the developer never quite knows how the game will react until it is plugged into the target console. Composers and sound designers were also given access to these development systems and often used them as part of the process when creating music and sound effects by tapping directly into the sound banks and features.

Aaron Marks recording in his home studio.

The specific tools available to composers and sound designers also have a significant impact on game audio. Music production took a big turn in the mid to late 1980s—allowing composers to record music in their own personal project studios instead of having to invest large amounts of money for the use of professional studios. By having unlimited access to recording equipment, often in a composer's spare bedroom, game music took on a new dimension as it became more accessible and easier to create. This method of home recording quickly caught on in the music industry, and hardware and software manufacturers rose to the challenge of creating high-quality tools at affordable prices. This was great news for game composers.

In the early years of game development, audio budgets were typically small or non-existent, and having the ability to create music and sound effects economically was primary. After game audio started to prove itself, and its acceptance by the public was obvious, budgets began to rise as quality audio actually became an advertised feature of the game.

With audio budgets on the rise, game composers could afford better recording equipment and software—which, in turn, increased the quality the player heard. This interesting relationship between manufacturers, developers, composers, and the player energized the progression that continues to this day.

Courtesy of Roland

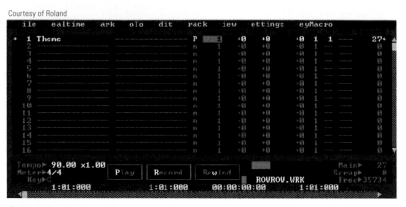

Cakewalk was the audio recording and editing software standard of the 1980s.

Let's not forget the development of audio recording, editing, and creation software. It wasn't until computers permeated society in the late 1980s and early 1990s that creative forces developed inexpensive yet powerful music production software that

Courtesy of Sony Creative Software Inc.

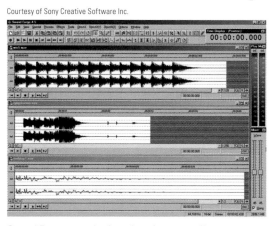

Sound Forge was the favorite of many audio professionals in the 1990s.

allowed entire tracks to be composed, arranged, and recorded at home on a PC or laptop. This allowed the traditional team roles to be performed by one individual, perfect for the lone game audio specialist. Game composers now had the ability to write, perform, record, and produce music—and sound designers could create, mix, and manipulate new sound effects ideas very easily. Both could edit and convert digital audio files to the required game formats instead of relying on the game developer—saving time and ensuring a higher quality of sound. As time progressed in this support industry, applications became increasingly cognitive—and more features became available to the user.

Game audio has benefited greatly from many different sources over the years. The advancement of computer technology has most certainly been the leading factor in its evolution—but discounting other elements would be unfair. The introduction of MIDI and downloadable sounds, the availability of computer software, the continuous education of the game industry, and innovative creative talents have all contributed to the overall increase in the entertainment value of games.

Current State of Game Audio

It's hard to believe that over 30 years have passed since the first video game was introduced to the public. What is more unimaginable is actually how far game audio has come during that time. What we perceive as standard quality and uses of sound in games today were literally unheard of in those early days. The constant progression of technology has allowed developers and players of today the ability to enjoy games played on immensely powerful gaming platforms, giving mind-blowing interactive experiences. The advancement of the tools and the talents of those who create them are indeed light years ahead of where they started.

Reprinted with permission from Microsoft Corporation   Reprinted with permission from Microsoft Corporation

More and more soundtrack albums are being released, including *Fable* (left) and *Mass Effect* (right).

Terms such as CD quality, surround sound, and interactive or adaptive audio are so commonplace today that no one gives them a second thought. These are the new criteria of the industry, and a game without them hardly has blockbuster potential. While not all games require such intense audio treatment, the AAA titles which are expected to earn millions of dollars do.

Game music is finally on par with the television and film industries. Game soundtracks are routine now that music is able to stand on its own—and, due to this, game composers even have the potential to attain Grammy award-winning status. Sound effects are being created by incredibly talented individuals who have gained experience either from years in the game industry or from film work. What about voiceovers? Today we are seeing more professional voice actors and celebrities lending their unique vocal style to game characters, which really increases their believability factor. It is indeed a great time to be involved in game audio!

Sample Rates & Resolution

CD quality audio, or 44,100 Hz sample rate and 16-bit resolution, was once considered an unreachable goal in audio quality—but the majority of game titles today utilize this very benchmark. Some game consoles can even playback at 48,000 Hz, giving yet another glimpse into the future. Sound quality is no longer an afterthought, and it is an important feature to players.

Sample rates and resolution are determined during the planning phase of development. The higher the sample rate and resolution, the larger the audio files—so size and quality concerns are often significant factors. There are many forces at play to get a game to the marketplace—and considerations such as the targeted game platform, type of storage medium, and even cost of the packaging can have an impact on how much space is available to the developer.

Nintendo

A tiny Nintendo DS game card (*Metroid*, actual size shown) is capable of holding 256 MB of data—but most DS games only utilize 64 MB or 128 MB to avoid slowing down the card access time.

The target game platform will establish the amount of digital information the system can handle, and its medium (like a CD-ROM or DVD-ROM) will set the limit of storage space. Music, sound effects, and dialogue all compete with other game elements—and not everything will fit on a disk or cartridge as it is. Concessions are often made in order to squeeze everything in, and decreasing the quality of the audio is typically considered the lesser of the evils. Simply reducing the sample rate from 44,100 Hz to 22,050 Hz (or reducing the resolution from 16-bit to 8-bit) will save half of the space.

Surround Sound

Stereo playback was once considered the ultimate, but today we find this as simply the minimum standard feature of games. Going a step beyond this, a major game release without surround sound today is almost unheard of—and 5.1 and 7.1 surround capabilities have steadily grown over the years, thanks in no small part to companies such as Dolby, DTS, and hardware manufacturers who have led the charge. Immersion is extremely important for players, and having game sounds that actually envelop you is indescribable; developers, players, and console manufacturers know this—and they have all embraced this form of audio playback.

Home theater systems that use multiple speaker arrangements and surround capable amplifiers are common. Since consumers have already made the often substantial investment and enjoy the complete movie experience in their living rooms, developers have taken advantage of this and target that specific audience. Home computer setups also typically include a surround capable sound card and multiple speakers as well, so the format is guaranteed to be around for some time to come.

Surround playback is the closest presentation of audio reality we currently have. When you think about it, having the capability to present sound in a highly directional format is extremely advantageous to those who create the game experiences. Games are pure entertainment, and what better way to take players on the ride of their lives than by sitting them in front of a large screen television and encasing them in a cocoon of sound? The field of vision is limited by the size of the screen and can be somewhat of a distraction to players—but there is no limit to what they hear when surrounded by speakers. Ambient sounds put players fully inside the game's environment—making them subconsciously believe they are indeed standing in a real jungle or cityscape. Directional sounds provide subtle clues to actions happening around them—often causing players to snap their heads to the side to see what is coming at them! Surround sound done correctly provides a tremendous experience for the player.

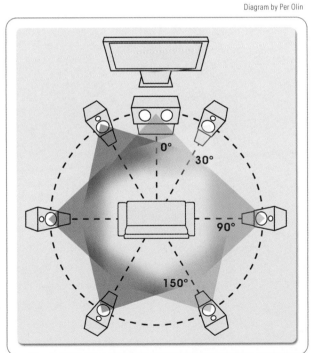

Diagram by Per Olin

Surround sound immerses players in the game from all angles.

Adaptive Audio

The greatest entertainment advantage of video games over film is that the experience can change every time it is played. Musically, this creates an incredible challenge because there is no way to actually know when an onscreen action will require musical punctuation. A film's linear format is predictable and much easier to score, with the music ebbing and flowing to the dynamics of the pre-determined action. However, the ever-changing video game experience has been unable to tie the music to the gameplay—until recently.

"Interactive," "adaptive," and "non-linear" are somewhat interchangeable terms that all describe the ability of the musical score to adapt to what the player is experiencing in a game. Much like how emotions are manipulated with music in film, game audio is now able to provide techniques such as foreshadowing an upcoming event, setting the mood and pace of the scene, and adding impact to a major occurrence—all through this new form of interactivity we'll refer to as *adaptive audio*. As audio engines are refined and more complex features are implemented, this new method is becoming more commonplace and is quickly establishing itself as the new standard.

Reprinted with permission from Microsoft Corporation

DirectMusic Producer's main segment editing window

Game composers, already used to creating music within the specific confines of a game's needs, are quickly becoming adept at this entirely new way of composing. Instead of simply composing a background music cue that plays behind the gameplay, the composer is now tasked with creating several different versions of the same music—all with a variety of intensities and instrumentation to suit any situation the player might face. This interactive music can transform at any moment to reflect a change in the action—from a player casually exploring an area to a bunch of bad guys jumping out ready for a fight; the music will adjust to fit the circumstance.

Orchestral Scores

Large game budgets, emerging composers with specific skills, and the continued demand for a more movie-like experience have brought game music to a point where full orchestras are often used to perform the score. It's not to say that an orchestra is always the right choice for a performance, but many games take advantage of this sound upgrade. While instrument samples are nearing perfect reproductions—and in the hands of a highly skilled composer and engineer they can sound like a live orchestra—there really isn't a substitute for the actual thing: a world class studio full of incredible instruments and musicians playing their hearts out! To have *this* in a game is magic!

Courtesy of Inon Zur and Vivendi Games

Inon Zur conducts the Hollywood Symphony Orchestra in the *Men of Valor* score at Eastwood Scoring Stage, Warner Bros. Studios.

Since digitized audio in games was first introduced, composers understood the potential of having their music performed by a live orchestra—including what it could do for their careers and for the game industry. The budget for orchestral performance was a hard sell; gathering an orchestra in a professional studio costs more money than game companies were used to spending. However, the idea was eventually accepted—slowly at first, and then gathering steam over time. Once game developers realized the profit potential when using orchestral scores, they were sold on the idea—and today we are seeing a large number of major game releases with them.

The largest stumbling block for recording an orchestra is typically the enormous cost involved. The few major orchestras that do high-quality film work have caused the game community to look elsewhere, due to their workload and high costs. Orchestras in Seattle, London, Eastern Europe, and Russia, for example, understand this need; they have priced their services according to the budgets of a game project and have gone out of their way to make themselves available. Orchestras in Los Angeles, recently becoming wise to how the game industry works, are negotiating contracts that will cover the needs of both orchestra and developer.

Available Game Platforms

Now is an exciting time to be involved in creating game audio. It's intoxicating to think there is no limit to what the current crop of gaming consoles and video games can do. Processing speed and memory capacity are at an all-time high, graphics are intense, and audio is finally at a place where it is well respected and considered to be a main feature. Players are serious enough about what the industry is doing that they are camping outside stores for days to get their hands on the next game console or widely anticipated game. That alone speaks volumes about the success and hunger for this type of entertainment.

There are dozens of *game platforms* available to the public today—more than ever before. Mobile, web-based, Java, and Flash games suffer most from processing, memory, speaker, and bandwidth constraints—but they are making rapid improvements. MIDI and low-quality digital audio—much like what the rest of the game industry was experiencing back in the late 1980s—provides the soundtrack to these types of games. Handheld game platforms such as the Sony PSP and Nintendo DS are currently similar in audio quality to game consoles in the mid to late 1990s—offering playback of compressed AAC, MP3, and WMA file formats. The Nintendo DS also utilizes "virtual surround sound" and even has a built-in microphone for chatting and gameplay. With portability comes unique technological issues to overcome—but as every other gaming console has done in the past, these platforms will make improvements.

PC- and arcade-based games have enjoyed non-stop leaps in quality over the years. As expected, today's audio is of considerable quality and on par with the major consoles—although the big difference is they aren't typically played on home theater systems. Arcade consoles are customized specifically to the game they contain, and players have no control over what they play or hear the game on.

PC games, on the other hand, require the serious gamer to be a little more proactive and upgrade hardware to keep pace with new features of the game. A large portion of PC players today own compact but powerful surround sound systems and sound cards with 96 kHz/24-bit playback capabilities in order to fully enjoy the experience. Since arcade consoles utilize the same computer-based technologies as personal computers, their audio quality typically keeps pace—although you wouldn't really know it, considering the other games in close proximity clamoring for attention.

The most anticipated game audio improvements appear when the three major console manufacturers release their latest offerings—and the current harvest has not disappointed.

The first in this current round is the Xbox 360, which was released in late 2005. The improved audio features include 256 audio channels, 320 independent decompression channels using 32-bit processing for audio, HDMI output—and support for 48 kHz/16-bit sound. Sound files are encoded in the XMA audio format and can play back in Dolby Digital surround sound. This is a very audio-friendly console.

Audio-wise, the clear winner for this generation of consoles is the PlayStation 3, which was released in late 2006. It not only gives the game developer more choices when creating a game, but also awards the consumer with some excellent features. It houses a dedicated audio processor that offers 512 audio and voice channels, 44.1 or 48 kHz sample rates—and playback in stereo, DTS, 7.1 Dolby Digital, and the latest surround format, Dolby TrueHD (not currently used in-game). In addition, the PS3 offers a 256 MB shared memory system that audio can utilize as needed.

Reprinted with permission from Microsoft Corporation   Sony Computer Entertainment America   Nintendo

Xbox 360 (left), PlayStation 3 (center), and Wii (right)

The Nintendo Wii was also released in late 2006, but its approach to game improvements didn't focus on audio. The main selling feature for this console is its manual interfaces (such as the Wiimote and nunchuk). These remote wireless controllers not only act as gamepads but as pointers and motion/rotation detectors that allow players to use physical gestures to control movements in a game. On the audio front, unfortunately, there isn't much difference from the previous generation platform (GameCube) other than the lack of digital surround capability. The Wii does have a dedicated audio processor, 64 voices, 44.1 and 48 kHz sample rates, 16-bit resolution, stereo, and Dolby ProLogic II embedded in the analog audio; it also utilizes a 512 MB shared-memory system and includes a speaker in the hand controller that adds a unique moving audio element.

Nintendo   Sony Computer Entertainment America

Nintendo DS Lite (left) and PlayStation Portable [PSP] (right)

It is interesting to note the various states of today's current game platforms. The major three home consoles typically set the standards by which all the others eventually follow. Due to this, PC and arcade games are always right on the heels of the newly released technology—often adapting new elements or upgrading their current features to match. Handheld devices such as the PSP or Nintendo DS are within striking distance of quality audio and will definitely have something worthy within the next few years. The most to benefit from recent technological advancements are cell phone games—as smaller, more powerful processors and storage are introduced—and web-based games, as higher Internet bandwidth and faster streaming methods are developed. Obviously, there are still certain limitations for some platforms because of speaker sizes and lack of lower-frequency playback—but sound will improve significantly. Quality game audio is here to stay.

Game Audio Specialists

When audio first appeared in video games, it was created by the same person who programmed the code. Music and sound effects were at the discretion of one person, and life back then was fairly simple. However, as development increased in complexity, it became overwhelming for that sole entity—and new job titles emerged in the industry. Today, it is sometimes difficult to understand the new division of audio duties completely. The lines continue to blur between the game, film, and music industries as more audio specialists are brought in to handle the new challenges.

There are essentially two branches of audio specialists that we'll explore in order to get the complete picture: in-house and third-party contractors. Between the two, there are myriad job titles, duties, and responsibilities unique to each.

In-House

Audio specialists who work as employees for a game developer or publisher are considered *in-house*. These folks work the proverbial 9-to-5 day jobs (although most companies don't hold creative people to specific start times) and utilize studios and equipment owned by the company. The advantage to the developer is that the employees are under tighter control, and tasking is less complicated. In-house audio specialists are available for meetings and can freely contribute to ongoing projects in real time, often giving their input while passing someone in the hall. Due to this, development time is faster and less frustrating as issues are dealt with quickly.

The major advantage to the developer deals with ownership of audio created by the employee on the job. Owning the rights to music, sound effects, and voiceovers can often be legally complicated—and contracts typically vary from composer to composer and sound designer to sound designer. Some only grant rights to the music for one game platform or for a specified period of time. Some only allow usage in a game but forbid inclusion in a soundtrack release or television commercial. Being an employee means surrendering all rights and interest in their work to their employer, as established in their employment agreements. Game developers will own all partial or completed work performed and created on their premises; some even stipulate they will also own any work created at home while the individual is employed by the company. This ultimately allows the developer/publisher to use the audio anywhere without being bound by contractual restrictions.

The in-house composer or sound designer is well compensated and often enjoys rewards far beyond what the average contractor will see. Most are partial to the steady income, health benefits, paid vacations, and the security of not having to constantly look for work. Others like being surrounded by many creative souls and the chance to concentrate on their work instead of dealing with administrative or business issues. Most even agree that having their employer purchase the incredibly expensive sound equipment gives their work a greater quality and allows them the chance to experience gear they could not afford on their own. These bonuses are substantial—but there is always the possibility of downsizing, corporate buyouts, or a game company closing its doors. Occasionally, there are grim possibilities to consider when working for someone else.

Job titles within a game developer or publisher vary, depending on the needs and workload. Large game companies have an audio department lead by a department head, audio manager, audio director, or audio lead. However, even these terms have meanings that vary from developer to developer. Let's take a closer look at various audio job titles you might expect to find within a game organization.

Audio Department Head

The *audio department head*—who might be an executive such as Vice President—manages all employees, assets, and administrative issues within the department; coordinates with other department heads for audio related concerns; and oversees all audio created. This is the type of job that requires years of experience and strong leadership skills.

Audio Director

The *audio director* typically oversees and guides audio requirements for a single project or multiple game projects—coordinating the creation of audio assets by both in-house team members and outside contractors. This individual might make last-minute edits or conversions before a game goes gold. This type of job can be extremely hectic when managing assets from multiple projects at once.

Audio Manager

The *audio manager* is usually responsible for music selection and licensing—working closely with record labels and/or artists to secure usage rights for projects where licensed music is used, such as a skateboarding or racing game.

Audio Lead

The *audio lead* is the primary point of contact on a single game project. This individual will attend regular development meetings, establish goals, and control equipment and personnel assets in order to meet established milestones. Since the audio director is often engaged in multiple simultaneous projects, audio leads are responsible for their specific projects and report directly to the audio director as required. Depending on the requirements of a game, a lead composer or lead sound designer could also fill this role.

Audio Editor

An *audio editor* is the workhorse of the audio department. While it is typical for composers and sound designers to record and edit their own work, the final task of editing often falls to the audio editor in order to increase overall quality and establish consistency in all of a game's audio assets. Audio editors often have strong studio engineering backgrounds or are experts in editing techniques. They can also be used as recording engineers—running the studio to capture music, sound effects, or voiceover sessions that they will edit later.

Voiceover Director

The *voiceover casting* or *session director* is extremely important in projects that utilize extensive dialogue. Voiceover directors will audition voice talent, make or recommend actor selections, write or review scripts, schedule studio time and actors, oversee the recording session—and, most importantly, direct the performance of the voiceover artists. Their primary mission is to ensure the quality and consistency of all voice assets.

Composer

The *composer* is the music creator on a game project. Composers are responsible for composing, performing, recording, mixing, and initial editing of all required musical assets. Most composers are multi-instrumentalists but will make use of outside expertise when needed. Extreme competence with music creation techniques and some serious talent is a must for this type of job.

Sound Designer

The *sound designer* is only in charge of sound effects—unlike the counterpart by the same name in film and theater who is responsible for *all* audio assets in a production. Sound designers are responsible for gathering sounds (either recording them or gathering them from sound libraries) and mixing a variety of these sonic elements to create appropriate sound effects for use in a game. They will perform initial editing and conversions and often work closely with the art team to ensure that the audio matches the visuals, and they will work with the audio programmer to implement the assets correctly.

Audio Programmer

The *audio programmer*, located within the audio or programming department, is responsible for implementing all audio assets into a game. Working closely with the audio team, the audio programmer ensures that: the audio is triggered correctly; the audio engine is performing as expected; and the effects processing, volume, panning and other playback considerations are addressed. This final, critical contributor to the audio chain can literally make or break the quality of the audio.

Third-Party Contractors

Game companies—those either without an audio department or with an overwhelmed audio team—call upon the third-party, independent contractor for their audio needs. The majority of these self-employed composers and sound designers are as skilled and creative as their in-house counterparts; the difference is they have chosen to go into business for themselves. Due to contractors' need to diversify, they can perform many additional services beyond music and sound effects to include voiceovers (such as casting and scriptwriting), editing, conversions, and surround sound encoding that the developer can exploit.

While it is nice to have a full audio team at the developer's immediate disposal, it can prove to be quite costly. Salaries (especially when between projects or during downtime in production), high-priced equipment purchases, and overhead ultimately affect the bottom line. This scenario often leads a developer to consider hiring contractors as a cost-saving alternative. Since contractors are not employees of the company, they aren't eligible for health benefits, paid vacations, sick days, or any other expensive enticements. Contractors are free from in-house administrative burdens and are able to focus on the project needs. Some overall control may be lost over the audio creation process, but the developer and contractor communicate regularly to compensate. There is some trade off between expense and convenience, but the audio quality does not suffer most of the time.

For the contractor, status as an independent is a double-edged sword. The obvious worry is keeping a steady flow of income, but other downsides can detract from the reason most individuals choose this route in the first place. Most independent composers and sound designers are incredibly good at their craft; understanding the quality of their work is key to being hired. However, what most never consider is that the skills needed to run a successful small business are just as important—if not more so. Tax obligations, legal matters, business costs: these all place a heavy burden on one person, and issues like these can severely impact the creative side of the business.

Illustration by Ian Robert Vasquez

Contractors are self-employed specialists ready to fill the holes in your in-house team.

Most that have chosen the independent contractor route are hearty souls and find that the potential rewards far outweigh any distractions or risks. There is a certain freedom to self-employment—and much can be said about being your own boss, working when you want to, and picking and choosing between a variety of projects. The only concerns developers will have is that the audio is done on time and within budget—and that it works in the game. As long as these criteria are met, how the job gets done is at the discretion of the contractor.

The independent contractor is usually supervised by a producer or audio department head, who acts as the single point of contact. This relationship ensures that the contractor receives focused direction and can get quick approval on submissions instead of having to please many masters. When developers do hire outside help, the job titles they seek are similar to the in-house team; however, their responsibilities are slightly different.

Composers & Sound Designers

For music and sound effects, external *game composers* and *sound designers* stand at the ready. Utilizing the developer's guidelines and requests, these individuals will compose, perform, record, mix, master, edit, and convert their work to its final, in-game format. They provide audio cues for all areas of a game—including menus, gameplay, and cinematics. The primary difference from their in-house counterparts is that they are responsible for final edits and do not use any developer assets while performing their tasks. Many times, one freelancer serves as both a game's composer and its sound designer.

Voiceover Director

When voiceovers are needed, the external *voiceover casting* or *session director* is retained to address this potentially cumbersome issue. Voiceover directors perform the same tasks as in-house directors—except they may use their own project studios, a commercial house, or one at the developer's location if available. Scheduling around dozens of busy voice actors isn't easy, and having a professional contractor who is up to the challenge can be a project saver.

Audio Editor

Most audio content is submitted to the developer already edited and in its final in-game format by those who created it. An external *audio editor* is occasionally brought in when extensive dialogue or sound effects require it. For example, most voiceover sessions are recorded from start to finish, and it is left to the developer to pick the appropriate vocal performances themselves and edit them. Weeding through thousands of lines can be time-consuming, and having an extra hand relieves the pressure.

Game Development Team

The game development team is organized to establish specific divisions of labor and responsibilities. Creating a game can be a complex, highly technical, and frustrating endeavor that, in a nutshell, is pure chaos and can spiral out of control if not carefully structured and managed. All members of the team are encouraged to be cognizant of their place in the arrangement—and familiar with the other components and how they affect the process.

Diagram by Per Olin

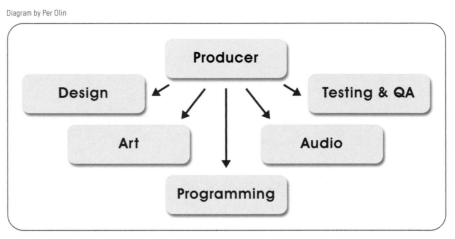

Typical organization of a development team

All sub-teams (art, design, tech, audio, and QA/testing) manage their individual departments and report directly to the producer. This structure may vary with the developer, but the outcome is the same. Within each department, there are from one to a dozen or more team members who work on their specific pieces of the big puzzle—with a complete and fully operational game as their end result.

Producer

The definitive authority over the entire development process is the *producer*—whose project management talents, leadership abilities, and creative vision lead the team to the completion of the assigned project on time and within budget. Working closely from the game design document (GDD) and from a knowledge of what makes a good game, the producer gives appropriate direction, sets deadlines, and manages resources carefully. Since the task is often too daunting for a single person, assistant producers are allocated to support the producer and the rest of the team as needed.

Design

The *design* team, led by the design director and/or lead designer, focuses its efforts on the game's concept/storyline, character development, level design, and gameplay. This team ensures that the complexity of the game is balanced between being entertaining and challenging, and it makes adjustments as necessary throughout the production. Simple things like assigning point values to injury hits will determine which weapons are more lethal and how many hits a player can take before being mortally wounded, for example. This team is lead by the head game designer with senior level designers overseeing the efforts of the level designers.

Art

In charge of the visuals of a game project is the *art* team, led by the art director and/or lead artist. This band of artisans is composed of concept artists, 3D modelers, 2D or texture artists, animators, and sometimes a technical artist, lead by a lead artist. They create everything from the landscape, structures, foliage, vehicles, and weapons to the characters, creatures, and game interface—using a mix of technical and artistic talent.

Programming

The overall functionality of a game belongs to the *programming* team, which is led by the technical director or lead programmer. This incredibly technical department ensures the game does what it's advertised to do, using specialized programmers with disciplines such as a game physics, artificial intelligence, gameplay, graphics, sound, scripting, user interface, input, network, game tools, and porting. The amount of effort needed to complete a modern game is inconceivable, something over which the lead game programmer will spend many hours toiling.

Audio

Led by the audio director, the *audio* team is responsible for everything a player hears in a game. Composers, sound designers, audio editors, recording engineers, technical assistants, and audio leads typically make up this crew. Most of the audio work will be handled by the in-house staff unless something outside their abilities is necessary, like composing for or recording an orchestra.

Testing & Quality Assurance

Assigned the responsibility of finding ways to break the game is the *testing* and/or *quality assurance (QA)* team. This group of testers focuses on the project from the player's perspective and ensures everything is working correctly—every bug they find before the game is released is critical to its overall success. This department normally has a manager, a lead tester, an assistant lead tester, and several game testers.

Marketing

The *marketing* team is the final element of the game production lineup that can have substantial influence on aspects of the game. Since this department is ultimately responsible for marketing of the game, they have expert knowledge of the targeted demographics, who will buy the game, and what they expect to experience when they do buy it. Because of this, they provide specific guidance how the game should be played, the features the game should have, and what it looks and sounds like in order to maximize sales. The producer would, of course, have the final say.

::

The video game, in one form or another, is here to stay. The incredible graphics, sound, and gameplay experiences available today are of astonishing quality—and they're only getting better and more popular. What used to take one person to create now requires a large team of highly skilled artisans, each with an education and experience to allow them to process and use cutting-edge technologies. Millions of dollars are funneled into development companies and billions of dollars are returned on these investments—because of it, this giant machine is gaining unstoppable momentum. One-third of the gameplay experience is the sound, and if that isn't done right, you can bet the success of the game will suffer. But now that you understand the progress game audio has made over the years and where it is today, a closer look at each element of audio content will help guarantee any audio you are involved in is of the highest caliber.

:::CHAPTER REVIEW:::

1. Imagine that you are a game audio developer working in the 1980s. Knowing the limitations associated with this era, describe the type of game you would most likely be working on—and discuss how you would use audio to the best of your ability to enhance the game's quality.

2. Play 3 games—one from the 1980s, one from the 1990s, and one released after 2004. Compare and contrast the way music, sound effects, and dialogue audio is utilized in all three games.

3. How does a game's genre affect the way its audio is developed? Choose one level from 3 games that are in current release—each from a distinct primary genre—and compare the way audio is used to create atmosphere, enhance immersion, and complement storyline and gameplay elements.

CHAPTER

Game Audio Basics

tools, equipment & skills

Key Chapter Questions

■ What is the primary purpose of the *computer* in the creation of game audio?

■ What types of *software* are used to create game audio, and what is the purpose of each type?

■ What types of recording situations require the use of *traditional* techniques and equipment?

■ What are the major *skills* required to work in the game industry as a composer or sound designer?

■ Why is knowledge of *copyright law* important for an audio content creator?

Just like any other specialized field, game audio requires a unique set of tools, equipment, and personal skills. While there is no specific list of obligatory gear to obtain or precise creation methods that must be followed, there are enough exclusive requirements that make game audio different from the audio used in other forms of entertainment. Music, sound effects, and dialogue can be created in many different ways. The needs of the game project and how the developer chooses to meet them will ultimately determine which equipment and methods are used. A great thing about game audio is that anyone with a background in music or recording, either as a hobbyist or full-time professional, already has much of the talent needed for this line of work. There is nothing inherently special about game audio, and anyone with an ear for what sounds good in a game already has the frame of reference needed to create appropriate audio. All you need are the right tools and skills to make it happen. Most audio professionals work on a variety of game projects in their careers and are prepared to tackle any audio style and deliver the results in any format. To accomplish this, many standard tools are found in game audio studios that help facilitate the process.

Computers

The personal *computer* is absolutely essential for creating game audio—and it is, without a doubt, the backbone of today's audio development process. A computer is not specifically required to create actual music or sound effects, but all game audio will eventually find its way into one for tasks such as editing and format conversions. These simple chores aside, most composers and sound designers find this tool incredibly useful and rely on it for much more.

Big Stock Photo

Your PC — an essential tool for creating game audio.

Considering the power and reliability of modern computer systems, it's totally plausible to compose, perform, mix, master, edit, and convert audio from start to finish without ever leaving the box. Due to this influence, composers and sound designers have fewer limitations and more flexibility to create when and where they desire. Instead of being holed up inside a commercial recording studio for weeks on end, the modern composer can take a laptop down to the beach and create a masterful orchestral performance while enjoying the sunshine. This new perspective can often lead to some incredible work!

The specifications of a computer used for game audio are heavily dependent on what it will be doing. For simple MIDI productions, an older, slower computer will work just fine. However, for massive, multitrack, full fidelity audio productions, the fastest processor and a full bank of RAM are highly recommended. Vital ingredients for a solid system also include: a high capacity hard drive system for storage; the capability to burn CDs or DVDs for final delivery or backups; and a high-speed Internet connection for file transfers.

Courtesy of MIDIplugins.com

MIDI Plugins (www.midiplugins.com) is one of many sites with a wide variety of plugins.

Interfaces

Having an appropriate computer system in place is only part of the big picture of audio production; a way to connect and control other gear in the studio is also important. *Interfaces* allow other computers, mixers, instruments, samplers, microphones, and storage devices to link to a central workstation—giving an almost unlimited set of creative options to the composer or sound designer. Typically, a good sound card will have analog and digital inputs/outputs—firewire or optical connections onboard for flexible routing of sound and information. Additional "break out" boxes and proprietary adapters also allow audio devices and controllers through USB and MIDI ports, which give added flexibility. A quality interface is important; one with good onboard pre-amps, multiple audio inputs/outputs, and multi-channel MIDI capabilities is worth its weight in gold.

Courtesy of E-MU Systems

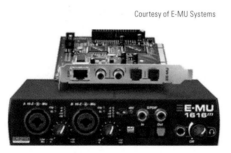

E-MU 1616M PCI audio-to-computer interface

"Lay Out the Roadmap"

Before writing a note, turning on the sound recorder, or talking to the voice actor, take a step back and look at the big picture. Lay out the roadmap and know the direction you want to head in. Sure, things can change and you should be open to change if it's beneficial—but without a roadmap, your soundtrack runs the risk of being incoherent or uninteresting. That's a shame when the opportunity exists for your game soundtrack to be so much more. For music, I suggest composing at the piano where the only limit is your imagination. Composing at the computer can mean you're pushed in the sonic direction of whatever samples you have. For sound effects, don't always go for literal. Throw a fun sound or two at the developers and see what they think. For voice, I suggest working on your own voice acting. One of the best tools you can have when directing voice is being able to say the lines exactly as you want the actor to say them. And one more thing: play lots of games! You have to be excited about games to be successful as a game audio content provider.

Matt Sayre (Owner, The Game Composer)

Plan Ahead for Audio

Be sure to involve audio in the game's development as early as possible. Don't put this off or cut corners on audio. It is no secret that most "AAA" games allot sufficient time for creating soundtracks, refining sound effects, and selecting the best voiceover actors for the job.

John Hight (Director of Product Development, Sony Computer Entertainment)

Software

The range of *software* available to game composers and sound designers determine what they are capable of doing and how they do it. It's often a personal choice of the content creator—balancing quality, features, and costs of the software and the processing capacity of their computer system—that decides what investments are made toward audio production requirements. Programs available on the market today range from simple freeware offerings to highly sophisticated and costly software suites—each of which serves its own purpose to achieve unique and fitting game audio. There are numerous selections within each category of computer programs to choose from, and often several are needed to do the job right.

Audio Editing

Audio editing software is an indispensable tool in today's audio production process—so much, in fact, that all game composers and sound designers use it on a daily basis. Audio editors perform most of the needed tasks—including recording, editing, mixing, effects processing, conversions, and playback—and as a host for many other sophisticated applications. Even if audio is created or mixed in another program, it will eventually end up in this type of software for final editing and format conversions. As with any software application, the quality of its features and sound is reflected in the price—and skimping on this type of software will have a direct effect on the overall characteristics of the audio. Examples of audio editing software include Sony Sound Forge, Adobe Audition, Audacity, Steinberg WaveLab, GoldWave, and Audio Editor Pro.

Courtesy of Sony Creative Software

Audio editing software (Sound Forge, shown) is indispensable.

Multitrack

Multitrack software essentially duplicates the capabilities of a multitrack tape recorder and is considered a definite "must have." Whether it is used for simple sound effects creation or complex music production, this software provides a flexible and non-destructive recording, mixing, and effects application platform with unlimited creative potential. Sound designers can perform complicated layering by controlling panning, volume, equalization, and effects processing for each element while creating sound effects with movement and interest. Composers can also accomplish the same thing with music—recording each track and later mixing the separate musical elements to create a cohesive piece of music. As further edits are needed, this type of program allows for quick recall of previous settings and makes easy work of revisions. Examples of multitrack software include Pro Tools, Steinberg Nuendo & Cubase, Sony Vegas & ACID, Cakewalk SONAR, Adobe Audition, and Audacity.

Courtesy of Avid Technology, Inc.

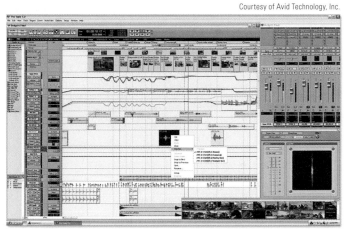

Pro Tools offers a wide range of multitrack capability.

Looping

Game composers working alone often turn to *looping* software to complement their abilities—usually for instruments beyond their expertise. Looping software has the capability to load various musical samples in sequence, adjust the key and tempo of the samples as required, and act as a multitrack program. Utilizing looping sample libraries is a fast and convenient way to present instruments such as drums and percussion, for example, which are more labor intensive to record. Whether working under a time crunch or looking for additional depth to a performance, looping software is an excellent tool—and the added features of multitrack recording or MIDI control make it quite powerful as well. Examples of looping software include Sony ACID, Cakewalk SONAR, Native Instruments Battery, and Propellerhead ReCycle.

Courtesy of Sony Creative Software

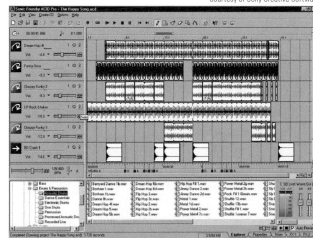

Looping software (ACID Pro, shown) makes life easier for a game composer.

Sequencing

High-quality MIDI control software is a valuable addition to any game audio creator's arsenal. As music and sound effects become more complex, *sequencing* software that allow simultaneous triggering of multiple electronic instruments, samplers, and effects processors are essential. Modern composers create evocative scores by layering multiple instruments and sounds—often in ways that can never be duplicated by a live musician. This method is faster and more cost effective than composing and recording a live orchestra—and coupled with quality samples, it achieves a solid performance.

Courtesy of Cakewalk

Sequencing software (SONAR 7 Producer Edition, shown) gives sound designers a variety of ways to manipulate sound.

Sound designers also invent new and exciting ways to manipulate sound by taking advantage of the precise control and features of sequencing software. They are able to mix various sounds together, apply effects processing, and manipulate them in real time to find the perfect blend for their application. Having the ability to bring this type of innovation to the process helps perpetuate the historical evolution of video games that we've come to expect. Examples of sequencing programs include Cakewalk SONAR, Steinberg Nuendo & Cubase, Sony ACID, Band in a Box, and Power Tracks Pro.

Mastering

When all of the music, sound effects, and dialogue are completed for a game, it is preferable that the audio goes through a final *mastering* phase before delivery. Time constraints or cost overruns may not always allow for this at an outside

Courtesy of Steinberg Media Technologies GmbH

"mastering" facility, but the content provider can utilize software-based applications to provide the final polish. Ensuring consistency in the "sound" of the audio is important. Volume, equalization, and sound quality should be similar enough so that none of the audio stands out unintentionally. There are many programs available to help the composer or sound designer deliver enhanced and fine-tuned audio at an affordable price. Mastering programs include IK Multimedia T-RackS 24, Sony CD Architect, Steinberg WaveLab, and BIAS Peak.

Mastering programs (WaveLab 6, shown) provide the final polish without an outside mastering facility.

Plug-Ins

Keeping the presentation of sound effects and music fresh and interesting is always a challenge in video games, and a myriad of audio *plug-ins* on the market today offer another solution. Plug-ins are auxiliary programs that run inside of host programs, such as multitrack or sequencing software, and allow creation of original sounds or manipulation of existing ones. These run the gamut from subtle treatment to outright mangling and destruction of sounds, with dozens of adjustable parameters to allow the sound creator total freedom. With literally hundreds of options to choose from, the sky is the limit. Examples of plug-ins include Waves Native & Platinum Bundles, Antares Auto-Tune, IK Multimedia Amplitude, M-Audio Producer Factory Bundle, BIAS SoundSoap, and BBE Sonic Maximizer.

Courtesy of Waves Audio Ltd.

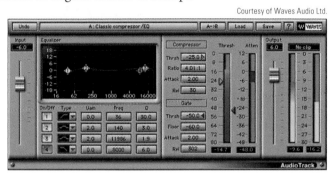

Many different plug-ins, such as Waves' Platinum Bundle, are available for game audio creation.

Surround Sound Encoding

As *surround* playback becomes more prevalent in the game scene, more composers and sound designers are tasked to deliver their goods in surround formats. For what used to be strictly a hardware-based process, where audio was routed through a dedicated encoding device, quality software applications have stepped in to streamline the process and make it more accessible. The software allows content providers to encode multiple formats (e.g., Dolby Digital, ProLogic II, and DTS) and deliver them as specified by the game developer's needs and the various target platforms. Examples of software-based surround encoding applications include Minnetonka SurCode, DTS Pro Series Surround Encoder, and Steinberg DTS Encoder.

Courtesy of Minnetonka Audio Software, Inc.

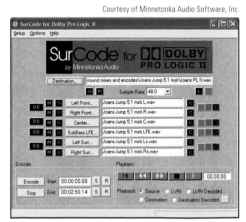

SurCode for Dolby Pro Logic II is one of several effective surround encoding applications.

Sampling

Quality reproduction and *sample* recording of instruments has led to some incredible software applications to trigger them. Game composers have embraced the ability to have an unlimited bank of instruments at their fingertips and instead

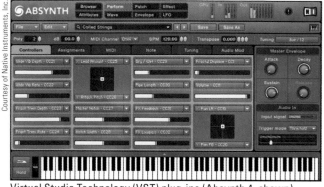

of stacks of keyboards and sound modules, now utilize *Virtual Studio Technology (VST)* plug ins and software-based samplers. Sequencing and multitrack software work in concert to provide the means to control and capture the virtual performances created by the composer. Examples of VST instruments and sampling software include Native Instruments Absynth, Battery, Kontakt, Kompakt, Intakt & Reaktor, Steinberg Halion, and Virtual Guitarist.

Virtual Studio Technology (VST) plug-ins (Absynth 4, shown) give the composer an unlimited bank of instruments.

Sound Libraries

When creating sounds is either inconvenient or overly expensive, game sound designers turn to pre-recorded *sound libraries* as a solution. These comprehensive collections of sounds provide a quick and expedient method to grab an audio ele-

ment that can then be edited to create a fitting game sound effect. However, since they can be used by anyone in the television, film, radio, and game industries, sounds from popular libraries can become overused and recognizable; this has the potential to break the immersive effect of a game. Most professionals insist on fresh sounds and typically only use sound libraries as a last resort. Sound libraries are available from companies such as Sound Ideas, Hollywood Edge, Network Music, and Sounddogs.com.

Online sound libraries such as Sound Ideas (www.sound-ideas.com) offer comprehensive collections of sounds.

Game Development Systems

In this modern era of game production, composers and sound designers are lucky. Music and sound effects can be created in a normal fashion and delivered ready, in their final formats, for the developer to simply drop into a game. Early game consoles actually required the use of a *game development system* to create, format, and test audio. These "dev" systems were expensive, difficult to obtain, and sometimes licensed for use only by the game developer and not the content provider. In an often arduous process, the composer would create music without the dev system and would only find out what it sounded like after the developer formatted and tested it in the game. The in-house composer had access to the dev system and was able to more easily create decent music, which required more work on the part of an independent contractor.

The era of the Xbox, PS2, and GameCube saw the introduction of software-based applications that allowed audio creators to implement and preview what the final audio would sound like in action. Software applications such as MusyX for Nintendo products, DirectMusic Producer for the Xbox, and SCREAM for the PlayStation also allow audio scripting; this streamlines the implementation process not only by giving credence to the creator's vision, but also by lowering the burden of the programmer—who simply drops the "script" into the game coding instead of writing it from scratch.

Courtesy of Factor 5, Inc.

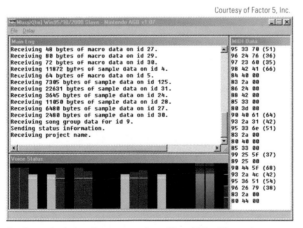

Audio scripting software, such as MusyX for Nintendo products, streamlines the final implementation process.

Working on older game systems compels the content provider to be proficient in the appropriate development tools to get the job done. Most composers and sound designers don't currently have to concern themselves with outdated consoles, but there is an existing subculture for these still popular platforms that present new opportunities and challenges. The current game systems are more developer friendly and provide an easier method for content providers to deliver the goods. Tools for the newer systems are usually just a quick download away, with registration and approval by the tool developer the only major step in the process.

Essential Game Audio Elements

From a studio GM perspective, there are a series of people and elements we're looking to combine in order to create audio that makes a great game even better:

1. A *top audio professional* to direct the audio in the project. He or she may also play another key role in audio design, composition, etc., but they have to have "the clear view of everything from 10,000 feet up."

2. A *composer* to adapt the music (in the case of a licensed game); re-create the spirit of the music (if, for example, a game ships and a movie premieres on the same date, which means the game music is done well before the movie music is written); or compose an original score. People underestimate how much musical talent is required to do adaptations and spirit-reproducing work, both of which actually require more skill than the more open original composition.

3. An *audio engineer* or *effects specialist* to create and mix the sound effects. As various Dolby systems come into wider and wider use, the power and complexity of this process grows.

4. The *audio hardware* and software to do all this work. Taking a brilliant pianist and having her or him play at a toy piano would be a terrible waste. Great audio people need to have the right tools to do their job.

5. The *studio space* to use those tools properly. For all of its complexity and sophistication, the process often comes back to taking a hollow piece of bamboo and rubbing it on the lid of an aluminum trash can to make just the right sound.

6. For dialogue, an experienced *writer*. At Stormfront we have consistently tried to use Emmy-winning talent like Bob Goodman and the late Hilary Bader, in order to have dialogue enhance rather than detract from the game experience. Why a professional writer? Because they can cover the same ground a good everyday writer can cover … in half as many words and with twice as much feeling.

7. For dialogue, an experienced *director* to guide the recording sessions in the studio—and, for that matter, a top quality studio in which to record.

8. Top professional *actors*. It should be noted here that being famous and being a top professional actor do not always go together. Some of the best performances I've ever heard are from studio voiceover professionals like Vanessa Marshall, whose names game players may not recognize … but who are widely respected in Hollywood.

9. Specialized *audio programmers*. How do you get the best sound out of a PS3? An Xbox 360? A Nintendo DS? The answer to each question is very different, and all the audio talent in the world cannot be shown off properly without having programmers who can make the machines play the right sounds properly at the right time. Imagine if all the dialogue were heard half a second too late to be in synch. If the sound effects were sometimes a little early, sometimes a little late. If the stirring music sounded like it was playing through the speaker of a radio that was manufactured in 1961.

Don Daglow (President & CEO, Stormfront Studios)

Equipment

Music and sound recording can be an incredibly complex and expensive undertaking. In today's game audio scene, computers and software are actually only part of the overall equation; in order to meet all of the potential requirements, more specialized *equipment* is often needed. Computers can accomplish much of the same results, but there are times when working methods or applications require a different approach.

Many game composers come from a traditional recording background—having cut their teeth in recording studios that utilize tape-based systems, enormous mixing consoles, and racks of outboard processors. Since they've grown into the business with these tools at hand, their comfort level is higher and they can create using very familiar systems. Sound designers, who have been around for more than a few years, have also followed similar paths and have made use of these established tools very successfully.

Grim Fandango is still one of my all-time favorites. Peter McConnell composed an entirely original, live jazz score that perfectly fit the game's film noir-meets-Mexican folklore setting.

Jamie Lendino (Composer & Sound Designer, Sound For Games Interactive)

Familiar territory aside, there are also times when a simple, computer-based system won't even come close to fulfilling the mission at hand. Recording a live band or full orchestra requires a professional facility with a mixing console, microphones, and multiple recording channels. A sound designer gathering sounds in the field usually requires equipment more rugged and less noisy than a laptop. There are many different situations in which only specific equipment will get the job done.

"Be Creative—Not Imitative"

The greatest responsibility in game audio creation is to be creative—not imitative. Be free from the past and start from square one with a new and unique approach. Experience may guide you through past unwanted obstacles in the technical process—as long as it doesn't lead you down familiar paths creating repetition and imitation. Engineering is quite distinct from the creative process; it can be creative but it always has audio playback considerations due to hardware limitations lurking in the background.

Larry G. Goldman (Music Producer, Lake Balboa Studios.net)

Traditional Recording

Whether it's a professional or personal project studio, a mixing console capable of handling multiple, simultaneous input and output channels is the centerpiece of a more *traditional recording* setup.

Courtesy of Tom Salta

Composer Tom Salta while recording *Tom Clancy's Ghost Recon: Advanced Warfighter 2*

A good console will allow multitrack tape or hard drive recording systems and outboard effects processing to run freely on this hardware-based arrangement. Additional equipment such as microphones, amplifiers, monitors, patchbays, power conditioners, cables, adapters, and acoustic treatment might also be needed to round out the gear list.

> The one game that made an impact on me was the music from the first *Katamari* game. Call me crazy—but after hearing many a sweeping score in games, this was like eating a mouthful of Starburst candy; it was fun! It reminded me what games were about again and how you can go totally and completely nuts with music in a game and still make it work. The tunes are catchy beyond belief.
>
> *Fernando Arce (Composer/ Musician, damselflymusic)*

Even though most game composers are "solo" artists, there are times when a room full of musicians becomes the better choice for a performance. For instance, a dozen channels can easily be utilized in order to properly mic a drum kit; this might prove a little more difficult on a computer-based audio workstation. There are also times when recording multiple voiceovers requires the entire cast to interact in real time. A variety of situations will lead game audio creators to turn to traditional recording equipment to complete their tasks. If the equipment isn't on hand, game audio creators will either rent the equipment or pay for time in a commercial studio.

Jon St. John on Voice Recording Tools :::::

Jon St. John is an American voice actor who got his start as a radio personality. He has most recently been heard on K-EARTH 101 in Los Angeles. Jon is one of the best-known voice actors in the video game industry because of his remarkable vocal range and long list of credits—including *Duke Nukem, Sonic The Hedgehog, Half-Life, Twisted Metal, Blue Stinger,* and *Balls of Steel* (just to name a few). Jon has been a voice actor for many years and is often heard on national radio and TV commercials and promos for clients such as HBO, Comcast, Toshiba, NBC, CNN, Nickelodeon, and others.

Jon St. John
(Owner, Jon St. John Productions)

A good microphone is essential. Often the audio is down-sampled considerably for the game platform, so the higher quality going IN, the better the OUTcome. I use a Neumann TLM 103 in my studio, with a Symetrix 528E processor. My preferred recording software is Sound Forge, since all of the tools needed for leveling, EQ, etc., are part of the package.

::::: *Ecco the Dolphin:* Using Audio to Engulf the Player

The *Ecco the Dolphin* series has one of the most comprehensive and well-designed scores. In order to fully immerse the player in an underwater, non-human environment, we used multiple sound designers to create unique samples as instruments with which I composed the score. We also moved specific sounds (e.g., whales, SFX) around the player using Q-Sound's real-time surround sound mixing controls. The beautiful thing about that system is that it only requires stereo speakers to fully engulf the player.

Spencer Nilsen (President & Creative Director, Ex'pression College for Digital Arts)

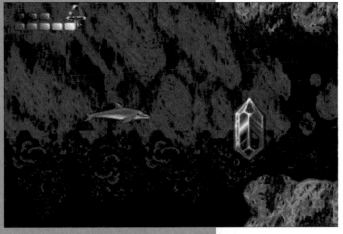

Game Audio Basics: tools, equipment & skills   chapter 2

Remote Recording & Capturing

Creating audio for games isn't always accomplished in the comfort of a climate-controlled and soundproof recording studio. More often than not, game sound designers will find themselves in the field recording and capturing sounds *remotely*, direct from the source, to use them as elements in original creations back in the studio. Obtaining common game sounds such as gun shots, car engines, aircraft, or exotic animals requires equipment that is mobile and able to deal with the unpredictability of the remote recording process.

Portable recorders, available with single or multiple channels, collect sound onto a variety of formats such as analog or digital tape, hard drives, or flash RAM. Specialized microphones are used to cover any situation—from focusing on a single

sound in noisy surroundings with a shotgun microphone to making a true stereo recording of an environment with a binaural mic. There are advantages and cost differences associated with the variety of equipment available to the sound designer; the budget and needs of the production will determine what is used. Since remote recording is common in the film, television, and game industries, there are many rental companies available that supply top of the line gear for any type of production.

Author Aaron Marks collects real-world samples.

Surround Encoding, Decoding & Playback

Creating audio that will be delivered to the developer in a *surround* format is best created within a surround environment. To do this correctly, a multi-speaker array consisting of at least five speakers and a subwoofer is a necessity. This arrangement covers center, front left and right, rear left and right, and lower frequency channels connected through either six separate mixing channels or a two-track mix of them routed through a surround decoding device. While there is available software to perform the encoding process, dedicated hardware encoders will do this in real time for better monitoring and control.

> For me, *Metroid* (NES) was one of the first games to really make me sit up and take notice of the audio landscape. Its "win" sting/cue especially sticks out in the minds of gamers everywhere.
>
> *Adam DiTroia (Composer/Sound Designer, DiTroia Audio Creations)*

Live Instruments & Noisemakers

Rounding out the equipment list is something that is not always obvious in this day of high quality samples and virtual instruments: *live instruments*. There is no substitute for the real thing—and game composers who are either proficient in certain instruments or have access to expert players tend to insist on using live instruments. Triggered samples lack the subtleties and nuances of live instruments—and using the real thing can result in a better emotional connection with the listener, which can have significant impact in a game setting.

Sometimes only the real thing will do.

Sound designers also have their own collections of *noisemakers* to keep things interesting. Items such as rain sticks, zube tubes, wooden train whistles, party favors, toys, novelty items, tools, mechanical gadgets, and junk are accumulated and kept well within reach. Besides being a useful variety of sonic elements, these objects also provide some appropriate creative inspiration.

"Try Everything": The Value of Experimentation

Try everything. Combine your comfort zone with new and laughably weird things and techniques. Don't get too caught up in your gear. Don't look around at X dollars worth of gear and turn your nose up at a cardboard mailing tube. Properly tracked and tweaked, it may open a variety of choices up to you. There will be plenty of gigs where your turnaround time is such that you won't have the luxury of taking the time to experiment. Value the ones that do have that time, by using it! Be willing to follow your ideas. It's a skill to know when to fold an idea, and when to persist—but allow yourself the space to develop everything internally, even if it gets abandoned fairly quickly.

Jed Smith (Lead Producer, betafish music)

Effective Game Audio Tools

One tool that I would be lost without is a piano. It's hard to go wrong with whatever technology you happen to be using when you start with a solid musical sketch on the piano and flesh it out in your imagination before heading to the computer.

Matt Sayre (Owner, The Game Composer)

For my electronic scores, I use live players whenever possible (drums, guitars, wind instruments) in conjunction with both hardware and software samplers and synthesizers. Live musicians will always interpret the music in ways I would have never imagined, which brings an important level of authenticity to the music—no matter what the style.

Spencer Nilsen (President & Creative Director, Ex'pression College for Digital Arts)

Many studios use the Sennheiser shotgun mic when the voice acting should sound like it's not in a studio—or when we're yelling. Neuman U87s or other large diaphragm mics are also good. As far as preamps, digital sound boards, and editing software—many people still use Avalon preamps or other quiet brands with good headroom. Motu interfaces help, and almost everyone has a digital sound board and decent editing software. It doesn't really matter if you use Pro Tools or Sound Forge. Developers need different file formats, and it's easy enough to provide those with most software out there.

Lani Minella (Master Creator, AudioGodz

I currently use a custom audio tool embedded into the Unreal 3 engine, created by our amazing audio programmers, and it has very few limitations. Based on the FMOD audio engine, it has been designed and expanded extremely well over the last few years and allows us to pretty much do whatever we want.

Rodney Gates (Lead Sound Designer, High Moon Studios)

Having a variety of real-world sound sources proves invaluable to me. Often, an odd world instrument manipulated through my Kyma capybara can provide me a truly unique solution to a getting a definitive sound. I do feel that Pro Tools is an essential medium to end up in, although many creative ideas that start in Ableton live for me as well. Soundtoys and Native Instruments make some really great tools for manipulating sound as well.

Jed Smith (Lead Producer, betafish music)

Skills

Having the appropriate tools and being proficient in their use is a good start to making worthwhile game audio. However, what goes into the creation of acceptable music, sound design, and dialogue is so much more than just having the right gear: there are certain personal *skills* that need to be developed and exploited in order to become successful in game audio. Some of these skills are indefinable qualities, such as having a good attitude or a "good ear"; others are more specific—such as musicianship or audio editing, which can be learned and honed with experience. Each skill can easily require a lifetime of study, but most people interested in pursuing game audio as a career usually have abilities from past audio endeavors to draw upon and aren't showing up unprepared.

Personal skills and talents usually determine an individual's primary audio focus and career path. Since most game audio folks have worn many hats over the years and are accustomed to working alone on projects, we will discuss the skills needed to make these types of individuals well rounded and ultimately successful. However, keep in mind that as game audio becomes more complex, it also becomes more specialized—which leads to more focused job titles and areas of expertise.

While it is best to have a handle on as many capabilities as possible, it's not as critical as it once was—and the chances of finding a job or a forming a creative partnership without knowing "everything" is actually pretty good. Not all composers are proficient recording engineers or producers. Not all sound designers have a musical background to draw from. Audio editors don't typically have an interest in copyright issues, and most musicians don't have technical knowledge of acoustics. Where one is lacking, an opportunity arises for someone else with complementary expertise to step in and fill the gap. Large game companies and established independent game audio houses do it effectively—and there is no reason it can't be done on any level, even on a small scale. Part of being successful in game audio is finding the right niche and exploiting it fully.

As far as an entire audio package is concerned, Rockstar's *Table Tennis* is an excellent example of great game audio. It has some simplistic music that kicks in after you rally for awhile, along with great subtle sound design; everything is appropriate. While there are games that contain "better" audio, this one has always stuck out to me as an excellent example of a complete package that doesn't damage the ears yet provides an immense amount of aural feedback to the player.

Matt Piersall (New School Beast Handler [a.k.a, Audio Director], OkaTron 5000)

Attitude

Attitude is one of those intangible qualities that will have the most impact on any-one's success in the game industry. Regardless of past knowledge or experience, a great attitude will open doors and help achieve things unreachable by those without one. Video games are a passion for those who create them, and those who can share in that enthusiasm are welcomed with open arms. What you know isn't as important as your eagerness to be a part of the process and learn the appropriate skills as you go. Many game development studios and publishers often have internship programs in place to feed on this phenomenon and groom individuals to meet their needs.

The interesting thing about a good attitude is how infectious it can be. When choos-ing between two potential candidates for a project, human nature will usually guide a development team to the one with the best attitude—even if the other candidate has a better resume. We want to be around people who are positive and energetic—to feed off of their energy and invigorate us. In turn, the renewed attitude we develop is spread through the team and carries them through the difficulties, frustrations and stress of the development cycle.

:::::: *Mage Knight Apocalypse:* Creating
        the Virtual Audio Department

Courtesy of NAMCO BANDAI
Games America Inc. and Wiz Kids

There was a title we worked on for Namco Bandai called *Mage Knight Apocalypse* where the developer was in Taiwan, and we acted as a virtual audio department. We recommended audio technologies and were given builds and tools so that we could deliver all the music, sound FX, and voiceovers for review actually running in the game. This is very rare for an audio team that isn't in-house; however, we received only a handful of requests for revisions over the whole development cycle, so I think we proved that it is possible to outsource audio a very complete way.

*Simon Amarasingham
(CEO, dSonic Inc)*

Don Daglow on Game Audio Management ∷∷∷

Don Daglow has served as President & CEO of Stormfront Studios since founding the company in 1988. At the 2008 Emmy Awards for Technology & Engineering, he accepted the award for creating *Neverwinter Nights*—the first graphical massively multiplayer online role-playing game (MMORPG); in 2003, he received the CGE Award for "groundbreaking achievements that shaped the video Game Industry." *Electronic Games* has called him "one of the best-known and respected producers in the history of the field." Stormfront's major titles include *The Spiderwick Chronicles*, *The Lord of the Rings: The Two Towers* (based on the film by Peter Jackson), *NASCAR Racing*, *Madden NFL Football*, and the original *Neverwinter Nights* on AOL. Prior to founding Stormfront, Don served as director of Intellivision game development for Mattel, producer at Electronic Arts, and head of the Entertainment & Education division at Broderbund. He designed and programmed the first-ever computer baseball game in 1971 (now recorded in the Baseball Hall of Fame in Cooperstown), the first mainframe computer role-playing game in 1975 (*Dungeon* for PDP-10 mainframes), the first sim game in 1981 (Intellivision *Utopia*), and the first game to use multiple camera angles in 1983 (Intellivision *World Series Major League Baseball*). Don co-designed Computer Game Hall of Fame title *Earl Weaver Baseball* (1987) and the original *Neverwinter Nights* for AOL (1991-97). He was elected to the Board of Directors of the Academy of Interactive Arts & Sciences in 2003 and again in 2007. He also is a past winner of the National Endowment for the Humanities New Voices playwriting competition. He speaks extensively on the topics of game design, interactive media, and the video game industry—and he has delivered keynote addresses in Canada, Germany, the UK, and the United States. Don holds a BA in Writing from Pomona College and an Ed.M. from Claremont Graduate University.

Don Daglow
(President & CEO, Stormfront Studios)

For the audio director or producer who pulls everything together, the most challenging part of the job is assembling a number of talented specialists, and then handling the dependencies of what needs to be done first in order for the next thing to be done second. For example, until you know whether a scene has World War II soldiers battling in a cobblestoned village, a big city, or open fields, you can't create the sounds of the bullets or explosions or even get the right echo on the voices of the actors. Until the designers have done most of their pre-tuning phase work and you know how the missions will play, you can't have the writer create dialogue—so you can't record the voices. But the programmers need to know how the timing and storage needs will work for the voices and sound effects before the voices are recorded. And so on.

Be a Team Player

Game development is an incredibly complex process that can involve dozens of people, several of which may have decision power over audio assets. It can be difficult at crunch time with looming project milestones, but bringing everyone in early and keeping the channels open usually resolves everything. Occasional email threads, conference calls, and in-person meetings can all help a great deal in resolving any issues.

Jamie Lendino (Composer/Sound Designer, Sound For Games Interactive)

At High Moon, we used a management process called SCRUM for *The Bourne Conspiracy* that generated a transparent view across the teams. We didn't feel as though we were in the dark during the game's development, and were able to work in tandem with the designers as the levels were created. This was a huge win over our previous title's development, which was much more 'reactionary.'

Rodney Gates (Lead Sound Designer, High Moon Studios)

When you sign on for a project, you are part of a team—frequently a very large one. You are a piece of the puzzle, and your music and sound effects need to fit within that puzzle. Your first concern should be making and keeping the development team happy and listening to what they want—*really* listening, not just hearing. :)

Adam DiTroia (Composer/Sound Designer, DiTroia Audio Creations)

Develop a good relationship with the producer, designer, and the rest of the team. Having a good team is like being in a functional family. It also shows in the work.

David Javelosa (Professor/Technologist/Composer, Santa Monica College)

Ear Training

Having a good ear is an extremely valuable skill. *Ear training* is essential to the recognition of high quality audio. In addition to having the technical competence to record, mix, and edit music and sound effects, the ability to hear beyond what is being recorded, getting a clean recording, knowing what adjustments are appropriate, and understanding how the audio affects other sonic elements in the overall soundscape of a game are all important subconscious decisions that impact the final product. As an example, could you record an acoustic guitar in the space you're sitting in at this moment? What does the space "sound" like? Are there background noises that would detract from the recording? Are you able to identify everything you are hearing? Do you hear the lights buzzing, a computer fan blowing, or traffic moving? Being able to hear past what you are capturing is the kind of attention to detail you need to have for a good ear.

Diagram by Per Olin

Four phases of a sound

Try this exercise to test your "ear": Find a large open room or a long hallway free of loud noises. Stand inside it, clap once, and listen to how many distinct sounds that are generated by your two hands coming together. At first, most only detect one sound—but once they understand there are other sounds to listen for, most people will easily hear an echo as well. However, if you're listening closely, you can actually hear four distinct phases of the sound:

1. *Attack* of your two hands hitting each other—the actual skin-on-skin contact.
2. *Body* of the sound where it intensifies and reaches its maximum volume.
3. *Echo* of the sound bouncing off another surface.
4. *Decay* of the sound as its volume decreases to nothing.

The final two phases can happen in either order depending on the size of the room. When you get to the point at which you can honestly recognize each portion of the sound, you are on your way to developing a good ear.

These simplified examples illustrate the process of *active listening* and are the basis of developing better listening skills. Creating music and sound effects by layering instruments and sound elements can be a complex issue. It's not as easy as throwing all the faders to zero and hoping they sound good together; it's a choreographed manipulation of volume, panning, and equalization, all of which require intense listening and an experienced ear to do correctly.

> Keep an eye out for creative ways to make and record new sounds, for both effects and music. Don't rely solely on pre-created instrument patches. Don't get caught up in the gear. Ultimately it's about the music and sound, and creative compositions always shine over mediocre ones.
>
> —*Eric Doggett (Owner, MoonDog Media, LLC)*

Acoustics

Acoustics is the science of sound—how it is created, controlled, transmitted, received, and affected. Understanding how these physical properties relate to game audio will be a great advantage, especially when the entire development team is looking to the sound designer for an "expert" opinion. What happens to a sound when there is an obstruction between the object and listener? What will the audio sound like from behind a closed door? Applying the knowledge of sound generation, sound waves, reverberation, and frequency filtering can really save the day—and it helps to have the basic scientific principles in mind when dealing with these types of situations.

For composers, musicians, and recording engineers, acoustics has a significant influence on the overall sound of the music being recorded. The actual space in which an instrument or orchestra is placed is important—but the types of microphones used and their placement in relation to the instrument and other microphones will also shape the sound that is captured. Simple knowledge of what a sound wave looks like and how the positioning of a microphone will determine what is collected can really make all the difference, especially when out of phase microphones work to cancel out the sounds that are being recorded.

Diagram by Per Olin

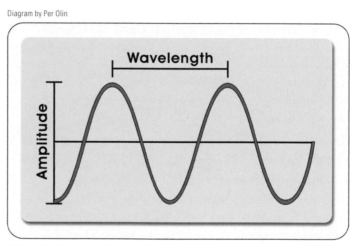

Understanding acoustics is a key aspect of a sound designer's abilities.

A sound designer considers acoustics during studio and field recording sessions—and also when layering multiple sonic elements to create sound effects. Positioning of audio in the stereo field and adjustments of equalization will influence whether each sound is clearly heard or is mixed into a glob of sonic mush. Similarly, since the soundscape of a game is a complicated and noisy place—with music, sound effects, and dialogue blending together—suitable adjustments will ensure a more polished presentation of game sound by applying the knowledge of acoustics.

Composition & Musicianship

Composers and musicians must be extremely proficient in their craft to create music that exudes professionalism. A billion dollar a year industry is no place to showcase amateur music productions, and those who find work on AAA game titles are the cream of the crop. In order to be considered for large budget projects, composers must have either years of experience or be particularly adept at the types of music they compose. Game composers are often called upon to create many different styles and genres, sometimes in a single game—and those who have a clear understanding of the various techniques and subtleties will have lengthy careers.

iStock Photo

For instruments that are more specialized or require a higher level of musicianship, composers will call in outside help.

Most game composers are also multi-instrumentalists. In the earlier years of game music, composers were "one-man bands" out of necessity—with small budgets and short deadlines forcing them to be efficient. This carries over into today's audio production mindset as needed—but for instruments that are more specialized or require a higher level of musicianship, composers will call in outside help. However, a game composer who is highly competent on piano and understands the mechanics of other instruments can usually fake it well enough to fool most people.

Engineering, Editing & Production

The game composer wears many audio hats. Since composing and recording go hand in hand, having the knowledge to record, edit, mix, and master the music is an essential skill. Unfortunately, it's not as simple as plugging an instrument in and pressing the record button. Understanding the technicalities of the recording process and the equipment or software being used can have as much impact on the sound of the music as the selection of instruments and musicians.

There are many technical issues that can degrade the quality of a performance, including:

- too much background noise
- a weak or overloaded signal
- poor quality interfaces and cabling
- incorrect signal paths

Whether the recording is software- or hardware-based, each system has specific methodologies that must be followed in order to capture high quality audio—and knowing how to do this is essential.

Game composers, sound designers, recording engineers, and dialogue editors will find themselves in front of an audio editing program on a daily basis. These programs do everything from recording the actual material, manipulating it in every imaginable way, to converting it to the final in-game format—and they will have high usage in any game audio studio. Due to this reality, it is imperative that anyone involved in the creation of game audio be completely familiar with the operations of these types of programs. Having their functions down will ensure that this valuable tool is transparent and not a hindrance to the process. Understanding the features of audio editing software is important, but it is also essential to be well-versed in how these features influence the actual sound:

- *What happens when noise reduction is applied to a recording?* The editor needs to know not only that the targeted "noise" is reduced, but also that it affects the remaining sound in some way.

- *What happens when a fade is used at the end of a recording?* The editor would need to listen closely to whether the decay sounds natural or appears to be cut off and would then utilize this tool appropriately for the application.

- *What happens when a low signal is boosted to a higher volume?* Knowing that any recorded noise is also increased at the same ratio as the target sound might determine a different course of action, such as recording the sound again.

What is done within the editing software has a direct impact on the quality of the sound, and understanding what each feature does to that sound can save time and significant headache.

Production skills beyond the technical aspects of recording are also important. Having the big picture in mind during the process will ensure that what is being created and each instrument being tracked will work toward the same end goal. The producer's role is also to oversee the recording sessions, coach the musicians, and supervise the recording, mixing, and mastering phases—all of which, coincidentally, are usually accomplished by the game composer or sound designer. Having the skills to successfully navigate the process will come into play almost daily.

Matt Piersall on Game Audio Implementation :::::

Matt Piersall started in the industry as an ADR engineer for FUNimation. He forced his way into a non-existent job (at the time) of doing music and sound design for anime trailers. From the start, his plan was to get into games—and that's what he's been doing ever since. His eighth-grade dream of being in an environment with a bunch of sweet gear and a massive library of video games is finally a reality.

Matt Piersall
(New School Beast Handler [a.k.a. Audio Director], OkraTron5000)

The real trick to great game audio is implementation. You can create amazing sounds and music—but if it isn't placed in the world in the right way, it will not be believable. Know your editor, your limitations—and even if you can't implement sounds yourself, be *fully* aware of the process that goes into it. The tendency of sound designers and composers is to create their assets in a way disconnected from the final product (myself included). Sometimes less is more, and sometimes more is not enough. You have to be aware at all times that the one-off moment that you're spending three hours on will play once—and those footsteps that you threw together in five minutes will be heard throughout the whole game.

Computers & Game Engines

Electronic games are developed through the use of *computers* and *game engines.*
Assets for computer games are created and designed with the use of computers.
Additionally, whether or not game audio is created on traditional recording gear,
it will eventually find its way into the computer. It then goes without saying that
understanding how a computer and its software work is a critical skill.

So much revolves around computers—such as music and sound design production,
editing and, implementation—that it is essential to have an above average knowledge
about them. Game developers don't have much free time or tolerance to train individuals on simple computer tasks, such as how to upload files to FTP sites or how to
install beta versions of their games. On the audio production side, knowing how to
install something like a new sound card or interface yourself will keep downtime to a
minimum. Basic knowledge will be relied on heavily.

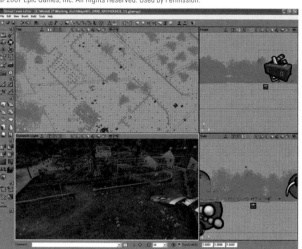

A game composer should be familiar with game engines and
level editors (Unreal Editor 3, shown).

In addition to comprehending how a computer works, it is essential to understand
how the targeted game platform functions and how audio is processed within it.
A general knowledge of whether music can be streamed from the hard drive or
disk—or whether compressed music files will be loaded into RAM and converted on
the fly—might also make a difference in the production process. Awareness of these
processes can directly impact how a game composer and sound designer approach
their work, and it will help them follow discussions with the development team over
other issues. It's not imperative to know minute details about how and why a system
functions, but a strong familiarity will do wonders to streamline the process and not
have the technology needlessly overwhelm creativity.

Copyright Law

In the midst of original audio creation for the video game market lies an often unspoken but incredibly important issue. *Copyright law* looms quietly in the back of the composer and sound designer's minds, influencing the end result of their music and sound effects creations. Laws are clear about the protection of previously created works, which include not only music but other recorded sounds and instrument samples. Due to this, it is imperative the music and sound effects created for a project contain original or properly licensed elements. Video games are a multi-billion dollar a year industry, and publishers and developers are particularly protective over it. The burden of originality is placed squarely upon the shoulders of composers and sound designers through agreements signed by them.

Ensuring that publishers and developers are unencumbered by lawsuits is significant, but what is additionally important is that they own all rights to the assets created for their projects. For developers who have an in-house audio team, these rights are secured through the conditions of employment. In exchange for salaries and benefits, content creators give up any interest in their material that is produced while on the clock. Independent contractors enter into a *work for hire* agreement that spells out the scope of work, compensation, and rights transferred by the creator to the developer; these contracts typically insist on complete ownership of all assets, but they occasionally allow creators to retain the rights if the audio is used in something other than the original game project (e.g., film). Understanding how copyrights and transfer of rights work will allow the composer and sound designer to achieve the best deal possible and stay out of any legal trouble.

:::

Having the equipment and knowledge to exploit game audio tools is a great start to creating quality game audio. Add personal skills, an unbridled passion for games, and endless creativity—and there is no telling what can be accomplished in a long and illustrious career. At first glance, there seems to be an impossible list of skills that have to be mastered, but this is not as bad as it looks. If you've been paying any attention to music or to the sounds surrounding you all your life, you're practically there. Much of the challenge in any audio career is not only about your ears but what's between them as well. Use the smarts you already have and fill in any weaknesses with study, practice, and experience. Every situation should offer something new: an alternate technique, the use of different equipment, or observing someone else at work. The pros refuse to become stagnant by constantly learning, and this attitude will serve you equally well. With this in mind, let's take a look at game sound effects and how to create them.

1. Begin designing your home recording studio. Take stock of your existing instruments, hardware, software, accessories, and other equipment. Draw a diagram of how you envision your setup (e.g., MIDI).

2. After taking stock of what you already have, consider what you still might need for audio creation (e.g., composing, recording, sequencing, capturing, sampling), editing, and mastering. Research the available hardware and software discussed in this chapter and decide which packages you'll need in order to meet your needs.

3. What knowledge and unique skills do you have that will be helpful to you as a game audio professional? Consider your existing knowledge of hardware, software, acoustics, and composition. Add personal skills that might benefit you in the industry. What areas do you feel might need improvement? Is it possible for you to enhance these areas through study, practice, or experience? Might it be necessary to team up with a partner who can complement your skills (e.g., orchestrator who wants to team up with a composer)?

Part II: Function & Process

Function of Game Sound Effects

bringing the game to life

Key Chapter Questions

- What type of *sound effects* can help reach the goal of total immersion of the game player?

- Where should sound effects be *placed* in a game?

- What are the distinct *disciplines* of sound design creation?

- What are some of the *methods* sound designers can use to produce original sound effects?

- Where does sound effects creation typically fall within the game development *process*?

Sound effects have an incredible influence on the overall game experience. While a game may be able to get by without music or dialogue, one without sound effects will be very disappointing. It's inconceivable to think of players firing "silent" weapons or seeing soundless conflagrations erupt in their paths. Early games may have been rudimentary, but their designers always understood that sound effects are more than just entertainment. The complexity of today's game sound has led to an entirely distinct job description and career path—involving the creation of nearly everything the player will hear. From environmental ambience to button presses to player feedback sounds, the sound designer imagines, records, creates, and edits sound effects. The term used for the creation of sound effects is referred to as *sound design*. The primary function of a game sound designer is to create sound effects and assist in their implementation. Effective sound can elevate a solid game to something even more fun and entertaining—but poor sound can bring a great game down a few notches. Keep this in mind as we discuss sound effects in this chapter—and focus your attention on creating high quality sounds that not only fit the game but actually set the bar high for the rest of the team to meet and exceed.

Purpose of Game Sound Effects

Sound effects exist specifically to give feedback to players, immerse them inside the virtual realm, and provide an entertaining experience—all of which are key ingredients to a successful video game. Since a game is nothing more than lines of code and pixels of colored light, the sense of sound is what adds warmth and familiarity to what is happening on the screen. Although many current games employ 3D and even hyperrealistic images, the player is still only looking at pixels; the only "real" sense fully experienced by the player is sound. Granted, players aren't hearing a "real" bird chirp or weapon fire—but the sound they do hear is an actual recording of the real object or a close reproduction of it. Whether it is a "real" sound or not, the impact is the same and the sound plays its specific role.

Reprinted with permission from Microsoft Corporation

Reprinted with permission from Microsoft Corporation

Forza Motorsport 2 (left) and *Gears of War* (right) immerse players in their environments.

To illustrate what sound does for the virtual experience, turn on a movie and mute the volume. Without the sense of hearing, clues to what is happening on screen are difficult to detect. While the actors and their surroundings may be visible, the subtlety of their actions and environments are missing and the personal connection you may have felt by being a part of the "scene" is completely absent. What is happening "off camera"? Is there a hurricane madly blowing outside? Are there tanks rumbling by? Is there gunfire or shouting? Often what is happening outside the field of view has a huge impact on the emotion of the experience—and if it's never heard, half of that "experience" is completely gone. Worse, with the audio absent from the onscreen visuals, sounds from the physical surroundings in which the film is being viewed will invade and detract from the immersive experience. That's why the sound of others talking in a theater during a movie frustrates many movie goers; the audience hates being forced back to reality by outside distractions.

Let's also take a look at this occurrence within the settings of a video game. Find a game that allows control of the sound effect volume and turn it off—leaving the music and dialogue untouched. Starting with the menu screen, press a button. Besides seeing the button press and the screen changing, what happened? The player has no aural feedback from pressing the button, and vital clues or emotional reinforcement to this simple action is missing. A good game experience is one that will totally immerse the player; something as plain as a button press can set the stage and convince players that they are actually doing something within the virtual setting. This minimal action still requires a sound—something which is true to the experience and makes it convincing. Button sounds for games such as *Halo* and *Medal of Honor* are not identical and incorporate the themes of their respective games.

> **B**urnout Revenge uses audio to convey an amazing sense of speed; it always feels as though you're accelerating, and I love the windy near-silence whenever you jump the car. *Rainbow Six: Vegas* has excellent weapon sound design; it feels powerful and punchy—whether you're taking out terrorists or your friends in multiplayer.
>
> *Rodney Gates (Lead Sound Designer, High Moon Studios)*

Reprinted with permission from Microsoft Corporation

Even the button sounds in *Halo: Combat Evolved* remind you of what game you're playing.

As you continue through the game, your mind expects to hear environmental sounds, feedback from any actions you may be engaged in, and sounds that match what your eyes are seeing. In the absence of these sounds, we are unable to receive clues or judge what is happening to us or around us. In reality, consider that even within a completely quiet room, we are always aware of the others around us, the mood and atmosphere that is present, whether we are safe or in danger, and other signals that would indicate what we might need to do. While there may be other forces at work here as well, such as visual or physical indications, the cues we hear play a huge part in determining our well being and what is going on around us. Yes, we may be sitting alone in a quiet room—but in the next room over, someone else may be hurriedly moving about, rustling through the medicine cabinet looking for aspirin. Outside, there may be emergency vehicles and sirens blaring, rushing to a nearby disaster. Screams in the hallway might reveal that the disaster is too close for comfort and that you need to take shelter or run for your life! But, sitting with headphones on with the sound blasting, you'd be completely oblivious. Sound effects in video games accomplish much in the way of setting the mood of the environment—giving clues to the surroundings and providing some great entertainment in the process.

Illustration by Ian Robert Vasquez

How deeply can sound effects immerse a player in a game?

Understanding the purpose of sound effects is a good first step to appreciating the objectives of a game. This broad knowledge will guide the production team and sound designer in the creative process to take full advantage of any features of the audio engine and to use sound effectively within it. Understanding which specific areas within the game environment require sound and the purpose they serve is equally important and will ultimately direct the audio production to a successful end. The purposes of sound effects include:

- *Setting the mood:* Whether silly or serious, sound effects can help set the appropriate mood of a game through everything from simple button presses to ambience tracks. For example, games designed for the younger crowd, such as *Putt-Putt Saves the Zoo*, use fun, cartoony sounds to keep the mood light—while horror-themed games such as *Resident Evil IV* and *Doom 3* make effective use of dark, eerie sounds.

- *Adding realism:* The *Medal of Honor* series utilizes era-appropriate sounds that create authenticity and help players feel as if they are participating in 1940s conflicts. Sounds associated with weapons, aircraft, and vehicles are specifically designed to match those heard during that particular time in history. Background ambience is also used extensively in these types of games, suggesting that action is taking place all around the character.

- *Providing clues to surroundings:* First-person shooters (FPSs) such as *Halo*, *Call of Duty*, and *BioShock* make good use of sounds to alert players to clues and other activity within the immediate environment. For example, players looking for a waterfall as a next waypoint would first hear it faintly in the distance; it would then increase in volume and from a more defined location within the sound field as they approached it.

- *Enhancing entertainment value:* A video game's primary purpose is to entertain, and sound effects are integral to the fun. Nothing beats hearing earth-shattering explosions, gunshots, or car crashes in direct relation to your actions. The shot sound in the casual game, *Zuma*, is so satisfying that players find themselves looking forward to the next click of the mouse.

- *Creating tactile and interface feedback:* Creating reality in a virtual environment is often a difficult proposition. In real life, something as simple as flipping a light switch produces a subtle sound that provides important feedback. These sounds are even more important in a game setting by notifying players that their actions have accomplished something that can't always be visualized. Consoles such as the Xbox 360, PS3, and Wii provide audio feedback for button presses and screen transitions.

- *Establishing brand identity:* Nearly every game produced today strives for a fresh and innovative identity. In attempting to develop an original look, feel, and sound of a game, the developer is inadvertently creating a recognizable brand identity that defines the game and any others within a series. Consequently, anyone seeing artwork or hearing a sound can instantly identify that particular game. Popular game series such as *Guitar Hero, Halo*, and *Need for Speed* are easily recognized by their "sound."

Placing Sound Effects

Each video game title has specific places where sound effects are a "must"—in start screens, active interface menus, cinematics, and gameplay. Every game—from simple puzzle games to full-blown, massively multiplayer online games (MMOGs)—uses audio in these places. Let's take a closer look at important areas to place sound effects.

Animated Logos

As a game loads, players are met with a variety of animated logos for publishers, key developers, and other creative forces. It's obvious these are there to promote the companies who are involved in the game's creation and distribution, but they also serve another more subtle purpose. Without knowing it, the developer is setting the stage for the player, building the excitement, setting the mood, and most importantly, making sure the sound is turned on. Grabbing players and absorbing them fully in the experience can't be done if the sound isn't working, and this is the last chance to ensure the player doesn't miss out.

These sounds don't have to be fancy or even that noticeable, really. A slow "whoosh" or simple "click" is subtle enough to do the trick. However, this doesn't mean the player can't be wowed from the opening screen. The sound designer can really have some fun creating these types of sounds!

Courtesy of Rockstar Games and Take-Two Interactive Software, Inc.

The audio for the animated logo in *Grand Theft Auto: Vice City* sets the stage for the player.

Cinematics & Cut-Scenes

Opening/closing and transitional "movies," respectively known as *cinematics* and *cut-scenes,* establish the story's background and drive it forward, set the mood, provide needed clues, and give praise for completing a difficult level. They are typically found at the beginning of a game, between each level and as the final sequence at the game's end. Occasionally, they are also found within each level or prior to an encounter with a "boss" character in order to highlight a shift in the story plot and add appropriate tension or excitement. Since these "mini movies" are non-interactive, it's also a good opportunity for a player to rest and mentally regroup before the next event.

Any major game release today uses a powerful opening cinematic to set the stage. *StarCraft: Brood War* is a classic example of a well produced opening movie that immediately grabs the players' attention and aggressively sucks them into the virtual experience. The sounds that accompany these significant features are usually of the highest quality and created by the most experienced sound designers within the team. Since the first impression of a game establishes its overall perceived quality, opening sequences usually hold nothing back.

In-game cut-scenes propel a story forward by summarizing what the player has already accomplished and alludes to things to come in upcoming game levels. *WarCraft III* uses this tool effectively to not only reward the player for recent victories but to introduce a major twist in the story when Arthas, the returning hero, betrays his father. These types of movies are often very dramatic and depend on audio to portray the mood—in this case changing from triumphant to dark.

With a player investing an incredible amount of time in a game, successful completion is a major accomplishment. Reward for this feat often appears in the form of an ending cinematic, skillfully designed to leave the player feeling good about a victory while revealing more of the plot. *Prince of Persia: The Sands of Time* is a good example of a finale that gives meaningful context to the game and heightens the overall game experience as everything is put into perspective. The audio remains true to the game and adds much to the sense of drama.

From a creative standpoint, sound effects are produced and integrated into this pre-scripted medium similarly to film. Background ambience, foley, and other required sounds are created utilizing a myriad of techniques with an edited sound file as the end result. There are no implementation issues or audio engine limitations to be concerned with, but there are specific post-production details to consider so that the work is effective.

StarCraft: Brood War is a classic example of a well produced opening movie that immediately grabs the player's attention.

Sound effects are mixed with background music and dialogue so that volume, panning, and equalization are adjusted appropriately; they are accurately synchronized to animations to match what the viewer is seeing. Sounds are prioritized to preserve the intentions of each scene, keeping the overall soundscape manageable and understood. Finally, the sounds serve a specific purpose—whether to add believability and a sense of realism, or simply for entertainment.

Interface & Menu Screen Effects

The *interface* is an onscreen menu area where adjustments to the console or game features can be applied. Interfaces can be either pre-game menus that appear during or immediately following the initial start-up sequence, or in-game controls and features that typically frame the viewing area; they can also be active menus that require feedback from the player, or passive *heads-up displays (HUDs)* that inform the player. In-game interfaces allow players to make quick adjustments during gameplay and provide important information regarding health and supply status, location, and clues necessary to successfully complete a sequence.

World of WarCraft utilizes an effective in-game interface. A usable interface is important in this type of game due mainly to the often incredible complexity of gameplay. Character and inventory management, player health and status, map, and messaging windows all are available on screen for quick access and to streamline play. Associated button, screen transition, and attention sounds, while subtle, are present to provide the needed tactile feedback and to audibly verify that the player has selected what was intended. Since interface screens depict what the character would be carrying in real life, their visual and audio qualities should reflect this in an understated manner.

Courtesy of Blizzard Entertainment, Inc.

World of WarCraft utilizes an effective in-game interface.

Menu screens can be simple or complex, depending entirely on the needs of the game; the sound effects created for these areas are usually fairly subtle and are always within the game's theme. Button sounds, ambience, environmental sounds, alarms, attention signals, and other audible indicators are typical for these areas. Music loops and occasional dialogue will also share the soundscape, and these elements must work together.

::::: Matching the Theme in *Call of Duty 3*

Sound effects should always match the *theme* of the game. There are many games within specific genres that utilize sound effectively and illustrate the concept of theme more clearly. *Call of Duty 3* is a good example of a 'World War II' based game series that recreates a variety of conflicts during that global struggle. This particular game not only portrays warfare associated with the era realistically, but it aims to accurately recreate weapon, vehicle, aircraft, and environmental sounds in their full glory.

Activision

Great care is taken to remain clear of 'modern' and other inaccurate sounds or any other sound that might break the spell. Everything from button sounds to ambience adheres to the theme of the game—making the sounds very effective.

Ambience & Environmental Effects

Background *ambience* and *environmental* sound effects are what give "life" to a game's virtual world. With total immersion as an objective, these sounds not only add a sense of realism to the visuals but also help mask any sounds in the player's living room or bedroom. Whether the scene takes place within a hectic cityscape or a quiet countryside, sounds indicating activity within the setting are a must.

The overall ambience is often complemented by specific environmental sounds from significant objects present in the location. A cityscape may have an ambience that includes the general "rumble" of the city—such as traffic noises, construction sounds, and airplanes flying overhead. Environmental sounds portray items that a player encounters while exploring this setting; a fire crackling inside of a trash bin, a buzzing street lamp, or a gushing water fountain are possible noise-making objects that players expect to "hear" as they approach them.

Any game in the *Medal of Honor* series contains ambient and environmental sounds that are both well constructed and well implemented. As players explore their surroundings, background sounds such as low-flying aircraft, barking dogs, distant explosions, or weather are often present. These sounds aren't associated with any specific object—and no matter where players turn or move within the setting, these non-directional sounds effectively suggest activity just outside of their view.

Environmental sounds are also depicted quite well in this series; the difference is that these sounds are based on important static objects a player can find within the game setting. The sound of these objects are anchored in a fixed position, enabling a player to aurally detect their location through the use of sound. In an actual mid-20th century battlefield, and in these games, players expect to hear the static of a military radio, hum of an electrical generator, or crackling of a shorted-out fuse box as they pass close by. These sounds, which are very easily implemented, have a tremendous impact on the realism and believability of the setting.

Electronic Arts, Inc.   Courtesy of Rockstar Games and Take-Two Interactive Software, Inc.

Medal of Honor: Airborne (left) and *BioShock* (right) have distinct moods, but both give life to what the player sees on the screen.

For games based in modern settings, such as *True Crime: New York City*, the sound designer will spend many hours in the field with remote recording equipment to capture various ambient elements that are edited together back in the studio. Fictional settings in games such as *Crysis* and *BioShock* require a bit more creativity when producing individual ambient elements, but an appropriate ambience can be developed after thoughtful layering. Sounds of specific objects are often collected in the field, but also can be recorded in the more controlled atmosphere of a studio when possible. For items that are cumbersome or impractical to record, other objects can be used in their place or taken from sound libraries.

> *Need for Speed: ProStreet* has some of the best engine sounds because we used the best field recordists, equipment, cars, and editors/audio programmers in the business.
>
> Watson Wu (President, WOOTONES, LLC)

Main Interaction & Player Feedback Effects

Main interaction and player feedback effects are the "meat and potatoes" of any game experience, and are the sounds that take center stage. These are the gunshots the player hears when the trigger is squeezed in *Halo 3*, the explosions in *Call of Duty 3*, the whine of a high revving engine in *Need for Speed*, the heavy clank of a sword in *EverQuest II*, the magical fireball in *Might & Magic*—these sounds players "feel" as they interact with the virtual experience. While music, ambience, and dialogue are important, a game cannot and should not ever be without these vital sonic elements.

These sounds are what primarily provide the audio entertainment. They are, without a doubt, a large part of the fun of playing games. For example, have you ever, fired a weapon in a game over and over again just for fun? Sometimes the sound is so perfect that it alone provides great satisfaction to the player. Imagine a game where all of the sounds were this incredible! People play games for amusement, and the sound designer has a great opportunity to deliver with these types of sounds.

Electronic Arts, Inc.

The whine of a revving engine in *Need for Speed ProStreet* takes center stage.

Secondarily, these key sounds give the player feedback to their onscreen actions. The sound often will not only validate that something is being done, but it will provide other subtle clues. For example, a player moves to open a closed door. As expected, the door handle or actuator mechanism will make a sound—but whether the door is open or locked is discovered by what is heard. With sounds complementing the visuals of the door opening or remaining closed, the player has the information needed for the next move.

:::::: Spell Effects in *EverQuest II*

Used with permission of
Sony Online Entertainment

Creating sound for the spell effects in *EverQuest II* was a challenge. It's tough to create sounds that are abstract with no reference to everyday life—and also ensure that they don't become irritating to hear over and over again. We also had limited tech on that game. It's difficult when you don't have full audio programmer support; your wish list ends up at the bottom.

*Chad W. Mossholder (Sound Designer / Composer,
Sony Online Entertainment)*

::::::Creating Sounds for Make-Believe Objects

Courtesy of PopCap Games, Inc.

Creating sounds for objects that don't actually exist can be a challenge if you want to keep the sound suitable and still evoke a sense of believability. Typically, the sounds are based on real objects, such as swords or pistols—but are manipulated to give them a more "alien" quality that marries them to their make-believe environment. Each sword strike or gun shot will be familiar to the player while also sounding "off" or different.

For objects that aren't based on reality, the key for the sound designer is to make them sound as if they *did* come from the object in question. Puzzle games such as *Luxor*, *Zuma* (shown), or *Bejeweled* utilize arcade style sounds in an effective manner to entertain the player while providing tactile feedback and clues to what is happening in the game. As game pieces are matched or bonus items are displayed, sounds provide important hints to keep the game engaging. These type of games are highly addictive—due in no small part to their skillfully applied sound effects.

Disciplines of Sound Design

There is a variety of disciplines requiring proficiency for a successful game sound design career. Since games utilize an assortment of sound styles, a good sound designer will need the knowledge to work expertly within each area to create sounds that are appropriate and of high quality. In the film and television industries, sound design disciplines are highly specialized and require specific talents and years of experience to be considered respectable. We've discussed previously that a career in sound design is within reach of those who have a good ear, engineering and production chops, and are proficient with audio editing software. The next step is to refine these skills further and apply them directly to a specific discipline.

Foley

Foley (named after Jack Foley, one of the earliest practitioners of the art in the Hollywood film industry) is the art of creating general movement and object-handling sounds that are in sync to onscreen actions. In film, this is used extensively to create or sweeten existing footfalls, clothes rustles, body falls, hits, weapon handling, and other general sounds a character would make while moving through a scene. Since the dialogue is the most important sound being captured at the time, these other movement sounds are missed or purposely deadened during each take with the knowledge they can be recreated later during foley. To accomplish this task, foley artists will gather suitable props and set up insulated "pits" with the appropriate surface types and make a few run-throughs before an actual recording. When the artists are fully practiced, they will then "perform" the scene and recreate the missing sonic elements in time to the visuals. Foley work is like working in "stealth mode" because it works best when it isn't noticed.

In games, "foley" refers more to the type of sound effects rather than the methods used to create them, although they can be captured similarly. Many games developed today require sounds such as footfalls, body hits, or object-handling noises for the purpose of adding a sense of realism to what the player is experiencing. The main difference between film and game foley work is how the sounds are "performed" and how they are ultimately implemented into the game medium.

Game cinematics are the most similar to film with regard to foley. The onscreen action is defined, happens predictably, and is the same no matter how many times it is viewed. Sound designers are tasked to create each sound within this mini movie—from simple footfalls to massive explosions to everything in between.

> The environment sounds and music, both licensed and original, for *BioShock* are fantastic in that they immerse the player into the creepy world of Rapture almost perfectly.
>
> *Chris Rickwood (Composer, Rickwood Music for Media)*

The foley sounds can either be "performed" to the pre-existing cinematic or they can be recorded and edited individually and later synchronized during the audio post-production process. Either way, the end result is nearly the same. The lines may be a bit blurred between the "types" of required sound effects, but this is where being familiar with each discipline of sound design really comes into play.

Courtesy of SAE Institute Sydney

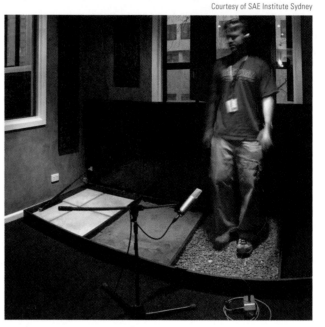

A foley pit allows sound designers to record samples used in post-production.

Footfalls are by far the most performed sound in film and a good example for discussion. Since they are recorded live while the foley artist is viewing the scene, each footfall is naturally distinct. The pitch, intensity of the step, and variation of the surface will change each time—whereas no two will ever sound the same. Within the game environment, memory constraints often limit the amount of sounds available—and for sounds such as footfalls that may be repeated continuously, there are sometimes only a few variations that are actually implemented.

Repetition is not the most preferred use of a sound effect, and every effort should be made to ensure that players never notice they are hearing the same sound repeatedly. For footfalls, having several individual sounds to trigger randomly is one way around this pitfall. The sound engine can also be programmed to alter the pitch and volume of each step or add effects processing, such as reverb, as the repeated sound is triggered. Either way, the production team should keep repetition of sounds to a minimum and strive to keep the playback of each sound fresh.

Remote Recording

Obtaining sounds *remotely*—outside of an acoustically treated studio and in uncontrolled conditions—is the extreme end of sound recording and something that game sound designers do quite frequently. Not only do they need the patience and skills to accomplish the job effectively, but specialized equipment is required to make the most of what can often be the absolute worst of circumstances. Game projects, like any other form of entertainment, rely on the sound professionals to give them their own "audio" identity; since everyone has access to the same sound libraries, the only way to ensure originality is to grab the remote gear and hit the road to capture previously unrecorded sounds. Not only does this fulfill the need for fresh sounds, but it also ensures that the copyright ownership of the recordings can be transferred to the game developer if required.

The game project will dictate the type of sounds needed and the preferred method for obtaining them, with budget constraints and contractual points further defining the path required by the sound designer. Large budgets will usually allow for field recordings to capture unique sounds; in this situation, the developer usually insists upon full ownership of any recordings the sound designer makes while performing work for the contract. Smaller-budget projects might rely more on sound library recordings or will allow the recordist to retain the rights to the sounds captured. Many options are possible to meet the needs of all parties involved.

Remote recording typically encompasses sessions that can't be achieved within a recording studio due to safety, health, or size issues, or even scheduling conflicts. It's extremely impractical to record a race car engine, cannon shots, or smashing debris in a studio for many reasons; the only reasonable solution is to take the studio on location. With battery operated recorders and microphone pre-amps—and a variety of sturdy field microphones, stands, booms, cables, and bags of necessary extras in hand—the sound designer is fully equipped to ensure that at least the technical requirements are met.

Audio director Will Davis prepares for remote recording.

Even with the right equipment, recording in the field can be fraught with unpredictability. The location of the objects or environment being recorded can also make a huge difference in the process. It is entirely possible to capture solid, useable sounds in between jet arrivals at the local airport, but this situation would be totally unacceptable for quieter, ambience effects. For those, selecting a better time of day or night might be the best way to avoid unwanted interruptions.

Remote recording can be quite a challenge regardless of the experience level. Rain or high winds can devastate recordings and equipment. Blistering heat or piercing cold not only affect the gear but the operators as well. Mechanical issues with the recording devices and the objects being recorded often bring the session to a grinding halt. Uncooperative bystanders can interfere at the most inopportune times, rendering takes unusable. Animal subjects almost never perform on cue—and when they do, the sounds they make aren't the ones needed. In the end, remote recording is a test of patience. Since the variables are great, almost nothing is under your control and it often takes an extraordinary effort just to be there in the first place. The sound designer has to be ready for anything.

In-Studio Recording

In-studio recording is the most desirable method for capturing quality game sounds. Not only are the conditions controllable and predictable, but studio gear is often of higher quality than smaller, portable equipment. Most large game developers have spent thousands of dollars on acoustically designed and well-equipped recording spaces for their in-house audio teams. Third-party contractors spend a large part of their budgets on recording equipment and also take great care with their own personal spaces. Even those who don't have defined areas understand the importance; they typically ally themselves with commercial recording studios when the need arises. Recording spaces are an important tool in the game development process.

Beyond sound effects such as car crashes, jet engines, and explosions, studios are useful for practically everything else. From the subtle sound of an expended shell casing hitting the ground to the dynamic strike of a crowbar forcefully colliding with an old car hood, the controlled conditions of the studio will make the job easier and give better results. Random outside noise is seldom a factor, and the sound designer can focus on creating the perfect sound instead of having to rely on luck out in the field.

The best part about working in the studio is the abundance of quality tools close at hand. Whether sounds are being recorded into a top of the line Pro Tools system or through an analog board to an analog multitrack tape deck, the chances are that the gear being used is far better than any remote gear available. Outboard processors offer choices of preamps and real time effects that can be invaluable during the creation process. Let's not forget the security of having backup equipment available in case something becomes inoperable. Studios are definitely the first choice when recording game sound effects.

Courtesy of SAE Institute Singapore

Recording session in a studio

Original Recording

Most creatures, vehicles, weapons, and alien planets depicted in games don't actually exist in the real world. Due to this conundrum, the simple task of sticking a microphone in front of something and recording it won't come close to producing the results a game may require. Using sounds that are associated with familiar objects in real-life risks breaking the immersive effect of the audio—something that must be protected at all cost—so it's not prudent to even consider that route. Instead, game sound designers turn to another one of their many skill sets to provide the answer: *original recording* and development.

Courtesy of SAE Institute Madrid

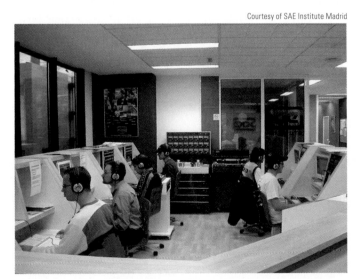

Workstations are used to edit recording and mixing sessions.

There are thousands of ways to create "make believe" sounds, but it takes a measure of skill to ensure that it is done believably. The type of sounds needed will drive the initial creative direction, whether it is based on something real or something completely fabricated. For example, we can assume an alien spaceship must have a power source to propel it through the depths of space. Creating the engine sound could easily be based on a pre-existing rocket or jet engine sound, or even sound from a vacuum cleaner—anything that gives a sense of "power." These sources could be driven though various effects processors or plug-ins to give the appropriate "alien" feel to them and then layered to create the final sound. These types of sounds, based on real objects, work well because they give a sense of familiarity but are different enough to be believably alien.

Contorting pre-existing sounds isn't the only route the sound designer can take in the original development process. Sounds can be generated entirely from scratch through a variety of sound sources such as keyboards, sound modules, virtual instruments, samplers, or tone generators and then processed and edited to create the needed effect. This method is often preferred in instances where pre-existing samples are unavailable or when the overall audio theme prescribes a more electronic feel. Using the previous alien spaceship engine sound as an example, this can also be created believably using this method. A simple low synthesizer note could be linearly pitch shifted (some audio editors refer to this as "pitch bend") and edited in such a way to replicate an electronic sounding "power up" effect to serve the purpose. There are also times when layering "electronic" with manipulated pre-existing sounds will produce the perfect sound effect. The key is to be open to trying whatever it takes.

Sound designers also have the option of utilizing specialized software or effects processors designed specifically to create unique, one-of-a-kind sounds. Sound-mangling software in particular generates its own signal, adds effects processing, and morphs it into the direction of the user for some often spectacular results. While the sounds created are unique, the disadvantage is that the amount of experimentation often needed to create anything useful can slow the creative process. Knowledge of the software's capabilities will streamline the effort and maintain productivity.

Sound Libraries

Sound libraries can be lifesavers when creating sound effects. The advantage of sound libraries is that they provide a wide selection of sounds in many formats (e.g., DVD, CD, or download). These high-quality recordings save massive amounts of time and place the expense of creating them on someone else for a change. The prime disadvantage is that everyone has access to the same libraries, and it can be tough to maintain any kind of originality. Many times an overused sound will actually distract players as their minds associate it with something else they've heard in the past. Breaking the spell of the game can be avoided by staying clear of such overused sounds.

Using sound libraries and being familiar with their content is a skill acquired with experience. Good sound designers can match particular sounds to their associated libraries (usually after hearing them on a movie or television program), and this familiarity translates well when knee-deep in a project of their own. Grabbing the exact library and file you need saves enormous time and keeps the creative process rolling, something which is appreciated with a rapidly approaching deadline. Knowing how to effectively use sound libraries is an essential skill.

Tommy Tallarico's SFX Kit

Sound libraries typically contain regular audio or digitized files (e.g., .wav) and are also available in CD, DVD, and occasionally hard drive formats for the large collections. While sound designers have the option of auditioning and saving audio tracks straight from disk, most will save each library as digitized files for easier archiving, faster auditioning, and streamlined use. Since sound for games is digitized as part of the sound design process anyway, doing this step beforehand can save an incredible amount of time over the course of a production.

Being familiar with each library is essential and will help make the creation process more efficient. A general knowledge of the sounds available—their quality, usability, and how they are labeled—will simplify the process. In order to manage literally millions of separate sounds, it's common for sound designers to make use of a variety of search tools—utilizing keywords such as "stab," "zap," or "whoosh" to find a specific sound. These functional search tools can be found online at vendor websites or packaged with each library.

Recommended Sound Libraries

Sound Ideas (www.sound-ideas.com) and The Hollywood Edge (www.hollywood-edge.com) are both major sound library distributors that offer extensive themed collections. Libraries range from common, everyday household sounds to all out, original creations from some of the top sound designers in the film, television, and game industries. These collected works can be quite expensive but are lifesavers when it's logistically impossible to record sounds such as explosions or jet fighters. As an alternative, several online storefronts such as SoundDogs.com and Sound-Effects-Library.com provide the option to audition and download specific sounds instead of having to license an entire library.

Production Cycle

In a perfect world, the sound designer would be involved in the game development process from the very start. As the rest of the production team solidifies the theme, objectives, and timeline of the project, the sound designers can establish early ideas and set a clear course for their role in the process. During the natural course of a game's construction, each creative production element lives, breathes, and eventually nurtures well-conceived stories, characters, gameplay, and programming to make it all happen. The more time the sound team has to experiment and develop their own content, the better the game experience will be. However, nothing is ever quite as perfect as we'd like to think in the chaotic world of game creation.

With the exception of larger game companies that have the luxury of an in-house sound department, content providers are brought in much later than you might expect. Partly due to the fiscal restraints against hiring a sound designer before sounds are needed and partly because artwork and programming aren't in place until the alpha or beta version, sound effects aren't usually even considered until late in the development process. For the developer, this can be a double-edged sword. Bring a sound designer on staff too early, and the company won't see an immediate return on the investment. Bring a sound designer in too late, and you'll might be left with missed milestones or hastily created sounds.

It's a different view from where the sound designer stands, for whom getting involved as early as possible is definitely the way to go. Ideas take time to grow, even for an experienced audio professional—and having time at the beginning of the production cycle to determine the appropriate way to proceed can save headaches down the road. As conceptual artwork and storyline are finalized, the best route to take sound-wise will present itself—but only if the sound designer is allowed to be close by. Is the game based in a real or fantasy world? Will the sounds need to be realistic or imagined? Will they be subtle or "over the top"? The answers become obvious and give the sound designer a solid direction to pursue.

Only after a firm course is established can the sound team get organized and prepare for the creation process. This is the time where we determine the needed sound assets, establish a plan of action, solidify a schedule, and begin initial sound gathering and recording. Since the game isn't ready for sound effects yet, these won't be created during at this point—but it's possible to purchase and set up equipment and software, make field recordings, acquire sound libraries, and refine the overall *sound palette*—a set of sound elements established as the foundation for a specific project's sound effects (narrowing millions of available sounds down to a manageable level, making effects easier to create, and giving the game a defined audio identity). This step can take anywhere from a couple of days to several months, depending on the scope of the game project—and getting it done before the pressures of looming deadlines will relieve a lot of stress later on.

As artwork and programming assets are implemented into a working version of the game, sound effects will finally be needed. Often in the early phases, placeholder sounds are used to test the audio engine, and scripted sound triggers are used to showcase ideas—both as proof of concept to investors and to give a life and momentum to the project. The sound designer is involved with these early tests and uses this opportunity to start developing ideas that might be pursued later. Sound effects created at this point may be rough and not specifically timed to any animations, since those will be amended before the game is done—but they will serve as a good foundation for the work to follow.

Diagram by Per Olin

Phase 1

(Concept Development & Pre-Production - design and production plan complete)

- Purchase and set up equipment and software
- Create field recordings
- Acquire sound libraries
- Refine sound palette

Phase 2

(Production - art and programming assets incorporated into game prototype)

- Implement placeholder sounds
- Test audio engine and scripted sound triggers

Phase 3

(Post-Production - design, art and programming final)

- Create final sound effects
- Incorporate sound assets into game engine

Typical phases in game audio development

Typically, the final third of a development cycle is where sound effects are created in earnest. Many elements have a tendency to change as ideas are considered or discarded, so it doesn't make much sense to waste time on sounds that won't be used or will be redone. Only after the artwork, animation, and programming are finalized, the sound designer can get down to business and create exactly what is needed—fully synchronized and ready to drop in the game.

Determining Required Sounds

"During the preliminary planning phases of game creation, the sky is the limit. The game will have brilliant 3D graphics, intuitive gameplay, a full orchestral score, *Star Wars* quality sound effects—and it will all be done in six months for under $100,000." If only the reality of game development were that optimistic. Plans change and compromises are made due to many stumbling blocks that present themselves along the way.

On the sound front, many developers feel that everything that looks like it can make a noise has to have a sound created for it. A *sound asset list* is fleshed out, and the sound designer is given the daunting task of producing each one according to this initial assessment. However, as the development cycle progresses, it becomes painfully obvious that this first plan is overly ambitious and adjustments have to be made. Initially, the game platform's memory and processor restraints become apparent, as artwork and other assets compete for a defined capacity. Not everything will fit through the pipeline efficiently, so the number and size of the assets are reduced. Disk or cartridge space on which the game is to be stored also has a finite volume— and, once again, assets are reduced or compressed. Unfortunately, the audio is usually the first to fall victim—and drastic steps are taken to make it work.

	A	B	C	D	E
2	KEY AUDIO ASSET LIST - WEAPONS, ATTACHMENTS AND EQUIPMENT				
4	TIER 1 - ESSENTIALS				
6	UNITED STATES MILITARY				
8	NAME	TYPE	NOTES	COMPLEXITY	DURATION (estimate
10	WEAPONS		* COLOR DENOTES HAS ATTACHMENTS		
12	MULTIPURPOSE BAYONET	BAYONET			
13	M4A1	ASSAULT RIFLE	* REUSED BY UK FORCES	3	3
14	M16A4	ASSAULT RIFLE	* REUSED BY UK FORCES	7	15
15	M249	MACHINE GUN		3	3
16	M240G	MACHINE GUN	* REUSED BY UK FORCES	8	20
17	M21	SNIPER RIFLE		7	15
18	M107	SNIPER RIFLE		7	15
19	AT4	ANTI-TANK MISSILE		6	12
20	JAVELIN	ANTI-TANK MISSILE	* REUSED BY UK FORCES	6	12
21	SMAW	ANTI-TANK MISSILE		6	12
22	M244 60MM MORTAR	MORTAR		7	15
23	STINGER	SURFACE TO AIR MISSILE		6	12
24	M92F BERETTA	BERETTA		6	12
25	COLT .45	PISTOL		6	12
26	MP5A4	SUB MACHINEGUN	* REUSED BY UK FORCES	7	15
27	MP5N	SUB MACHINEGUN	VARIATION OF MP5 A4	8	5
28	MP5K - PDW	SUB MACHINEGUN	VARIATION OF MP5 A4	8	5
29	MK16 MOD 0	ASSAULT RIFLE	* REUSED BY UK FORCES	7	15
30	MK17 MOD 0	ASSAULT RIFLE	VARIATION OF MK 16 MOD 0	8	5
31	MK48 MOD 0	MACHINE GUN		8	20
32	MK 23 MOD 0 SOCOM	PISTOL		6	12
33	MK11 MOD 0	ASSAULT RIFLE		4	5
34	M67 FRAG GRENADE	GRENADE		4	5

Part of a typical sound effects asset list

Sound effects that were presented in the first sound asset list are reevaluated with the idea of reducing the amount needed. It's often an unpleasant task, but there are obvious choices that can be made. Footfalls, gunshots, explosions, and any other sound that may be heard multiple times can be strategically cut back. It may have been a great idea to reduce repetition by having a dozen different footfalls for each surface, but this could easily be cut in half if needed. The same could be done for gunshots or explosions as well. Since these types of sounds can be coded to trigger randomly, the development team can get away with using fewer of the same types of sounds in order to save space.

A simple test can be constructed to determine how many variations will give the illusion without being repetitive. During chaotic gameplay, typically found in action games such as FPSs, a player can easily suffer from sensory overload. With explosions, gunfire, screaming, ambience, environmental sounds, dialogue, music, and everything else playing at once, the soundscape can quickly become a nightmare. Even if everything has an associated sound to it, this doesn't mean they have to all play at once!

Developers select sound effects based on their entertainment value and those that best convey what is happening in the game at that moment. When sound effects are implemented, they will be prioritized in order of their importance with these ideas in mind. In an FPS, gunshots, explosions, voice commands, and character sounds will have a higher priority than sounds which occur in the distance or off screen. As a game moves further into its development, sounds that are consistently tagged as low priority and serve no specific purpose might be dropped in order to save processing power or space. There's a delicate balance between creating a believable soundscape and confusing the player with the bombardment of sound. This is an issue definitely worth considering for the sake of a game's quality.

The sound engineering in *Tom Clancy's Rainbow Six: Vegas 2* keeps players from being overwhelmed, even during intense action.

:::

Sound effects serve a very specific role in video games; they entertain, provide feedback, present important information, and breathe life into the virtual world. Without them, the experience would be far from satisfying. Sound designers have a huge responsibility to the development team, the game itself, and the player, to create and implement an effective soundscape using a wide variety of unique skills and tools. Game sound design is not an easy job by any stretch of the imagination, and doing quality work takes effort. By establishing a solid knowledge base—and having the appropriate equipment and the skills to do the job well—the sound designer can be a powerful force on the game development team. While past stigmas still haunt the audio side of this business, players are pleasantly surprised and impressed with the utility and quality of today's sound effects. All it takes of the sound designer is well-directed effort and the desire to do the job well.

Function of Game Sound Effects: bringing the game to life   chapter 3

:::CHAPTER REVIEW:::

1. Play 3 games currently available and identify the purposes of the sound effects in each game. How do the sound effects set the mood, add realism, provide clues to surroundings, enhance entertainment value, create tactile and interface feedback, or establish brand identity?

2. Referring to the same 3 games you chose in Exercise 1, discuss the placement of the sound effects in each game. Do the sound effects appear in association with animated logos, cinematics/cut-scenes, interface/menu screens, ambience/environmental effects, or main interaction/ player feedback effects? How appropriate are the sound effects in these areas?

3. Describe the various sound design disciplines—including foley, remote recording, in-studio recording, original recording/development, and sound libraries—and discuss how well-suited you are for each. What are the pros and cons of each discipline with regard to game audio?

4

Creating Game Sound Effects

the art of sound design

Key Chapter Questions

■ What are the main *technical* aspects that must be determined prior to the creation of game sound effects?

■ How does the psychology of human *emotion* influence the creation of game sound?

■ What is the process of *creating* game sound effects?

■ What are the main objectives of the sound *editing* process?

■ What is the importance of *beta testing* during the sound design process?

After months of planning and preparation, the game is at the stage where sound effects can be implemented—and the sound designer's creative powers are unleashed. Most of the animation, art, and programming are in place—and what was already a busy pre-production period for the sound designer has just turned chaotic. The pressure is on, and the sound design team will be busy. The sound design document or sound asset list will be resolved as the development team makes its final assessment—now knowing exactly what sounds are needed and the storage or processor constraints that are available. Even with this final list in place, sounds will still be added, changed, or removed. The game assets, animations, coding, and art are revised and tweaked right up to the last minute. The sound designer's work often doesn't end until the game goes "gold."

Pre-Production

With the finalization of assets, the sound designer will have a solid idea of what needs to be accomplished during *pre-production*. Game production relies heavily on meeting milestones in a timely manner. Unfortunately, the sound designer is placed in an awkward position while the rest of the team waits for the sound effects—which can only be done correctly after the other assets are in place. If the rest of the game is already behind, it becomes the hope that sound effects can be completed without pushing the release of the game. Obviously, the solution to this is to have most of the sound elements organized and sound effects that don't require synchronization already created. An in-house sound team might have this luxury and may have already planned for this inevitability, but this doesn't happen by accident.

Certain steps should be taken before any sound effects are created. In Chapter 3, we discussed the need to record or collect required sounds and elements that will be used to form the final sounds. This should definitely be completed prior to this point in the development cycle, since time becomes a critical factor later. The collected sounds then need to be logically organized, preferably as high-resolution sound files on a central hard drive or server, and made accessible to the members of the sound team. It is essential that the team only use these pre-selected sounds and sound elements to ensure consistency in the other sounds that will be created.

If more than one sound designer is working on a project, it is important to define a clear division of labor. Dividing a large project into smaller, more manageable pieces will make it easier on each sound team member and prevent any overlap. With assigned tasks, sound designers can maintain more focus on their work—and this in turn will produce more creative sounds and increased consistency. For example, a sound designer might be tasked with all sounds in a particular level—including environmental sounds, ambience, and any other sounds found only in that specific level. When these sounds are heard during gameplay, they won't stick out because none will contain odd characteristics that make them appear different. By having these sounds handled by one person, they will have a better chance of blending in with the quality of the other sounds in that level. Another suggestion would be to assign work that takes advantage of each individual's creative strengths and skill sets. If someone else is better at creating ambience, why not have that person do it? Either way, the game will benefit.

Creating a schedule and sound team milestones is another critical step to ensure that sounds are completed on time. This task is a little more "administrative" than what some creative people typically enjoy—but sitting down with the sound asset list, the divided tasks, and a calendar will give the process an entirely new perspective. A rush job is not conducive to quality work, so there is no need to blast through the creative process if there happens to be plenty of time. Conversely, if the team is on a tight schedule, it might plan on all-nighters or hire an extra hand to see that the job is finished by the deadline.

◇	A	B	C	D
1	PERSON	ROLE	TASK (green tasks refer to detail sheet)	DAYS
2				
3	**Michael**	Audio Director	Hire audio programmer & sound designer	3
4	**Michael**	Audio Director	Assign Khartoum, Marrakesh, Kilimanjaro levels to editors	2
5	**Adam**	Audio Manager	Contract rights to Hatari and other Mancini works	5
6	**Trip**	Audio Editor	Edit cinematics for Marrakesh level	2
7	**Trip**	Audio Editor	Edit sound effects for Khartoum level	3
8	**Will**	Composer	Complete Prehistoric suite for first three cinematics	5
9	**Jesse**	Sound Designer	Complete foley for Marrakesh level	1
10	**Jesse**	Sound Designer	Begin foley for Prehistoric level	4
11	**Evie**	Voiceover Director	Record Khartoum cinematics and level dialogue	5
12	**Travis**	Audio Engineer	Assist in Khartoum recordings	5
13	**Angela**	Audio Programmer	Check format compatibility with all current audio files	5

Example of a simple weekly task sheet

Contracted sound designers have an entirely different perspective due to their involvement later in the process. If they have been afforded the opportunity to preview and prepare beforehand, their course of action is similar to that of the in-house team—and they will have completed any pre-recordings, gathered and organized sound elements, and created any basic sound effects. However, more often than not, none of this will be accomplished until the contracts are signed and the sound designer is given the green light. This can be an extremely intense period for the contractor, who must cover a lot of ground in a short time. Even in this tight production schedule, pre-planning is a crucial step to success in meeting the required timeline.

Technical Considerations

With pre-production accomplished, there is one final aspect that must be taken into account before the sound designer gets too involved in the creative process. Any endeavor that involves technology always requires the establishment of specific boundaries so that everything works predictably. Game platforms have their individual constraints, audio engines manage sound assets in specific ways, and even playback systems have their limitations. A sound designer has the opportunity to take advantage of an audio engine or a console's touted features—pushing the quality of the work. Just as great features can be exploited, recognizing the boundaries will help the sound team steer clear of many obstacles and decrease the number of headaches along the way.

Mono, Stereo & Surround

Will the final sound files be delivered as single-channel *mono* files, two-channel *stereo* files, six-channel raw *surround* files, or encoded two-channel surround files? Sounds can be delivered in a variety of formats for the same project, and it is important to have these spelled out in advance. Games that utilize spatial or directional orientation of sound in the soundscape will use mono; this way, the sound remains in the same location despite any change in the direction of the player—who may use these cues as points of reference. Sounds that are tagged as priority sounds or are specified as ambience will most likely be either stereo or surround. A sound designer has to know what these parameters are in order to create a sound that works effectively.

Diagram by Per Olin

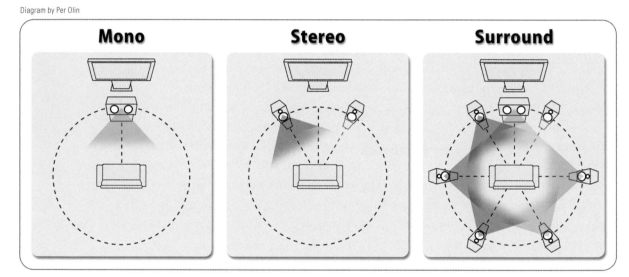

The number of audio channels through which a sound will be played will affect how the sound is created.

Ambience, for example, is intended to surround the player in a believable environment and must be created in stereo at the very least. In the real world, sounds are in constant motion—and a sound designer may simulate this effect by panning between the left and right channels. A fast moving object, such as an aircraft, will normally start on one side of the stereo field and move to the other—giving players a sense of action beyond any direct input they may be providing. Surround sound is obviously the best choice for this application, but you can quickly see why mono wouldn't normally be considered.

Beyond the actual sounds being created, knowing the final format will ensure that a sound designer's valuable time isn't wasted on the wrong approach. Creating mono sounds that must be surround—or spending large amounts of time creating surround sounds only to find out they are needed as single channel—will definitely add pressure to the process.

Sample Rate & Resolution

The standard in today's game production is considered to be 44,100 kHz *sample rate* and 16-bit *resolution*, but many projects still use lower settings such as 22,050 kHz or 8-bit resolution for various reasons. It is important that sound designers create sound effects for each project at the required fidelity at the very least, but it is strongly recommended that sounds are produced at the highest possible quality and then later down-sampled if needed; more sound designers are doing this at 96 kHz/24-bit, which produces incredible clarity and quality to the sounds themselves.

Diagram by Per Olin

File Type	44.1 kHz	22.05 kHz	11.25 kHz
16-bit Stereo	10.1 Mb	5.05 Mb	2.52 Mb
16-bit Mono	5.05 Mb	2.52 Mb	1.26 Mb
8-bit Mono	2.52 Mb	1.26 Mb	630 Kb

Memory required for one minute of digital audio

Down-sampling to 44 kHz/16-bit, for instance, will degrade the sound slightly—but much of its characteristics will still be preserved. Sound designers can get into real trouble if they incorrectly build sounds at a lower sample rate and resolution and have to up-sample later. Since the initial files are of a lower quality, they are still the same "low" quality sound—just saved at a higher rate. There are many occasions in which these parameters can change—mostly after some heavy campaigning by the sound designer who might convince the developer that a higher resolution is better. Always create sound effects at the highest sample rate and resolution possible.

Although it's important to create sound effects at the highest standard, the most influential element is the down-sampling rate. You can save space with 22 kHz/8-bit, but the sound quality is noticeably degraded. Knowing this ahead of time will allow the sound designer to create sound effects accordingly and make them sound their best. Noticeable artifacts are introduced with 8-bit resolution; these are especially prevalent when the sound becomes quieter, such as during a fadeout. Occasionally, a 22 kHz sample rate is used for some lower priority sounds or casual online games; these will have a degraded higher frequency band that is very noticeable for sounds with most of their focus on the higher range, such as shell casings, bells, or dings that will sound dull or like clicks. By understanding what the final sample rate and resolution does to the sound quality, a sound designer can work around any limitation and still create great sound.

Final Format Requirements

The game developer will always specify the required configuration of the final delivered sound files—including sample rate, resolution, number of channels, and file format. As expected, the *final format* will dictate how a sound designer approaches the work in order to maintain the high quality of sound a game demands. Uncompressed formats such as .wav and .aiff are used by most creators to construct sound effects, since they offer the best fidelity. If plenty of memory and processing power are available, these uncompressed formats will actually make it into the game as the final versions. However, there are instances where compressed formats such as .mp3, .ogg, or .au are the better choices, and conversions need to be performed before delivery.

While it may save a tremendous amount of space, conversion to a compressed audio format is not accomplished without consequence. The actual act of conversion discards data that is determined by the compression algorithm to be unnecessary, which in most cases includes high and low frequency sonic data. Most listeners can't detect gentle compression, but it becomes quite obvious as more compression is applied and the bit rate to which it is converted declines. Smart developers will use compressed audio files for background ambience or sound effects that are buried in the soundscape to keep from publicizing their lower fidelity. This is a great method to keep sound files small and save space for more important assets without drawing any attention to a lack of sound quality.

When comparing a compressed audio file to an uncompressed version, it becomes clear that compression algorithms greatly affect the sound. Most noticeably, high frequencies are degraded—which defeats subtleties and gives it a certain dullness. The low frequency range is also affected but it isn't as noticeable, although some degradation is present in the perceived bass. If a low bit rate is used to keep the files small, this will also produce sounds that weren't present in the original recordings, known as compression artifacts.

Sound designers can still work around the limitation of compressed sounds by spending a little extra time with them after the conversion process. Lightly boosting the upper and lower frequency ranges can restore some of the loss, but they unfortunately can't do it completely. The μ-law (pronounced "mew-law") compression algorithm (.au), for example, has no frequency above the 8 kHz range—and any important subtleties that might reside there will be completely lost even after adjustment attempts. The only way around these types of limitations is to have the final file format in mind when creating compressed sounds and working around them from the start.

Playback Expectations

Part of a game's development involves researching player demographics and current game platforms. A sound designer can use this knowledge to create material that sounds best on the most prevalent type of platform. This is not to say that the material won't also sound good on other systems—but by planning for the average platform with its minimum/recommended requirements, the sound designer ensures that the majority of the players will get their money's worth and feel better about their purchase.

Big Stock Photo

A surround sound home theater system is one of the best ways to enjoy a video game.

Sounds created for a subwoofer-equipped home theater system will be approached very differently than a handheld console with a single, tiny speaker. A home theater system is the standard for consoles such as the PlayStation 3, Xbox 360, and Wii—so sounds are expected to be high fidelity, directional, and perhaps surround encoded. Computer/PC games are more stereo oriented due to the typical setup of these platforms—but while hardcore players do have surround systems and large budget games plan for this, making the sounds work in a stereo field is the priority. Games that might appear on a handheld device focus more on mono sounds, but do utilize stereo and surround files as needed. Overall, sound effects should be created with the final playback system in mind in order to take advantage of any features and not be unduly hampered by any limitations.

Platforms

There are dozens of game *platforms* on the market; each of them has a unique method of storing and managing sound assets, which can occasionally become a factor to the sound designer. Will the sounds be compressed? How will they be decompressed: on the fly or preloaded into RAM? Are there memory constraints that require smaller sound files? What type of onboard effects processing is being utilized, and how will it affect the sound? Will the sound files be converted to a proprietary format, and what will these do to the quality? Questions such as these will continually narrow the creation parameters and should be answered before sound effects are even created. With the facts clearly established, the sound designer can effectively manage any side effects.

Nintendo Reprinted with permission from Microsoft Corporation

Platforms such as the Wii (*Endless Ocean*, left) and the Xbox 360 (*Halo 3*, right) have distinct features that affect game sound design.

With the many game platforms and audio engines available to the developer, audio options are plentiful. Much will depend on the needs of the game and how the assets will be managed by both the programming and the hardware. Even when creating different games on the same platform, the sound designer will often find significant differences among them that will force another approach to their work. The key to a successful sound design process is to have an open dialogue with the audio programmer and understand exactly how the sounds will be managed.

This doesn't change how the sound effects will be created, but it can have an impact on how they will sound. Game audio is affected by everything from the circuitry of the game console to the audio engine and the playback system—so while some of this can be managed, other factors can be unpredictable. The best thing the sound designer can do is to ensure that the sound quality is consistent through the majority of possibilities. When working closely with the developer, the sound designer will have access to the target platform and can have direct influence on the use of the audio engine; the only unknown factor is the playback system used by the consumer. This can be dealt with in the final stages after the game is finalized and not still undergoing major changes. The current next-generation game platforms have predictable hardware features that help set the stage for the audio provider.

Sound Design Thought Process

There is a certain mindset the sound designer will employ as the actual creation process begins. Understanding the purpose of sound effects will serve as a good start, but going back a little further into the human psyche will shed additional light on the subject. What distinguishes average sound designers from great ones is their use of sonic elements to actually influence how players feel when they hear the sound.

A little understanding of human psychology can allow the sound designer to create sound effects with emotional impact. We have been conditioned all our lives to respond to sound—such as answering the telephone when it rings, going to the door when there is a knock, and running out of the classroom when the bell sounds. A siren, scream, or loud bang elicit a specific response: to immediately evaluate any threat and our well-being. Other sounds cause us to react physically—such as fingernails scraping a chalkboard, a snarling dog, or the grinding crunch of a breaking bone; these can cause discomfort or fear. A great sound designer will take advantage of these pre-conditioned responses, creating intense and emotionally charged sound effects.

As the sound designer reviews the sound asset list, the next step is to formulate an approach to creating them. Professional sound designers are always listening to the world around them. This simple act hones their creation skills and helps them determine how to go about capturing or recreating any game sounds from scratch. Can the needed sound be captured, or will it have to be manufactured? Is the sound of the object being portrayed "real" enough, or should another sound be used instead? Unfortunately, not all actual sounds are interesting enough for entertainment purposes and will often need a little enhancement to make them work. Either way, these types of creative decisions need to be made early in the process.

A gunshot in a film is typically a loud, forceful sound that portrays the urgency and power of the situation; it grabs your attention and makes a very influential statement. In reality, a gunshot may carry the same strong statement in the action itself—but its sound is nothing more than a simple, unexciting "pop." A game that is trying to engage a player and evoke a strong emotion can't do it with a toy gun that goes "pop, pop, pop." Instead, it has to convey the fury with something much bigger such as a "BLAM!" However, if the goal of the game is to be as realistic as possible, then maybe other sounds or musical accompaniment will be designed to provide the emotional statement.

Creating a gunshot that provides guttural satisfaction every time the trigger is pulled requires a little creativity. It would be logical to start with an actual gunshot, but this is not always necessary. Finding or creating other elements with the same sharp, explosive characteristics is all it takes to make an exciting and satisfying sound effect. One or several of these can be layered appropriately to create an original sound effect that will do the trick.

When faced with any sound effect, it is a good idea to strip the sound to its basic elements and create with these in mind. A gunshot is a quick, explosive sound that has a loud, fast attack and then decays rapidly. What other more available sounds contain these types of characteristics and could be used to create or enhance the sound? Consider the crack of a high pitched snare drum, the hit of an oak axe handle, the burst of a balloon, the smack of an empty tennis shoe on a concrete floor, the slam of a wooden cabinet door, or a pre-recorded explosion pitched higher all as acceptable elements. Layer these sounds, apply appropriate *equalization (EQ)*, add a little reverb—and it'll start to sound pretty good. By shifting the focus away from just simply recording the gunshot, experimentation will lead to better, exciting sounds that really make a statement. This fundamental thought process will lead sound designers down some interesting roads throughout their careers.

Courtesy of Adobe

A machine gun burst is a series of quick, explosive sounds that have a loud, fast attack and then decay rapidly (Audition, shown).

Foley Possibilities

There is an abundance of sounds that can be created using items and methods you might not immediately consider:

- *Crackling fireplace:* This sound can be created by kneading loosely wadded paper or cellophane, crumbling potato chips, or slowly pulling apart Velcro.

- *Breaking bones:* This sound can be created with a quick snap of a stalk of celery or carrot, a dry branch, or anything that crunches when it's destroyed— such as dried walnuts.

- *Bloody stabbing, slashing, or punching:* These sounds can be created by striking a watermelon or piece of raw meat.

- *Heavy stone being moved:* This sound can be created by slowly scraping the lid of the toilet tank and pitching it down to taste.

- *Footsteps on grass:* This sound can be created by unrolling a cassette and stepping on the mound of tape.

- *Wings flapping:* This sound can be created by waving leather or rubber gloves.

It all starts with listening to the world, paying close attention to the characteristics of the sounds, and discovering ways to recreate each of them. This is an incredibly important mindset to master and the key to being a successful sound designer.

The best way for a game sound designer to get into the proper mindset is to be completely immersed in the game—to live and breathe it. The sound effects creator needs to fully understand the game's intentions, characters, and environment in order to create sounds that are appropriate; being totally consumed by the virtual world they will portray is the best way to do this. Obtaining copies of any artwork, storyboards, rough versions of the game, and completed music will serve this purpose well and is highly recommended. Most sound designers find this look into the world they are creating gives them much needed inspiration.

Game Sound Development Cycle

With the boundaries fully established, it is time to get to work. This phase is highly subjective due to the variety of opinions that saturate the production team. If the sound designer is lucky, the producers will recognize the talents of the audio experts they hired and let them create unencumbered. The pressure is already immense, but having a nervous producer constantly breathing down one's neck can really turn up the heat. Since the producers are ultimately responsible, it is understandable why they are so concerned—but if the sound designer remains professional and does some extraordinary work, there will be more room to do the job.

Sound designers approach the creation of each sound effect differently, based on their personal working styles. Some will record or gather sound elements that they feel can be used during the creation process and use these as a foundation for most of their sounds. Others will approach each sound individually, confronting the logistics as they appear and deciding on the more purposeful approach instead. Others will have a good idea already worked out in their minds and manage it methodically, while some prefer to accidentally stumble across a workable idea. There are as many approaches to the process as there are sound designers; it's just a matter of finding what works best and leads to the best results.

Not everything can be planned—and even if it is, there are no guarantees that the final sound effect will even work within the confines of the game. It's a good idea to remain open to doing whatever it takes to create appropriate sound effects, even if the methods seem unconventional or are a bit outside of the comfort zone. A sound designer's identity is not only about how well the job is performed but by the flavor and style of the designer's unique personality and working methods.

> I record my own noises in the field and come back to mix them with sound libraries in order to create something entirely new. It really comes down to being completely dialed into the game's realm.
>
> *Ben Long (Composer/Sound Designer/*
> *Singer-Songwriter, Noise Buffet)*

Robert Burns & Rodney Gates on the Role of Lead Sound Designer:::::

Robert Burns
(Lead Sound Designer,
High Moon Studios)

Robert began his career in the game industry in 2002 as a quality assurance associate at Interplay Entertainment. In 2003, he was promoted to Assistant Sound Editor—and to Sound Designer soon after that. In 2004, he was hired as Sound Designer at Neversoft Entertainment. Later that same year, he moved to San Diego county and took a position as Sound Designer at Sammy Studios (now High Moon). Robert has worked on *The Bourne Conspiracy, Darkwatch, Tony Hawk's Underground 2, Baldur's Gate: Dark Alliance 2,* and *Fallout: Brotherhood of Steel.*

My job is to create a clear vision of the game's audio based on the game director's overall vision, and to work with other sound designers and programmers to implement it. I work closely with a pair of audio programmers to develop new proprietary tools to be used in the game engine, as well as creating and implementing the in-game sound effects, dialogue, and music with the other sound designers on the project. The biggest challenge I find in game audio is coming up with a good mix. The games I work on tend to have the excitement level turned to 11 all the time, which translates into "everything trying to be louder than everything else" audio-wise. In order to get a more dynamic audio mix, I work closely with the audio programmers to create mixing tools that allow the game to dynamically mix itself based on what's currently happening in the game.

Rodney Gates
(Lead Sound Designer,
High Moon Studios)

Rodney grew up in Phoenix, Arizona, and attended the Conservatory of Recording Arts & Sciences. The traditional path of music production engineer did not appeal to him. After picking up *Medal of Honor: Allied Assault*, he was immediately impressed with the quality of the audio and began considering video games as a career choice. In 2004, Rodney began working at High Moon as Associate Sound Designer; now Lead Sound Designer, he has had the opportunity to work on some great games—including *Iron Phoenix, Darkwatch,* and *Robert Ludlum's The Bourne Conspiracy.*

As Lead Sound Designer, my role consists of managing the sound designers working on a title with me, meeting with the other leads on the development and scope of the game, and creating content for the project.

We try to record as much new material for our custom library as we can, usually during the pre-production stage. My responsibilities include:

- organizing field recording trips
- inspiring creativity
- providing solutions
- conceiving of ideas and challenges for the audio programmers
- helping to determine the project's musical direction
- co-directing voice talent

There are many similarities to audio post when it comes to a game's linear cinematics, but there are several other disciplines we get to work with that are unique. There are usually hundreds of animations that require audio. We have memory as well as voice channel budgets to work within, priority schemes to manage, and DSP (digital signal processor) effects to design and integrate. We also get to design and implement the audio for everything as simple as footsteps on up to complex destructible physics props, crossfading vehicle engines, and bellowing monsters—in addition to creating an interactive music system, since you never know what the player is going to do. It's sort of like working on a totally blank canvas similar to an animated feature film—though in a very technical way.

Sound Recording

The most common technique of creating sound effects is to *record* them directly from their source. This ensures their originality and increases the chances of capturing the exact audio the sound designer hopes to achieve. Available sound libraries fulfill this role as well, but there is always a necessary compromise in having to settle for a sound that is "close enough." This method is a logical approach to sound design, and maintaining creative control is a definite advantage. The main rule to respect when pursuing this particular option is to make recordings incorporating the perspective in which they will be played back in the game. It's tempting to record everything close up to capture cleaner recordings, but the end result is that everything will ultimately sound just that: close up. Volume, panning, and reverb effects are tools that may be used to add air and provide additional depth—but nothing expresses the intent of the sound better than capturing it from the viewpoint of the player.

Background sounds and ambience should be captured from a distance as a stereo recording to take advantage of any natural spatial interaction. When heard within a game environment, these properly recorded tracks will provide a more realistic atmosphere and make the entire experience more believable. These can also be taken a step further by recording them in surround, assuming they will be played back in the game in this format. Any games can benefit from this type of treatment, especially those that depict a living environment.

Electronic Arts, Inc.

Half-Life 2 makes heavy use of sounds that directly concern the player.

Sound effects that are part of an onscreen character's immediate vicinity are best when recorded from a medium perspective as either mono or stereo. First-person shooters (FPSs) such as *Medal of Honor* or *Half-Life 2* make heavy use of sounds such as weapon handling, footsteps, body falls, and injuries that directly concern the player—and their realistic representation is necessary for the immersive effect. These sounds can be recorded from a closer distance and adjusted with volume, EQ, and reverb if necessary—but in order to produce sounds of the highest possible quality, this should be avoided.

Close miking is a technique that serves its own specific purpose in sound effects production and often yields interesting and sometimes unexpected results. A sound that is recorded close to the microphone brings out exaggerated elements that under normal circumstances wouldn't be noticed. This practice not only allows for a cleaner recording—but the recorded object can be used for something entirely different, resulting in a unique presentation and a previously unheard sound.

Listening Up Close

Operating a retractable ball point pen from arm's length produces the standard "click click" sound associated with a standard pen. However, when held against the ear, the simple "click" becomes more complex—and the sounds of scraping plastic pieces and the "ping" of the spring is very apparent. This closely miked sound could be used as a toggle switch or, if lowered in pitch, as a weapon loading sound. This method can completely change the approach to creative sound design and is well worth the effort.

Steve Johnson on the Importance of Technical Knowledge⁙⁙

After graduating from the University of Richmond in 2002 with nothing but a degree in English and a lot of student loan debt, Steve decided to take a shot at what he already knew was his passion: sound design. He returned to his hometown of Chicago and got his feet wet working on student films before landing a post-production internship at Chicago Recording Company. The experience proved invaluable, resulting in an assistant engineer position at David Axelbaum's audio post studio, Airstream Audio, in December 2003. As much fun as commercials and the occasional documentary were, sound design beckoned—and Steve headed to San Francisco in 2005 with DVDs in hand for the Game Developers Conference. One of the DVDs hit the mark with Sony Computer Entertainment America's Sound Design Manager, Dave Murrant. Steve moved to San Diego to join SCEA as Associate Sound Designer in July 2005. He was given the opportunity to work on several titles in a wide range of capacities: sound design, mixing, effects recording/editing, foley, walla, voiceover, music, and motion capture dialogue. He had a blast on titles such as Sony's *NBA, MLB, God of War*—and ATV franchises *Warhawk, flOw, Blastfactor, Lair*, and *Pain*. In July 2007, Steve transferred to SCEA's Santa Monica studio to focus on sound design for PlayStation Network downloadable games and the upcoming *God of War III*.

Steve Johnson
(Sound Designer,
Sony Computer
Entertainment America)

Learn Pro Tools. It is pretty much the de facto digital audio workstation (DAW) in all audio industries. Some argue that there are better alternatives, and they're probably right. In truth, what mostly matters is that you learn a DAW so that your "canvas" is second nature and all the ins and outs and shortcut commands are under your fingertips—freeing your mind to focus on the real work. If that's your goal, why not choose the DAW you're likely to find in most every studio and mix stage around the world? . . . If you're interested in sound, then really get into sound. There are so many crazy sound programs floating around on the Internet. Force yourself to seek out new tools all the time. And keep the cool stuff you make organized. Sound designers are only as good as their sounds—and your sound library is your paint, so start building it. . . . Audio technology, especially in the game industry, is constantly evolving. You should be passionate about what you do and always strive to be learning something new. If you've been learning a lot—but start thinking that the more you know, the less you actually feel like you know—then you're on the right path. . . . If you plan to work in audio, you'll work in studios, and you'll be around gear—a lot. Being able to make your own cables or solder a patch bay, understanding voltage and impedance and signal flow, etc., are things that will make your life easier—and make you a more valuable, respected resource to the increasing number of people who lack that knowledge.

Synthesized Sound

Games often center around futuristic or science fiction themes; since the accompanying sounds don't exist in the real world, unique methods of creating them are necessary. Synthesized sounds, whether created from synthesizers or other electronic tone-generating tools, allow the sound designer to produce a wide variety of electronic or "spacey" effects such as laser zaps, computer bleeps, sirens, white noise, and tuned notes to use alone or as elements in other sounds. Synthesized tones begin with a specified frequency and waveform shape (sine, square, triangle or saw wave) and are manipulated to create the needed sound effect. These tones can be generated directly from an analog or digital synthesizer, sound module, or sound producing software using one of many presets—and further adjusted by controlling oscillators, filters, envelopes, and voltage to create a foundation for the rest of the sound. Once generated, these tones can be further manipulated using processing such as pitch shifting or bending, delays, chorusing, and reverb to give the sound personality and purpose. It's astonishing the variety of sound effects that can be created using simple tones and a little creativity.

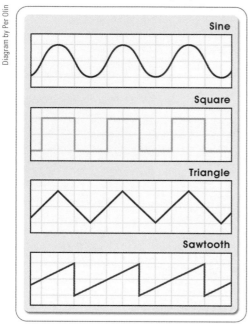

Diagram by Per Olin

Sine

Square

Triangle

Sawtooth

A sound's waveform gives it a distinct character—from a smooth sine wave to a harsh sawtooth.

Creating an Electronic Button Press

Button presses are typically very short and subtle sounds. Generate a 0.1 second, 440 kHz, sine wave tone in any audio editing program. This should be a very quick and very plain monotone sounding "boop." In order to spice it up a bit and give it a button press quality, apply a pitch bend effect. Open a pitch bend tool and adjust it so that at the beginning of the file, the pitch is lowered to -24 semitones and the pitch rises to the end of the file to +24 semitones. This is the equivalent of a four-octave range from the start to the finish of the sound file—and, because the sound is very short, it will produce a fast change from low to high (something like a "bwip!" instant button press sound effect). This new button press sound can also easily be turned into a laser weapon or engine sound by copying and pasting it so that it repeats about 10 times. This laser/engine sound can be further manipulated to sound like large fan blades rotating by pitch shifting the entire file down by 30 semitones. Apply a reverse tool to the entire fan blade sound and it becomes an electronic bass drum beat. Pitch shift the bass drum beat file up by 50 semitones and it becomes another laser weapon sound. Apply the same pitch bend settings used on the button sound to this new laser sound—and another, "meaner" laser weapon sound is created. It's incredible to think that all of these sounds were based on the same monotone "boop" sound.

Audio Morphing

Audio morphing (or *mangling*) is a relatively new term that has become prevalent with the introduction of specially designed software applications. While some may refer to the act of manipulating and modifying sound as "morphing," the use of this term is more specific to the technique where the alteration of the sound actually drives the creative process. Software applications such as Camel Audio's Cameleon or U&I's MetaSynth are examples that work well for sound design creation and give the content provider powerful tools to bring fresh and truly unique sounds to the game experience.

Courtesy of U&I Software

MetaSynth gives the content provider powerful tools to bring fresh and truly unique sounds to the game experience.

Atmospheres and textural ambience creation benefit greatly from these types of tools. These programs are capable of creating complex and moving soundscapes with unlimited rhythmic elements—affecting the mood of the environment using unfamiliar sounds. Importing pre-existing sound files is also permitted—allowing plain sound effects to be morphed or re-synthesized into fresh and exciting sounds far beyond the capabilities of standard processing.

Creating truly unique sounds is always one of the goals of the sound designer, and these programs will certainly deliver. Unfortunately, there is also a huge learning curve associated with these particular applications—and much experimentation and familiarity is often needed to create predictable results. However, this does not prevent the designer from stumbling upon something very usable during experimentation. Once the creative faucet has been opened, anything can happen.

::::: Exploring Cameleon 5000 as a Sound Design Tool

Camel Audio's Cameleon 5000 is a powerful and highly functional software synthesizer. To the musician, it brings a fresh musical perspective and offers a wide range of instruments. However, in the hands of a sound designer, this "musical" program becomes a pliable morphing, additive synthesis, and re-synthesis tool that allows the creative manipulation of any imported sound. It is particularly useful for creating an uneasy or dark ambience, such as found in the game *F.E.A.R.*, or when something recognizable but a little off the wall is needed.

Courtesy of Camel Audio   Courtesy of Monolith Productions, Inc.

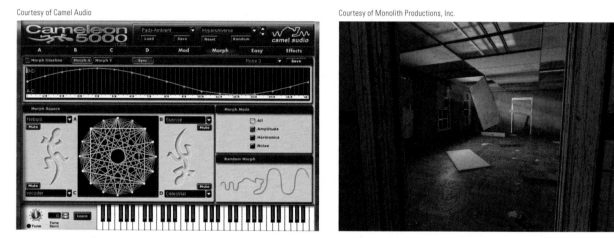

Cameleon 5000 is particularly useful for creating an uneasy or dark ambience, such as in *F.E.A.R.*

All the sound designer needs to do is to import 1-4 sounds, adjust their parameters on the interface, and establish how these sounds will evolve on their own or morph together. Not only can these sounds be manipulated using standard synthesizer functions, but effects processing such as reverb, chorus, or delay will give the creation even more uniqueness. For those who are more unsystematic in their approach, this program offers a "random" feature that adjusts the morphing and effects parameters arbitrarily—which can be used or manipulated further to meet the needs. This type of program can really be an asset to the sound designer.

Samplers

Samplers and other sound sources give the sound designer further creative options. Imagine loading several gunshots and similar elements into a sampler, key mapping each sound over several notes and then auditioning how they work together in real time. The simple action of pressing notes on a musical keyboard allows the sound designer to test each element, and then layer and tune them until the sound works appropriately. Elements can easily be added or discarded as they are auditioned.

Samplers also allow the sound designer to "perform" sound effects in real time, adding a human element to the production. This particular system is handy when creating audio for cinematics and animation, giving the content creator the ability to visually follow the onscreen movements and manually synchronize the sounds to them. Game animations cannot always be imported into audio software, and it becomes a hit or miss process for the sound designer to match them. The ability to perform while observing them in action gets the job done faster and with better results.

It is not always possible or practical to have the developer create separate animation files for every object that moves. This can sometimes present a challenge to a sound designer responsible for creating a sound that will synchronize perfectly. Depending on the time available, the "hit or miss" approach using a multitrack program is used—or the sound elements are loaded into a sampler and performed in real time by the sound designer. By watching the animation work within the game—and with a little practice—the sound can be "performed" in sync and recorded to an audio editor for final editing. The only real difficulty in this technique is to keymap each sound element appropriately and choose the correctly pitched note during the performance.

Courtesy of Native Instruments, Inc.

Kontakt is a powerful VST software sampler that can produced incredible results in game sound design.

Tuning Techniques

All audio in casino games is created in the key of C major specifically to ensure a pleasant, harmonious sound emanating from the casino floor. This means the C, E, and G notes will be in primary use throughout the array of games. Creating a spin sound effect with a prominent "hum" will require a little tuning to make sure this hum is in key. Auditioning this sound, and then pitching it up or down as necessary, will help the sound designer create a sound that blends well with the rest of the game. This technique can also be used in nearly every game project to create sounds that mix well together or purposely stand out from any music that may be playing. Let's say that the music playing in a level is in the key of D and the main evil character's sword strike doesn't quite sound nasty enough. Instead of tuning the sound to match the music's key, like you might do with the "good" characters, you could show how vile the bad character is by de-tuning the sword strike to something like a D flat or A flat on purpose. Auditioning this sound using a sampler and keyboard as the game's background music is playing will help the sound designer determine the absolute "worst" sound to use.

Samplers also have adjustable parameters, similar to synthesizer functions, which can be applied to pre-recorded sounds with some interesting results. Whether it is an instrument sample, a sound effect, or other audio element, the sound can be manipulated using various oscillators, filters, and any onboard effects processors once it is loaded into the sampler. Consider this technique as similar to what can be done with a generated sound wave on a synthesizer—only these sounds are created separately and then manipulated within the same type of device. Much of sound design relies heavily on experience and the predictability it brings to the process, but there is much to be said about experimentation and the originality it can bring as well; these techniques encourage more spontaneity than most and are yet another way to create great sound effects.

Sequencers

Sequencers enable the sound designer to control the many samplers, sound modules, and keyboards they may have in their inventory, and allow the creation of highly complex and effective sound effects. Once sounds are loaded and selected, they can be triggered and mixed as with a multitrack recorder—and mixed down and recorded as final once the results are satisfactory. This technique allows for a bit more impulsiveness than other methods—since sound selection, non-destructive effects processing, and parameter adjustments can be considered before any final decisions are actually made. Often, an interesting mix of audio is discovered in the process that adds the desirable flavor of uniqueness. This technique essentially automates a "real-time" performance and permits corrective timing, volume, or panning adjustments that can't be done on the fly.

Courtesy of Roland

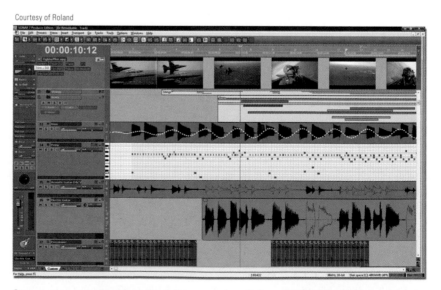

Sequencers embedded in audio software such as Cakewalk SONAR are all very robust and have far more capabilities than they ever did as standalone products.

The sequencer is widely used in other forms of music creation. Instruments and corresponding notes are triggered, layered, and mixed to create many forms of music. Sound designers also benefit from the features and flexibility of these applications, whether they are musically influenced sound effects or other types of audio. Novelty, casino, and other casual games profit from this particular method since they rely on a more musical feel to the sound effects and are often tuned to a specific key so that all games in the same location produce a pleasant harmony. Since this has to be applied consciously, the sequencer and its key tuning function can ensure that this need is met.

High energy and rapid playback of sound influences the energy level of the player and builds excitement. In musical terms, this is achieved by heavy use of 1/16th and occasionally 1/32nd noted arpeggios played in a strict cadence. Flawlessly performing these types of sounds in real time is difficult, if not impossible—but with the assistance of a sequencer, these sounds can be perfectly quantized to a specific timing and tempo. Players will hardly notice the perfectly played notes, but a note that plays slightly before or after the beat will catch their ears and distract them from the experience.

Consider the technique of creating a button press sound by pitch bending a short tone from a low note to one four octaves higher. Creative use of a sequencer can create a similar but more interesting button sound—by a quick, perfectly timed sequence of programmed notes. Instead of sliding the frequencies over a four-octave spread with a pitch bend, the sequencer allows the succession of frequency jumps that specifically hit each note instead of just ascending through them. This button example only begins to showcase the types of sounds that can be created via a sequencer and the nearly infinite instruments available.

Using Sequencers in Casino Game Sound Effects

Spins on retro casino slot games appear to have a certain randomness to them, which ensures that the player isn't distracted or annoyed as the sound repeats with each pull of the handle. Producing a spin sound with a sequencer gives the sound designer the ability to adjust the notes, timing, and instruments for the best sequence—all without committing to any of it until completion. This type of sound creation often requires much experimentation, and the capabilities of a sequencing program allow the sound designer some flexibility.

Multitrack Recording

Next to audio editing software, multitrack programs are easily the most utilized tools in sound design. The flexibility in recording, layering, effects processing, and organization of sound elements is the definitive highlight of these applications—and most sound designers are extremely proficient in their use. Sound effects with multi-dimensional interest may easily be created with nearly unlimited layering of pre-recorded sound elements on individual tracks. Each element may be adjusted individually, giving total control over each sound within the final sound effect. This especially comes in handy when the sound effect needs reworking; the offending sound element can be isolated and dealt with appropriately.

Courtesy of Steinberg Media Technologies GmbH

Multitrack software such as Cubase Studio can provide the sound designer with an unlimited amount of audio tracks to layer, process, and combine.

Instead of triggering samples and other sound sources as a sequencer does, multitrack software allows the sound designer to either record sounds directly to the open project or import existing sound files. Obviously, a little preparation is needed before using this particular creation method—but one of the benefits of creating a sound palette in pre-production is that most of these sounds are already available and ready to use.

> Know what your system is and the limitations that it presents. Also think variety: No one wants to hear that same footstep or gunshot when they play a game for hours.
>
> *Tom Graczkowski (Composer / Graphic Designer, TDimension Studios)*

Most multi-channel audio programs also include MIDI instrument control that enables the sound designer to utilize a hybrid of pre-recorded audio and triggered sounds during the course of the process. With these abilities combined into one package, the procedure becomes a bit more complicated—but the sound designer can ultimately create some incredible sounds with a little more effort. Reworks can be a bit more difficult, since samples and sound modules have to be accessed and set up again—but a little organization will go a long way.

:::::Creating a Gunshot Using a Multitrack Program

A single gunshot from a large caliber weapon may easily be created using a multitrack program. To accomplish this correctly, a substantial "shot" sound suggesting the power of the weapon will necessitate creative layering of several sonic elements from the pre-selected sound palette. The sound of a real weapon doesn't always communicate its power—but for the sound designer, it can be a good starting point. Opening a new file and importing a recorded gunshot, a short powerful explosion, and a sharp snare drum hit to individual tracks will provide appropriate elements to work with. Over-modulate the recorded shot sound to give it a more fierce presence (by setting the volume to a very high setting just shy of detectable audible distortion) and apply a limiter to the track to keep the final signal below digital zero. This will give the shot a solid "punch" and something the player will almost "feel" every time the trigger is pressed. The snare and explosion tracks will be added as necessary for the desired effect—something very powerful in this case.

Courtesy of Adobe

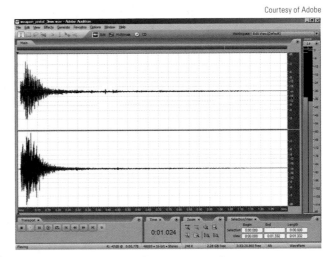

Start with an actual gunshot (Audition, shown).

A good explosion exudes power, and adding this element to the gunshot will give it a larger than life depth. Depending on the sound, the explosion can be used "as is" or manipulated to mesh with the other sound elements. Some sound designers will apply a pitch shift—increasing the pitch an octave or so—and then equalize as needed. Others may decide to let the attack of the recorded gunshot ring, then use only the tail of the explosion mixed in with the fade of the original shot sound. Experimenting with the possibilities will eventually lead to the sound that is most effective for the scenario. The snare hit is another element that can be added to suit the needs of the sound designer. The solid crack of the drumstick hitting a tightly tuned drum head can provide even more punch to the shot. This sound can be pitch shifted up, equalized, compressed, and affected by an appropriate reverb setting—then mixed for the desired sound. To finalize the mix, align the attacks of each element, adjust their volumes, apply a short reverb, and then render the file for final editing to complete this fairly simple process. The flexibility provided by a multitrack program is even more appreciated if the final sound requires later changes. The sound designer has the option of reopening the project file to make minor fixes or replace entire elements as needed, without having to start from scratch or reset levels and effects settings.

Editing

When creating sound effects for games, it is inevitable that the sound file will pass through an *editor* somewhere along the line. Even if the audio was created, mixed, and edited outside of a computer on a multitrack tape deck, the sound has to eventually be saved as a digital sound file in order to work within the game environment. Most sound design work is currently done completely in the digital realm, so this is accomplished as part of the process but isn't completely necessary until the final step.

Before any digital sound file is delivered to the development team, it must be cleaned up, finalized, formatted, and appropriately named. This is often a natural part of the creation process, and minimal time is required to accomplish this stage. However, some sound designers purposely leave this administrative phase until the very end, preferring not to disrupt any creative momentum that they may be enjoying.

The physical act of editing audio files may impact the character of the final sounds. It is imperative that the sound designer understands the potential of each action and the influence it has on the process. If multiple sound designers or audio editors are involved with the same sound effects, guidelines must be established and adhered to so that no time is wasted.

The recordist will purposely capture "silence" before or after the actual sound being recorded. This will allow the editor to have a decent chance of sampling any subtle activity and applying noise reduction if needed. Silence is never absolute; it's a varying degree of background noise. Whether it is the slight buzzing of a fluorescent light or the general din of an environment, steady silence can be neutralized so that the actual sound effect is clean. If the audio editor cuts any silence before applying noise reduction, the ability to do so becomes significantly reduced. Silence used at the beginning of a sound file to synchronize with an animation has bearing on the final sound. Any change by an uninformed editor will cause the sound to fall out of sync. Each member of the team working on sound effects should stay informed and be mindful of the effect they may have on the process to keep additional work to a minimum.

Unreal Tournament 3 makes good use of scripting and editing tools.

Audio Editing Software

Powerful *audio editing* software is by far the most important tool a sound designer can have, and it is nearly impossible to do the job without it. Not only does it act as a recording medium, but it can prepare the sound for use in the game once the sound is digitized. The ability to visualize sound in this type of environment is a significant feature, enhancing the already practiced sense of hearing.

The most basic function of an audio editor is to either record the performance of the sound designer or import audio from remote or other media. The sample rate and resolution of the new file should initially be set reasonably high—at least 44 kHz/16-bit. If storage space or processor speed isn't a concern, it should be set even higher—at 96 kHz/24-bit. The file should also be established as either mono or stereo (depending on the application) prior to any recording. Once these initial settings are primed, input levels from an outboard mixing board or effects processors and the recording input on the computer's sound card should be adjusted. The sound should be significant enough—obviously louder than the noise floor, but not so loud that clipping or unplanned saturation is present. Several checks and sample recordings can be made to further adjust settings prior to the actual performance—all of which should be performed at full volume, full speed, and at the planned energy of the recording. Simply hitting a hammer lightly on a concrete block, for example, will give false level readings during the test. If the plan is to completely obliterate the block, make sure there is enough headroom available for the sound to work and be captured correctly. Once everything is set, make the recording and save the rough file for later editing.

Typically, the best way to conduct a session is to record many takes at once within the same file, or on several files if the length becomes difficult to deal with. By allowing for several chances to collect that perfect sound, the sound designer has sufficient time to discover the best way to hit, bend, mangle, stomp, smack, or manipulate the object in question so that it produces a workable sound. After the recordings are complete to everyone's satisfaction, the next part of the editing process is to identify the best takes and begin the cleanup process.

A good practice is to always save the initial recorded audio as a rough file and conduct any processing on a copy. By doing so, the original recording remains available if something happens to go wrong in the editing process. If the entire file is to be used, rename the copy and save it as a new file. If only a portion will be selected, copy that piece to a new file and save it before any work is started. When working and creating sounds within an audio editor, it is always a worthwhile consideration to save each version as a new file, since undoing edits several iterations prior could be problematic. Saving time is important during a hectic development cycle, and having something to go back to if changes are needed can save the day. Some advanced editing programs can track each step in its history and allow for targeted changes, but saving these after significant adjustments is always a good idea.

Once the newly created file is opened and ready for editing, it is a good time to take a visual inventory of what needs to be done to the sound. A close listen to the "silence" before and after the target sound will divulge any unwanted noise that might need to be dealt with. If it is significant, sample as much of the steady noise as practical (leaving out any random sounds such as pops or clicks) utilizing a noise reduction application, and apply only the smallest correction required to reduce the unwanted noise. If too much is applied, it will affect the targeted sound as well—which should be avoided. Once the noise reduction has been completed, and assuming there are no specific timing issues to consider, remove the silence before and after the sound. Be careful not to cut any needed part of the audio, and apply a slight fade in or fade out if necessary. Extra care should be taken on the tail of the sound; its decay should sound natural without any abrupt ending, which could produce a noticeable "click."

The next issue is to consider the overall loudness of the sound. Is it loud enough? Is it too loud? Apply any needed volume adjustments to bring it to the correct level. This assumes the initial recording was done correctly and that the audio is at a decent level to begin with. If the noise floor is overbearing, re-recording may be the only option. Is there a volume peak or clipping that is causing distortion? Reduce the overall volume level and apply compression or a peak limiter to tame the offending intensity. Did these applications work, or is the distortion or clipping still noticeable? Apply clipping or peak restoration, utilize EQ, physically redraw the wave form, or delete the single sample if you can do so cleanly. If these efforts are still unsuccessful, listen to the file prior to any volume adjustments and attempt to isolate the cause; if it cannot be isolated, another recorded sound from the original session may have to be selected—or in the worst case scenario, the sound will have to be re-recorded. Overall, the sound file should look and sound healthy.

Additional EQ and effects processing could be applied at this point, based on the expected playback and overall soundscape needs. Similar sounds should be handled in the same way to ensure consistency between them, employing matching EQ and identical effects accordingly. Priority sound effects will be enhanced using these applications; other sounds that might compete with music, dialogue, or higher priority sound effects will use these to help minimize any competition between them. After any supplemental embellishments, the sound should again be reviewed for clipping, volume issues, and overall quality of the sound. The sound effects at this point are ready for conversion to the final in-game format.

In addition to general sound cleanup as described in this section, audio editors are useful for synchronizing to animations and audio post production for cinematic sequences. With an animation or cinematic in a playable movie format imported into an editor, sounds can be aligned to the exact frame—giving a nearly perfect representation. Audio editors with multitrack capability perform this feature more easily during complex mixes, but it can also be accomplished with great success in a stereo track environment. With the audio completely mixed and aligned, a stereo or surround audio file is rendered and reopened for the general cleanup process. Synchronized sound effects are saved appropriately, and the audio files that are created for cut-scenes are submitted to the designated individual who will eventually import them into the animation sequence.

Courtesy of Audacity Team

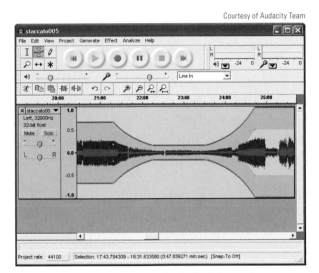

Audio editing software such as Audacity is by far the most important tool a sound designer can have.

No matter how sound effects are created—whether mixed in a multitrack program, developed on a sequencer, or performed by a live foley artist—they will inevitably be edited within an audio editing program. Mastery of this type of software is critical to the sound designer—but even with intimate knowledge, the sheer size of a game project can become an issue. For games with thousands of individual sound effects files, the job of editing them can be quite daunting. Fortunately, software developers understand the plight of audio creators and outfit their wares with a convenient tool known as the *batch converter*. This program within a program allows the sound designer to apply the same edits and effects processing to multiple files in a specified order and then save them all to same file format in a designated directory. This is incredibly handy when blanket adjustments must be made to multiple sound files, allowing the computer to expend its energy instead. Overall, sound designers appreciate the power of good audio editing software programs and have come to rely heavily on their capabilities and potential.

Multitrack Software

The complexities of today's game audio demand formidable tools. Multitrack software, while initially developed for and used by music creators, quickly found prominence within the sound design domain. It is a natural fit, since sound effects are a conglomeration of various sounds and sound elements mixed together to create something interesting and exciting. With nearly unlimited tracks available, the sound designer can create almost anything imaginable through creative layering, crossfading, panning, and effects processing.

Like audio editors, multitrack programs are used as robust recording media well-suited for multiple microphone placements and surround recording needs. Combined with the ability to import unlimited pre-recorded audio files, this powerhouse allows the creative energy of the sound designer to really shine. From simple button presses to background ambience to audio post for cinematic sequences, this incredible tool can handle most sound designer needs. Despite the advantages of this type of application, there is a major pitfall to consider and avoid. It is important to always be attentive to the final outcome and work specifically toward that goal when creating in this environment. Since it is so easy to import or record dozens of sound elements, audio chaos might ensue if the sound designer isn't paying attention. Just because 100 sounds *can* be layered, it doesn't mean those 100 sounds *must* be used. Choices must be made to ensure that the sound effect works well within the game environment—with the understanding that a single sound element is sometimes the best choice. The experience of the sound designer and the needs of the game will dictate whether their creations should be subtle or if they should go all out.

Each fresh creation within a multitrack setting should be saved as a new project, and any sound used in it should be kept in a separate and easily accessible directory. There will be many instances during a development cycle when a sound effect will need additional editing months after it was created—and maintaining an organized system will keep the revisit brief. If a logical routine is made part of the creation process, opening the project file should immediately restore all contents and settings without wasted time searching for wayward elements. When backups are performed, it will be easy to copy information in an organized fashion as well.

With a new project opened, audio can either be imported or recorded directly to the project. Unlike an audio editor where every sound element must be immediately integrated into a single file, this situation allocates each sound its own "track" where it can be individually manipulated without affecting other sounds. This principal advantage gives a sound designer the ability to shift each element within the stereo or surround field, from panning hard left or right to creatively repositioning as the file plays. This simple act can liven up even the most basic sounds. However, there is no need to stop here. Add in the capability of individual EQ, volume control, and effects processing— and the sky is the limit.

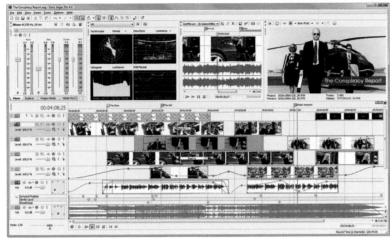

Good multitrack software (Vegas Pro 8, shown) allows the creative energy of the sound designer to really shine.

After each sound element is placed and appropriately manipulated, the project must be mixed as the final sound effect. Each program is slightly different—with some referring to this process as "exporting" or "rendering," and some approaching it simply as a "save file as" function. Whatever the process, this final phase will create the file that will be sent to the audio editor for final cleanup and formatting. With multiple tracks engaged, care must be taken to render the sound without clipping or volume issues. Adjusting the volume of each sound element appropriately will produce the intended mix, but it will often result in an overloaded sound. By regulating the master fader to relieve the intensity, the sound can be tamed before it reaches the editing process. Situations with multiple sound effects created on a multitrack program will also require attention to the consistency of the volume of each file relative to another—ensuring that the volumes of like sounds are uniform. While this can be taken care of in a later stage, it's always a good idea to deal with any potential issue before it can create more work.

Multitrack audio programs also have the capability to import video files, making them perfect for audio post production associated with cinematics and synchronizing to animation sequences. Unlike audio editors, where each sound must be immediately mixed into the final file, this gives the sound designer the flexibility to adjust each sound individually. Having the ability to fine tune each individual sound—not only how it is synchronized to the animation but its volume, panning, EQ, and added effects processing—makes this method a far better choice. When everything is in place and sounding good, the project will be mixed to a single audio file, cleaned up in an audio editor, and delivered to the developer as appropriate.

Audio Scripting

As game development techniques advance, methods of implementing and presenting sound are also greatly improved upon. One of the biggest concerns of sound designers is the lack of control over their work once it is delivered to the developer. Sound designers become attached to their creations after putting their heart and soul into the work. More importantly, the sounds they are receiving public credit for are a direct reflection of their abilities and influence whether they get the next job or not. Outside of this consideration, the audio programmer and sound designer may not have the same audio skills, sensibilities, or ideas—and their visions may conflict. The end goal is to have the audio sound great, no matter what reason is given—and audio scripting has emerged to achieve that goal. Audio scripting allows the sound designer to create flexible, non-repetitive content. Parameters are programmed, depending on the activity within each game setting; this, in turn, will tell the audio engine what to play and when to play it. The language, referred to typically as "human readable" code, allows the content provider to be involved without having to learn and write a complicated computer language—although there may be a bit of a learning curve for some of the interfaces. The beauty of this feature is that once the sound designer has developed a vision for the audio presentation, the script and sound effects are delivered to the programmer who will simply drop them into the game. Programmers will still have input, with the guidance of the sound designer and producer, and they will additionally set parameters such as the dynamic volume and manage uploading and downloading of audio assets. The programmer is usually not involved in major creative decisions but specifically ensures that the scripting works as planned. In the end, this enhances the use and playback of sound—saving valuable time in the process.

Courtesy of Audiokinetic

Middleware applications such as Wwise allow the sound designer to define audio behaviors, edit, and mix in real time within the game, and manage sound integration across multiple game platforms.

There are many uses for scripting as a sound effects management tool. It can mix sound effects on the fly during gameplay in each level or scene, dynamically adjusting volume levels or effects processing based on what is immediately transpiring. For example, as a player character becomes injured and loses health points, an audio script can adjust the output of sound effect volumes to indicate that the character is losing consciousness and about to pass out. This could accompany visuals that darken the screen or cause a red haze to slowly blossom.

Scripting can also create active changes in mood, time of day, or weather variations depending on what is set by the sound designer. Sound effects can be triggered based on variables such as the number of bad guys present in the scene, whether the weather is changing from a sunny day to something more dark and ominous, or to indicate the sun has set and night time has arrived. To the player, these transitions would be seamless and give an incredible sense of realism to the experience.

Audio scripting can be accomplished in several different ways, mainly through proprietary tools developed in house by the developer. Since one size does not fit all, this allows developers to create an application that best suits their needs and to take advantage of a game's programming features. A PC game utilizing Microsoft's DirectX will have the application DirectMusic available which, while initially designed for music, allows sound designers to create audio content with interactive, variable, and adaptive playback properties. Other specific programs are available to those working under license for game platforms such as the Xbox 360, PlayStation 3, or Wii. Typically, these are only available to in-house audio teams.

Formatting & Conversion

Preparing the sound effects for their final delivery to the developer is one of the last steps a sound designer will perform. Since these audio files were created in the highest resolution possible, they will first be converted to the correct sample rate and resolution. A 96 kHz sampling rate and 24-bit resolution indicates very high quality sound properties, but it also means very large file sizes. Until storage space and processor speeds grow, developers look for 44 or 22 kHz/16-bit as today's current standards. Content providers may expect to utilize their audio editor's conversion features and convert down to the requested sample rate and resolution.

Once conversions are successfully completed, it's necessary to save the files to their final format. Normally, the format will already be what the sound designer has been working with throughout the process, such as .wav or .aiff. However, with .mp3, .ogg, or an obscure format, an extra step will have to be performed. Most audio editors have the capability to save to most standard formats; it's often as simple as clicking "save as" and the formatting is completed. For special formats, a specific program, development kit, or encoder will be necessary—or the developer will handle this separately. The sound designer will have addressed this requirement early on in the process, so it shouldn't be a surprise or a great concern.

Sony Computer Entertainment America

Convert audio to .aac for PlayStation 3 games such as *Killzone 2*.

With hundreds or sometimes thousands of sound files to deliver, the tasks of converting and formatting can quickly become a burden. Once again, the batch conversion feature of a solid audio editor may be utilized with great success. Normally, all it takes is scripting each step in order, re-sampling, adjusting the resolution, and saving the files to their final format. Simply tag the files to be manipulated, identify the directory to which the files should be saved, start the script, and take a break while the machine does the work. It's that simple if the right tools are available.

Before the final files are sent, it's a good idea to give them one last critical listen. Occasionally, due to the type of conversion performed or some inherent property of the final file format, sonic properties may have changed. If this is the case, some minor editing, EQ, volume, peak, or fade issues may need to be re-addressed before the files are ready. These kinds of adjustments will be made on the final converted and formatted files, since these are the ones that will be implemented into the game and need to sound their best.

Courtesy of Adobe

Audio editing software such as Audition is the primary formatting and conversion tool used by sound designers, although other specific programs are also available that only make conversions. Older game consoles such as the PlayStation 2 require a proprietary development kit to make the appropriate conversion to the final game format (in this case, VAG).

The final consideration before delivery of the files is how they are labeled—referred to as *naming conventions*. For any scripting, programming triggers, or other coded references to work, the name of each sound file has to exactly match how they are labeled in the code. The creative process is often a focused endeavor, with the sound designer typically creating multiple files while ideas flow quickly. Sounds such as explosions or laser shots won't be associated with any specific action until later on. The developer will identify file naming conventions, usually in the sound asset list, which must be followed to the letter.

Beta Testing

Beta testing is the point in a development cycle where all of the project's assets are pieced together to form a nearly complete, working game. This is the official test phase, where in-house or contracted beta testers put the software through its paces and essentially try to "break" the game. The sound designer's unofficial role in this particular process is to determine whether any sound issues need to be fixed.

Through the expert ears of the sound designer, it is important to listen intently to the sounds in the game. Do they work? Are they appropriate? Is the timing correct? Are the volume and EQ adjusted properly? Will any alterations need to be made in the programming or to the sound file? These are the types of questions that should be considered when making this important evaluation.

Modifications will always need to be made to ensure a perfect fit; rarely is anything flawless the first time around. It is wise to be organized during this process so that each sound can be heard and remain in context with other existing sounds. Playing a sound by itself won't guarantee anything; only after hearing it with music, dialogue, background ambience, environmental sounds, and all the other sounds that might be playing is it possible to make an appropriate judgment. A high-priority sound should cut through the rest of the mix; if it's intended as a background sound, it obviously shouldn't be the loudest. Once the determination is made, the sound file can be adjusted—or if other programming factors need to be considered, it can be fixed in the coding.

Illustration by Robert Ian Vasquez

During this phase, the sound designer can expect to hear terms such as "rework" and "redo" as the developer and beta testers discover flaws and express their opinions over the quality and appropriateness of the sound effects. As it implies, "rework" means that the existing sound is good but some minor corrections are needed to make it right. These could be anything from slight timing issues to volume or EQ adjustments. "Redo" means just that: The sound isn't working, and it needs to be completely redone—possibly using an entirely different approach. There are many reasons a sound might have to be redone, but these can be kept to a minimum if the sound designer has maintained an open dialogue with the development team throughout the project.

Creating sound effects for video games can be a huge undertaking. However, whether the sound team is made up of a single person or several sound designers, there are time-honored steps that can be taken to ensure that the process goes smoothly. Pre-planning is essential. A solid understanding of each sound effect's purpose is a must. Genuine knowledge and skill to operate the tools to perform the job are both critical. Sound effects are not created by accident nor with crossed fingers; an extreme effort must always be made. With the sound effects complete, the sound team can now focus on the next audio task: the music.

1. In this chapter, a gunshot sound has been described as a quick, explosive sound that has a loud, fast attack and then decays rapidly. Analyzing the characteristics of real-life sounds can help you create them using other tools (e.g., snare drum, balloon). Play 3 games currently on the market and identify the characteristics of at least 3 prominent sound effects in each game. Knowing these characteristics, how would you create these sounds from scratch without using their real-life counterparts?

2. How does "close miking" (or listening up close) to the sound made by a certain object, such as a retractable pen, change the perception of that sound? Choose 3 everyday objects and compare how they sound up close vs. mid-range (a few feet away).

3. Create and edit at least 7 sound effects for an original game idea—using foley during the recording process. Your sound effects should consist of at least one interface (e.g., menu button), environmental (e.g., fire, water, erupting volcano), human (e.g., breaking bones, falling), and machinery/weapon (e.g., grenade, trash compactor) element.

CHAPTER

5

Function of Game Music

building the atmosphere

Key Chapter Questions

- What are the primary functions of *music* in video games?

- Where should music be *placed* in a game?

- What are the practices that allow for the effective use of *adaptive* or *interactive* music?

- What are the main advantages of utilizing music *loops*?

- What are *ambient tracks*, and how are they effective elements of a game soundtrack?

Game music has made an incredible journey in a relatively short time. From the early days of simple electronic beeps to today's full orchestral scores recorded in multi-channel surround, game audio's continued evolution has been incredibly exciting. Gone are the days when game music was thought of as a series of unenthusiastic bleeps and bloops; today, game composers even have the potential to capture Grammy awards for their efforts. Game scores rival those of big budget films, and players are finally getting the full cinematic experience they've been yearning for. Music within visual media such as film, television, and video games plays a tremendous role in the overall emotional experience of the viewer or player. When the action is fast paced and full of non-stop excitement, music is energetic and charged with adrenaline—driving the events forward. During more touching moments, such as the death of a character or a love scene, the musical tone matches the poignancy of the event. Big adventure themes demand a huge, upbeat, full orchestral production to support immense storylines. An uncomplicated, playful score provides a sense of fun to a casual puzzle game. Regardless of the game's genre, music is designed to serve a very specific purpose and enhance the overall experience.

Purpose of Game Music

Game music has several purposes, including setting the mood and overall tone, identifying the era and setting, establishing gameplay pace, and increasing immersion. Let's take a look at each of these functions in more detail.

Setting the Mood & Overall Tone

The primary goal of game music is to set the mood and overall tone of the gameplay experience. Much like music used in films, the score can speak volumes about what is happening—often in a completely subconscious way. It can be a challenge for the player to emotionally connect with onscreen characters or to comprehend the significance of what is happening without effective musical accompaniment. Music is a powerful force in our everyday lives, and a game that capitalizes on this phenomenon is guaranteed to be a great experience.

During the course of production, the development studio will be very specific about how players should feel during their journey through the game—and it will dictate how the soundtrack will be used to express the onscreen emotion. It is the job of the composer to translate this vision into appropriate music that is fitting to both the game and the requested mood. The only restrictions to this process will be the pre-established standards that have been used in games of the same genre.

A prime example of how the mood of a game can be specifically established by music is in the original game, *Myst*. The music was very basic by today's game standards, but it successfully managed to use this simplicity to evoke intense feelings from the player—and effectively enhance the game experience. The selection of instrumentation and their specific sound provided a sharp contrast to the visuals. Interestingly, the game developers (Robin and Rand Miller) had first planned to only utilize sound effects and ambience to create the mood—but they discovered how powerful the emotional characteristics of music can be and quickly changed their strategy.

The music in *Myst* was very basic by today's game standards, but it successfully managed to use this simplicity to evoke intense feelings.

Matching the genre of the game to the type of music that the player expects to hear is an unfortunate impediment to the creative process, but it is something that is often necessary. Since film and television have influenced our expectations, games must be consistent with the usage of music in other media. This is not to say that creativity must be stifled or new uses of music can't ever be tried—but that established standards, whether a game developer likes it or not, will have better success if they at least attempt to respect them. For example, a high-intensity driving game such as *Need for Speed* works best with music that is fast and energetic. A slow, depressing soundtrack would completely destroy the fun of the game. A horror-themed game such as the *Silent Hill* series has a score that is dark and foreboding instead of happy and upbeat (although sometimes the latter tone could be used to "trick" the players or serve as an interesting contrast). Naturally, a children's game such as *Putt-Putt Saves the Zoo* contains music that is light and fun instead of complex or dark. (It should be noted that many games in the Mario franchise use fairly complex scores that contain more foreboding motifs in dramatic moments; however, as a rule, using music that is expected by the market will help avoid confusion and make the gameplay experience more enjoyable.)

> Without the sound and music, the *Silent Hill* series would not be as scary as it is. Beautiful yet eerie pieces. Very dark and creepy sounds. Especially effective considering they were working around the limited memory constraints of the PS1 and PS2 for the first 3 games.
>
> *Chad W. Mossholder (Sound Designer/ Composer, Sony Online Entertainment)*

Identifying the Era & Setting

In addition to establishing the genre of the game, music can also be used to subtly identify the era and location of the game setting. Exotic locales and other foreign surroundings are popular venues for games, sometimes due to their historical significance or being designed to influence how players feel when they are there. Unfamiliar territory can make players feel uncomfortable as they explore a strange land, while the tropical backdrop of a white sandy beach and palm trees can evoke fun and relaxation. The music that accompanies these environments will reinforce and contribute to those feelings.

Courtesy of NovaLogic, Inc.

The music in *Delta Force: Black Hawk Down* helps identify the era and location of the game setting.

Similarly, games set in a certain time period will require a soundtrack appropriate to that period. For example, World War II games such as *Medal of Honor* and *Call of Duty* must use suitable music from that era to accurately move the player back in time. These two particular examples shine by utilizing the music style and instrumentation within the high quality score and incorporating other era specific music elements into cinematics and sound effects. The sound of old radio and phonograph recordings from the 1940s can be an extremely powerful reminder of that era and will influence the perception of the player. Modern popular music here would definitely be out of place, even though it would work very well for a war game based on today's conflicts. A game such as *Delta Force: Black Hawk Down*, which encompasses a more recent conflict, uses a modern score and incorporates musical elements that suggest the exotic African setting of Somalia. Through the music alone and without knowing anything else about the game, players could easily identify their locations. The power of suggestion can literally transport them there, making for a remarkable experience.

Establishing Gameplay Pace

Music also has the ability to set the pace of the gameplay. Faster music gives players the feeling of speed, the need to be quick with their reactions, or a subconscious sense that they need to rush. Racing games such as *Midnight Club* and *Need for Speed* typically utilize upbeat alternative rock or dance soundtracks as a way to imply speed. Their fast tempos help keep players on the edge of their seats as they madly maneuver through busy city streets. Simple arcade games such as *Zuma* increase the tempo of the music to indicate a sense of urgency and to suggest players need to speed up their play in order to successfully complete the level. It also uses an increased tempo to inform the player that the complexity of the game is increasing—just in case, in the middle of the gameplay, they hadn't noticed. As the chance of failure passes, the music will slow to the standard, more relaxed music. Slower music allows players a chance to explore, to enjoy their characters' environments, and experience a feeling of safety. Whatever the tempo, the music is designed purposefully depending on the type of game and the intentions of the gameplay. Development teams can further use music to lull players into a false sense of security—getting them to drop their guard just in time to be surprised by a monster hiding around the corner. This usage cleverly sets players up for an entertaining shock and a quick change of pace.

Courtesy of Rockstar Games and Take-Two Interactive Software, Inc.

Racing games such as *Midnight Club 3: DUB Edition* typically use upbeat alternative rock or dance soundtracks as a way to imply speed.

Increasing Immersion

Finally, music is designed to help mask real-life sounds and to completely immerse the player in the game. Part of the appeal of most genres—including first-person shooters (FPSs) such as *Halo* or *Half-Life*, real-time strategy (RTS) games such as *WarCraft*, or adventure games such as *The Journeyman Project* —is the ability to fully transport players to another reality and allow them to escape from their current surroundings.

Certain games will totally envelop players in sound with background ambience or music—whatever can effectively drown out the sounds that may be happening around them. While it is next to impossible to fully mask life as it carries on around a player, effective use of both music and ambient sound effects will conceal most of it.

Reprinted with permission from Microsoft Corporation

The music in games such as *Halo 3* can fully transport the player to another reality.

Placing Music

Similar to sound effects, most game titles have specific places where music is used—including credit sequences, opening and closing cinematics, in-game background, cut-scenes, level transitions, and victory and defeat cues. Creating appropriate music is often an artistic challenge to a composer but simpler if the objectives are clearly understood. Much like the flow of a film, the score will take the player on a journey that often occurs from the opening sequence to the final credits and every rise and fall of emotion in between. Each segment of the adventure has a defined purpose, and the music is intended to fully support each one.

The creation, application, and implementation of a soundtrack can vary greatly depending on the needs of the game. Some music is designed to adapt and seamlessly crossfade between assorted cues as the onscreen action changes. Some music has to continuously loop without any obvious repeat, while others have to provide subtle clues to the significance of what is happening or is about to happen. Unlike music for film, game music must be able to adjust as players navigate through the game environment and menus regardless of what order they do it in—and ultimately without bringing undue attention to itself.

The original *Super Mario Bros.* really hooked me with its jazz and Latin tinged music. It was a classic example of rising above technical limitations and coming up with some real creative stuff. I will never tire of this game.

Ben Long (Composer, Noise Buffet)

Introduction, Closing & Credit Sequences

Music within the introduction, closing, and credit sequences is typically created as the main musical theme of the game. The opening sequence of music and animation initially sets the tone of the entire experience and is often the largest production in the title. The composer will pull out all the stops for this first sequence and work hard to establish a great opening experience. Whether it is a huge orchestral performance or something a little lighter, additional time is spent with this theme in order to give a highly polished, well produced sound and a skilled composition. Since this is the first music the player will hear, these initial impressions are important and serve as the basis of their opinion for the rest of the game. Games such as *BioShock*, *Halo 3*, *Heavenly Sword*, *Hellgate: London*, and *Mass Effect* are all excellent examples of opening sequences where the music really shines and gives tremendous impact to the rest of the game experience.

Sony Computer Entertainment America

The music in the opening sequences of *Heavenly Sword* really shines and gives tremendous impact to the rest of the game experience.

For closing or end credit sequences, variations of the main theme are often used to signify the end of the "experience" and give a congratulatory salute for completion of the game. It's not a hard and fast rule that the theme is used in these areas—often seen in films that instead place licensed music to convey the mood they want moviegoers to have as they leave the theater. Other types of music can work well but will depend on the direction the game producer wishes to go. The composer should definitely have this issue solidified before beginning work on these final music cues.

::::: Licensed Music in *Skate*

EA's *Skate* makes excellent use of licensed music. The loading screens are accompanied by cheesy "elevator" arrangements of the music that actually made it fun while waiting for the game to load. Also, music is placed in important skate areas that work as an audio GPS as you skate around the city. It's refreshing to hear licensed music used as more than just audio wallpaper.

Chris Rickwood (Composer, Rickwood Music for Media)

Electronic Arts, Inc.

Cinematics

Cinematics are similar to their big screen counterparts and are scored in the same fashion: linearly, predictably, and to complement the depicted emotions. They can be used at any point in a game—but they are typically created for the main title sequence that builds the excitement of the game and as cut scenes used to propel the storyline forward or conclude it. The composer requires diverse skills to create distinctive musical cues that may be timed specifically to each scene and hit precise visual marks. Underscoring for linear media is not about predictable chord progressions and staying within an established tempo such as most mainstream music, although it does have its time and place. Scoring for cinematics or film is an often challenging pursuit due to the unique structure and arrangements that are necessary; hitting specific timings *isn't* difficult, but making it all sound musical *is*.

Typically, a cinematic is first created in its basic form and then furnished to the composer. In order to keep the process from any bottlenecks, some developers will first render a mockup of the movie and have the composer, artists, and animators complete their work simultaneously. While the music is being created, the art team will finalize the animation, characters, and background settings until a fully realized movie is completed—and all of the finished graphic and sound assets will eventually be assembled to conclude this effort. Occasionally, the process is conducted in reverse with the music completed first and the animation team assembling scene changes or poignant moments around the beat, existing flourishes, or swells. This is typically done when the producer feels strongly about a particular piece of pre-existing music that conveys the needed emotion and tone of the scene.

Electronic Arts, Inc.

A masterful score accompanies the grand cinematics in *The Lord of the Rings: The Return of the King.*

At some point before working on a cinematic score, the composer and game producer or audio director discuss initial ideas and goals in a *spotting session.* Specific topics during the session might include discussions about each scene, placement of transitions, and timing issues that need to be met. The spotting session is a chance for the composer to glean appropriate information about the intentions of the movie and to get on the same page musically as the rest of the team. If the music will also share sonic space with sound effects, dialogue and voice overs, this is the chance to ascertain their role and tailor the music appropriately around them. Music is more complex than sound effects and is not as easy to change, so it is important that the composer understands what is expected and get it right the first time.

There are many masterful scores accompanying cinematics in games such as *Medal of Honor: Rising Sun, The Lord of the Rings: The Return of the King* and *WarCraft III: Reign of Chaos.* These scores strictly follow film scoring techniques—and even though they are created for the game medium, the respective composers apply the same passion and skill as their big screen counterparts. By not seeing a cinematic game score as inconsequential, the player is able to experience something almost larger than life due to the intensity and care taken by the composer to make high-quality music.

> **S**plinter Cell: Double Agent has a really rich score. Mike McCann really honed in on a sound, and its color works so well with the game. Also, the music isn't over the top—so it's not annoying to the player.
>
> *Tim Rideout (Executive Hit Writer &*
> *Groupie Herder, Tim Ridout dot com)*

Menu Screens

Next to gameplay, a player will spend a good deal of time within the menu screens adjusting controls, selecting features, or simply taking a break from the action. Music for these areas will generally be unobtrusive with consistent dynamics. The introduction sequence and cinematics will have already presented the player with a heart pounding opening, and the gameplay music to follow will have its own intensity—so it is not necessary to continue this within the menu screens. Instead, the music should be within the theme of the game—something foreboding or in a fashion to build tension or anticipation. These are obviously generalizations and should not be considered rules that have to be followed, but the majority of current games use these ideas.

The music for the menu system in *Medal of Honor: Allied Assault* provides an unassuming thematic backdrop to player choices. While it is initially a modest accompaniment, the music builds to a powerful and memorable composition as the player remains within the menus—making it well worth the time spent there. Interestingly, this menu cue is universally recognized as the theme of the game series. *Deus Ex*, *Hitman: Blood Money*, *Morrowind*, and *Max Payne* are also excellent examples of games with menu music that hits the mark—both in appropriateness and quality. All of these menu cues enjoy a certain popularity among players, which further supports their suitability to the franchises they represent.

Electronic Arts, Inc.

The music for the menu system in *Medal of Honor: Allied Assault* provides an unassuming thematic backdrop to player choices.

It is difficult to predict just how long a player will spend within the menu screens, what buttons they will press, and what other menu features will be activated. Since storage and processor capacity are always issues, developers solve this unpredictability by continuously looping music within the menu. As a composer, the task of creating seamless loops that are musical and unnoticed is a major concern. Noticeable repeat points or instruments and notes that stand out can ruin the effect, and extra care must be applied. If the style and characteristics of the music don't allow this to be done smoothly, increasing the length of the piece will make the repeats less obvious. Within menu screens, 30–60 second loops are used—but these can be longer if needed.

Multiple menu levels and sub-levels can add complexity to the job of the composer. If the music remains the same throughout the entire menu system, the job is relatively simple—but if multiple music cues are used, there are other issues that develop because of this. Transitioning between one menu cue to the next can be done effectively in three different ways, ensuring musicality and smoothness:

1. The programmer can activate a fade out of the music as the menu screen disappears and activate a fade in as the new menu appears. This allows music with a variety of keys, tempos, or instrumentation to be used with little concern for the transition.

2. Instead of a fade out, the programmer could trigger a short ending cue or transition piece to match the piece being faded. The composer would be required to create a short piece of music that could be crossfaded anywhere in the menu cue and bring it to a natural end. Depending on the number of menu cues, this has the potential to add a few more days to the music production cycle.

3. Each menu cue could crossfade directly into the new one being triggered. This would require the composer to be mindful of the key, tempo, and instrumentation of the menu cues and ensure that they can transition smoothly and musically.

A final consideration for the composer when creating menu music is to be fully aware of other sonic activity that may be taking place. Obviously, sound effects will be triggered—but environmental sounds and dialogue are possible as well; if this is the case, additional planning is necessary. Similar to the process of mixing a piece of music, the menu cue can be adjusted to allow the sound effects and dialogue to break through. Volume and equalization are the first obvious solutions, but the audio programmer can also implement volume changes known as "ducking" to permit dialogue or sound effects to be heard. This will entirely depend on the density of the music; simple music with plenty of air will naturally allow for this and will need little adjustment.

And the Loop Goes On . . .

When creating menu music, keep in mind that your goal is to ensure that the player doesn't turn the sound off! Looping music has a tendency to drive anyone nuts after a while, and extreme care should be taken in the choice of instrumentation and anything that might be bothersome after several repetitions. Squealing horn or guitar riffs are examples of what to avoid in the menu screen environment. The less the music draws attention to itself, the better. The Wii console menu music is a good example of looping music that is most often enjoyable rather than irritating. We suggest that you listen to it yourself and determine what works (and what doesn't) for you!

In-Game & Background

The score that accompanies the actual gameplay is far and above the most important music of the game experience. Players will spend the majority of their time deeply involved with the unfolding story, and the primary goal of the music is to set mood and pace. There are many ways in which a developer and composer can approach this audio backdrop, depending on the type of game. Unless the game centers around playing rhythmic sequences or music, such as *Guitar Hero* or *Rock Band* , in-game music will take a more subtle role.

It is has been said the best film score is one that is never noticed. This is a powerful statement that is often difficult to attain, but it is something that should always be in the back of your mind as the ultimate goal when adding musical enhancement to the game experience. The *Halo* and *Medal of Honor* series come close to achieving this accomplishment at times. Due in part to the often intense action taking the focus and because the music is designed to lay back during the slower, exploration phases, the game developers are able to realize the perfect blend of stimuli. In games such as these, understanding that the music is not the centerpiece and only present to enhance the emotional impact is the key to creating a superior playing experience. Music is specifically intended to create a mood and stir feelings in a listener. Used within the video game setting, music is an incredibly influential tool that can be calculated to enable the player to connect personally to the game. This basic idea should be the driving force to the developer and composer when in-game music is being considered.

::::: Fusing Music & Rhythm in *Patapon*

The PSP title *Patapon* is a very interesting and original example of fusing music and rhythm into its gameplay design. The gameplay is a little subtle because it involves trying to throw the player off time by adding out-of-time sounds and rhythms as the gameplay gets harder. *Patapon* is an interesting title for a musician to play!

Simon Amarasingham (CEO, dSonic Inc)

Electronic Arts, Inc.

There are several different ways to approach a game score, and each has a place in the experience; sometimes several styles can appear in the same game. Subtle, barely noticeable music that quietly evokes specific feelings is perfect for slower-paced exploration or when a player's ears need a bit of rest after a recent violent, noisy confrontation. A high musical intensity shouldn't be sustained for too long of a period due to the fatigue it can cause a player, and unassuming music is essential to provide a break in the audio action.

As gameplay intensifies (e.g., a battle ensues or a dramatic shift in the storyline is revealed), the music should follow suit. This is one specific area where the music should stand out and be noticed as it calls attention to the change in gameplay. The composer can create this action by an increase in complexity and volume, a sudden key change, instrument and tempo changes, or any other musical method that causes the player to notice something different and dramatic may be happening. This type of music can be sustained for a longer period of time without causing weariness but should eventually shift either back to the subtle soundtrack or to an even higher intensity as the action increases. Since this type of music is only being used to make a specific point, the music should change to fit the action once the point is made.

Loud, "in your face" music that demands to be a part of the experience is used primarily to support intense or adrenaline-driven moments in a game. The music will need to be louder and more energetic during a final boss battle, fire fight at the end of a level, or mad race toward the finish line. *Race Driver: GRID* utilizes an intricate music layering system specifically designed to increase and decrease in intensity as the energy of the game shifts. Racing is an inherently adrenaline-driven activity, and the music for most racing games is up tempo and energetic. However, as the end of a timed race approaches or when another player is battling the player for first position, the music in this game is designed to include additional instrument layers such as heavy drums and extra percussion to increase the tension. In these instances, the music takes center stage and energizes the player. Most game levels are designed with

Courtesy of Codemasters

The music in *Race Driver: GRID* is designed to increase and decrease in intensity as the energy of the game shifts.

short bursts of intense action; the purpose is to keep the player interested and add dynamics to the gameplay. The music accompanying these moments will imply the increase in pace and intensity—and it will emotionally invigorate players, supporting their activities by providing a sort of fanfare.

::::: *Halo*'s Use of Musical Styles

The *Halo* series, which has won numerous awards for its sophisticated and ground-breaking use of audio, is a perfect example to study as it utilizes several styles of music very effectively during gameplay. In an early level, after the player lands on an unknown planet surface, the music is initially tranquil and serene. A gentle arrange-ment of music drifts unobtrusively as the player begins to explore the new surroundings. At times, when onscreen action is slow, the music will also pur-posely fade to silence as a way to prevent the player from growing tired of it. As the music returns, it is a refreshing reappear-ance that is noticeable and welcome. At a point further into the level, the Covenant ships appear in search of the player as the music grows a little more intense and foreboding to subconsciously put the player on edge. As they begin their

Reprinted with permission from Microsoft Corporation

Halo 3

attack on the player, the music grows in intensity, the tempo increases, drums and other percussive instruments appear, and the player's emotional state changes with the accompanying score. After the bad guys are defeated, the music returns to a more relaxed and positive tone to reflect the ensuing calm.

Without the players specifically knowing it, the music has influenced their emotions during the experience—taking them from a relaxed and unhurried state of mind to a heart-pounding, adrenaline filled fight for their virtual lives and then back again. Even the subtle use of musical silence has an incredible impact on the game experience—disap-pearing during neutral emotional states and then reappearing as the situation changes.

Players will spend the majority of time engaged in the game experience—and the mood, genre, and instrumentation of the music must all add up. An FPS based in Somalia such as *Delta Force: Black Hawk Down* will have African undertones no matter what style of music accompanies it. The same type of game based on American soldiers in World War II, such as *Call of Duty* will likely have music from the late 1930s and early 1940s American landscape. A western themed game could use instruments such as guitar, har-monica, or player piano to help sell the time and place of the story. A racing game such as *Project Gotham 4, Forza Motorsport 2,* or *Gran Turismo 4* will likely have up tempo rock, electronica, or dance as the musical backdrop. A space game will utilize electronic instruments in a futuristic arrangement. Creativity doesn't need to be hampered by these perceived restrictions, but straying from the expected style and instrumentation could cause some distraction to the player and should be avoided.

A racing game such as *Project Gotham 4* will likely have up tempo rock, electronica, or dance as the musical backdrop.

During gameplay, background music can be managed in a variety of ways depending on the needs of the game. If memory, storage, or processor restrictions are in play, the music will either be compressed or reduced in quality to keep file sizes small—but it can also be looped to extend the use of the limited amount of these tracks. If storage space isn't an issue, a variety of music tracks will be created and can be triggered to play randomly or in a planned order and continue as long as the player remains in that specific level. More advanced programming will allow for interactive or adaptive music to transform as the gameplay dynamics change. Game titles today use many of these techniques to ensure that players remain interested and, most of all, entertained.

Plot Advancement, Cut-Scenes & Tie-Ins

Games that rely heavily on storytelling require additional features to assist advancement of the plot and link connecting levels of gameplay together in an intelligent and logical manner. These can take the form of a text screen, still graphics, slideshow—or something more considerable such as a cinematic production to offer praise to the player, maintain the momentum of the game, or provide the setup for the next round. The composer will often be required to provide appropriate musical accompaniment to these elements. Games such as *WarCraft III: Reign of Chaos, Bloodrayne,* and *Resident Evil* all show remarkable examples of these done effectively with skillful musical productions—offering a cinematic experience between game levels that players don't encounter during gameplay. Not only are the cut-scenes created with greater detail and with a specific purpose, but the music is perfectly synchronized and of a higher quality.

> The music in *Outcast* (composed by Lennie Moore) helped "save" the game to an extent. The graphics were not up to par (surprisingly low resolution for the time), but the gameplay and terrific orchestral music drew me in and kept me playing regardless.
>
> *Matt Sayre (Owner, The Game Composer)*

The needs of the game and the use of the tie-ins will ultimately determine the
format of the music. Cinematics will be scored in the typical manner to the visuals. Music created for the other visual methods such as text screens, still graphics,
or slideshows will convey the desired mood
of the moment and will either be a single cue
or loop that ends or fades as the next level
or scene opens. Whether these tie-ins occur
within a level as part of a significant change in
the storyline or at the conclusion, the purpose
of the music will be further influenced. Music
may be required to help lead in to the next
scene, provide a slight change of pace from
the background music, or act as a finale. Each
of these instances would require a different
musical approach that the composer should
fully investigate prior to beginning work on
them.

Courtesy of Blizzard Entertainment, Inc.

I'm sorry for eavesdropping, Master, but...

WarCraft III: Reign of Chaos offers a cinematic experience between
game levels that players don't encounter during gameplay.

Victory & Defeat Finale Cues

Small musical interludes that are used to applaud, razz, or provide closure to the
end of a game level are referred to as *victory and defeat finale cues*. These are usually
short, one-shot bits of music that may or may not be tied to animation, graphics,
or text. Much will depend on how elaborate the setup is at the end of the level and
whether a short cinematic or a still graphic is used. However, regardless of the visual
method, the music for these cues will have to say it all and provide complete emotional influence.

Winning cues will be upbeat, triumphant affairs that congratulate the player on a job
well done. The more intense the level, the more musical applause will be given in order
to provide the appropriate amount of praise. A bugle call of three or four measly notes
after a huge battle that took 45 minutes to complete will not contrast well at all, but a
full orchestral fanfare that lasts 5-10 seconds would fit the bill perfectly. The larger the
accomplishment, the bigger the fanfare. The same applies in the reverse; small achievements only require small flourishes to make the point.

Losing cues can reflect either a total defeat or offer encouragement to the player for
the failure, depending on the attitude of the game. An edgy game designed specifically for adults will inevitably be hard on any thrashing the player gets and will use
this opportunity to tease and torment the player for sub-par performance as part of
the entertainment. A children's game will instead attempt to give support and cushion
the loss so that the younger player won't be discouraged and will want to try again.

Function of Game Music: building the atmosphere

chapter 5

Both of these cue examples follow an unsuccessful attempt to complete a level but with very different methods and intentions. The type of music created for a defeat cue can run through a variety of emotions depending on the purpose; the tempo is generally slower and not as compelling as the victory cue. On rare occasions, a developer will bypass the losing cue altogether and rely on the power of deafening silence instead as appropriate punishment.

Used by permission from id Software, Inc.

Doom 3 (victory cinematic, shown) contains effective victory and defeat cues.

Super Mario Bros. (NES), *Mario Kart 64* (N64), *Suikoden* (PS1), *Final Fantasy XII* (PS2), *Contra 4* (Nintendo DS) and *Doom 3* (PC) are all popular games with excellent examples of victory and defeat cues. Even those games dating back to 1985 and earlier utilize musical bonuses to either reward or tease players (sometimes letting them off easy).

Adaptive & Interactive Music

As the complexity of video games continues to increase, music has become more tightly integrated into the experience through the use of interactivity. Instead of a detached linear score merely accompanying players through their journeys, such as in film, adaptive and interactive techniques enable music to adjust in real time to what is happening in the game. It is almost impossible to predict what a player will do in every situation—but by utilizing this technique, music has the ability to morph into the level of intensity and involvement the situation demands.

> *Super Mario Galaxy* for the Wii does a great job of smoothly and musically reacting to onscreen developments.
>
> *Jed Smith (Lead Producer, betafish music)*

Tools for the creation and implementation of interactive audio range from proprietary, in-house applications such as those created and used on the *Halo* series to those developed by third-party middleware companies for a number of purposes. Audiokinetic's Wwise, Firelight Technology's FMOD, and RAD Game Tools Miles Sound System are strong third-party applications that allow audio creators to define sound behaviors within the game, build interactive music structures, and edit and mix in real time. Microsoft Cross-Platform Audio Creation Tool (XACT) is another powerful tool that is specific to the Xbox console and Windows PC—allowing control over many implementation issues and including multiple musical stems for interactive use.

> The *Halo* series contains one of the best implementations of interactive arrangements, due to the Direct Music system and the orchestral content. The procedural music engine in *Spore* is also along these lines, but it generates musical performance on the individual note level.
>
> *David Javelosa (Professor/Technologist/ Composer, Santa Monica College)*

Courtesy of Audiokinetic   Reprinted with permission from Microsoft Corporation

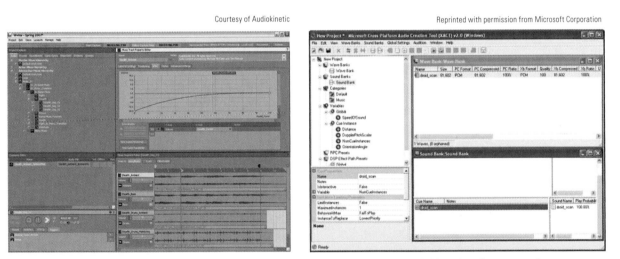

Wwise (left) and XACT (right) are two of the powerful middleware tools available to handle game audio.

Two popular methods are used to achieve the goal of adapting to the player's movements throughout a game: horizontal re-sequencing and vertical re-orchestration. Both methods provide a feeling of interactivity and the illusion of a score that is following the player's every move—a powerful application that brings an entirely different level of musical accompaniment than ever seen before.

Horizontal Re-Sequencing

Horizontal re-sequencing is the practice of utilizing pre-composed cues or small musical segments that are shuffled according to the in-game movement of the player. Any game that makes use of emotional influences on a player will benefit from a score that can change its mood accordingly—from simple puzzle games that increase tension as time runs out to huge multiplayer free-roaming environments with a variety of gameplay possibilities. Since music is created to evoke emotion, a piece of music that accompanies relaxed play will not provide the proper sense of uneasiness when a difficult situation presents itself. Horizontal re-sequencing allows for a change in music to reflect the new state by introducing music that is more in tune to what the player is experiencing.

For example, a simple puzzle game could easily include three different music segments available to complement what is happening. The game may start casually as the player makes decisions that are not stressful; the music would be unhurried and upbeat to match the carefree mood. However, as the allotted time begins to run out, perhaps with the appearance of a one-minute warning, the music could become more tense—with a faster tempo to increase the pace and match the now hurried feel of this portion of the game. Finally, as the final 10 seconds begin to count down, the music might turn ominous, chaotic, and stressful as the player encounters the last chance to make it to the next level. Each piece of music is designed to match the feelings of the player or to induce those emotions as part of the entertainment. How they are implemented and employed is another matter.

Asteroids, the popular arcade classic created by Atari in 1979, is an overly simplified example of horizontal re-sequencing. This early game didn't have any accompanying music, but it did utilize a two-note sequence that cleverly established the mood of the gameplay. At the beginning of each level, the two tones would alternate every couple of seconds as a casual, hardly noticeable background. As more asteroids appeared onscreen, the tempo of the alternating notes increased—creating a very effective sense of urgency and danger. The tempo increased gradually until the end of the level or until the player's ship was destroyed. When the player successfully moved to the next level, the tempo slowed to its normal setting and the sequence was repeated.

Courtesy of Atari Interactive, Inc.

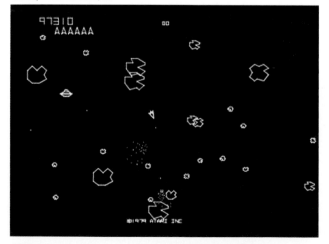

Asteroid's two-note sequence established the mood.

Final Fantasy VIII is another example of interactive music that utilizes horizontal re-sequencing. As players maneuver throughout the story, the music follows their actions. Exploring in a relaxed state provides a compatible soundtrack, while segments that produce a change in the storyline result in another. As a boss character is engaged, the music changes dramatically—increasing in tempo and drama as the battle ensues. A large majority of games have used this particular technique and continue to do so in a more dynamic and purposeful manner.

Crafting solid music cues that can crossfade at any point or musical "stingers" that hit when appropriate can sometimes be a challenge for the composer. Using the previous puzzle game as an example, the main level music is the basis for everything else. No matter what the music consists of, there are several methods that can be used to create a "one-minute warning" cue. Planning everything in advance is a good idea, even if just to imagine how the cues will work before beginning work on these final musical cues. Obviously, an increase in tempo from the main cue is an acceptable way of adding tension and a hurried feel—each cue faster than the one previous. However, dramatic key changes, different instrumentation, or an increase of notes (from quarter to eighth notes, for example) are perfect ways to get the point across. An industrious audio programmer might take the concept further by adding markers to the cues so that the new cue will only hit on the downbeat or at the end of a measure. It's not always critical that the new music hit exactly at "one minute to go"; a second or two will hardly be noticed, which isn't a bad tradeoff for a musical sounding transition.

Vertical Re-Orchestration

Vertical re-orchestration takes horizontal re-sequencing in a slightly different although highly effective direction. Instead of transitioning between pre-composed bits of music as the situation dictates, this technique manipulates the mix of a single ongoing piece of music—either a long cue or loop—to match a player's activities within the game. Essentially, this equates to enabling or disabling specific tracks or layers of music in a mix—similar to a recording engineer doing so on a mixing console. Instead of a live person controlling the mix, it is done fully within the programming in reference to where the player is at the time or what the player is about to encounter in the game.

An FPS with a large, free-roaming environment and an extensive storyline would benefit from this technique. A player begins the game calmly exploring the surroundings; the music is simple, with a sense that there is an entire world to freely discover. There is no sense of urgency or threat, and the player can travel within the environment without fear.

As players round a corner, they subconsciously note the subtle change in the music and become more alert. The music hasn't changed drastically—perhaps an addition of a light percussion track or a new instrument layered into the mix—but they know something has changed in the experience. As they creep into a dark hall, a low synth pad is introduced—adding a taste of apprehension and hinting to the player at what is about to come. Suddenly, an evil creature leaps from the shadows—baring its teeth and slashing through the air with its razor sharp claws. The music, as expected, is heart pounding and dramatic—exuding a sense of extreme danger. Now the adrenaline is pumping—and the music changes again to provide the motivation to stay in the fight and defeat this nasty creature. As the player finally overpowers the creature, the music calmly returns to the feeling of peace and the exploration continues. In all of these instances, the same piece of music is used as layers of instruments are added and disabled to suit the occasion.

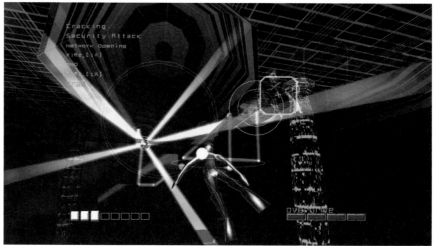

Rez is a phenomenal example of vertical re-orchestration.

Creating music that can be effectively used in these instances isn't as difficult as it initially seems. Once the variety of emotions for the level is established, it's a matter of creating a selection of layers that will fulfill each one; the only difference is that the same piece of music is being used to do this. Many composers will work backwards in this process by first creating a dense cue that could be used for an elaborate battle scene. Since this will be the busiest and most complex bit of music, it makes perfect sense. To create levels of music with less intensity, layers can easily be subtracted for a basic exploration or discovery cue. From these basic elements, additional tracks can be triggered as the situation dictates.

To increase the tempo of gameplay, or for a change of dynamics, enable the percussion tracks; whether they are light or intense will depend on their intention. If a happy mood needs to change to dark, alter the same bit of music by disabling tracks that are happy and enabling those that are dark (e.g., using minor chords). The composer can easily create a track in a major key and another similar one in a minor key. Changes in key are also a way to evoke a dramatic change, and the composer can easily create a track in an appropriate key and have the programmer toggle it off or on as necessary. As the pace of the gameplay increases and becomes more intense, more tracks can be enabled until the majority of tracks are playing in the final battle cue. As long as the composer and audio programmer work together, or if scripting is being utilized, each transition will remain musical—and players will only take notice of each subconsciously. Games such as *Need For Speed 3: Hot Pursuit*, *Gauntlet: Seven Sorrows*, *Rez*, *Guitar Hero*, *Rock Band*, *Dance Dance Revolution*, *Karaoke Revolution!* and *Parappa the Rapper* are all phenomenal examples of vertical re-orchestration that demonstrate the effectiveness of this type of implementation.

Jamie Lendino on Adaptive & Interactive Audio :::::

Jamie Lendino is an independent sound designer and music composer with 10 years of experience in the game industry. He has created audio for over 30 games, including *Monopoly: Here & Now*, *SpongeBob's Atlantis SquarePantis: Atlantis Treasures*, *Elder Scrolls IV: Oblivion*, *Zoo Tycoon 2: Endangered Species*, *Mage Knight: Apocalypse,* and the mobile version of *True Crime: New York City*. When he's not creating alien sound effects or working out drum parts for his next composition, he is busy indulging his other passions: writing, reading (both fiction and non-fiction), fast cars, and astronomy.

Jamie Lendino
(Composer/Sound Designer, Sound For Games Interactive)

Adaptive audio is either music that adapts to onscreen gameplay, swelling and ebbing in intensity level, or sound design that is randomized or "mixed" in real time to 5.1 so that it sounds as natural as possible—such as when using Microsoft XACT or Creative Labs ISACT. When done correctly, adaptive audio solves thorny issues such as endlessly looping the same tracks while a character explores a level, using long periods of silence or ambience to fill audio space, or hearing overly repetitive sound effects. Adaptive audio can really take a game to the next level, especially with today's available tools.

Adaptive Audio

Adaptive audio allows a composer who is talented enough to know how to use the technology to "make the music suit the mood." You're walking down the country lane when six barbarians leap out and attack you. One player may kill them off in 10 seconds, and another may take 45. Adaptive music keeps the frenzied battle music going naturally and without the perception of excessive repetition for either case—and then winds down the energy level when the last villain expires. Did you use your supercharge attack? The special high-energy music can't just replace the notes that were playing; it has to merge in at the right moment and fade away at the right time—sounding like that's what was intended all along. Describing it here makes it sound straightforward, but it requires both talented composers and skillful engineers to pull it off without sounding like three people taking turns plugging your headphones into their iPod and then unplugging it again.

Don Daglow (President & CEO, Stormfront Studios)

Adaptive audio can help create more immersion. Being able to adapt the pace and tone of audio to game flow allows for larger swings of emotion during critical moments of gameplay.

Mark A. Temple (Founder, Enemy Technology)

Adaptive audio heightens the game experience. The player feels more and more enveloped in the game if the music is directly connected to events and situations.

Henning Nugel (CEO, Nugel Bros Music)

When players have a direct effect on what they hear, it's like they're the developers in some small way. They control the environment and have an audible impact and effect on it. This in turn heightens the gameplay experience by adding suspense, intrigue, or motivation as a result of what players do.

Lani Minella (Master Creator, AudioGodz)

Adaptive audio is particularly important for horror/thriller games. There is nothing more lame than having an unchanging menacing drone underneath moments where suspense is building and moments where it is released.

Jed Smith (Lead Producer, betafish music)

Loops

Music *loops* in video games are complete musical cues that appear to play indefinitely. These gems with their relatively smaller lengths were initially the answer to storage space and processor speed restrictions but inadvertently solved the unpredictable nature of the player and how to keep music playing as long as they lingered in an area. Menu screens and certain gameplay applications, such as the interactive methods just discussed, benefit most from the creation of musical loops allowing for continuous accompaniment for a few seconds to infinity. Most games, including simple puzzle games and intensive multiplayer games, have use for loops as part of their musical makeup.

These bits of music can be short or lengthy depending on the duration a player may have to listen. To reduce the likelihood a player will notice any repetition, the loop should be as long as possible. When created successfully, there will be no indication of the actual repeat point—and the music will play on until a transition is triggered. Composers have to use care in the creation process (e.g., starting a loop on a beat or ensuring a cymbal or reverb tail doesn't get cut off as the cue ends and restarts). There are many ways to accomplish this, but how it is done effectively is entirely dependent on the style of music.

Long loops aren't necessary when the expected duration of a player's presence is short, but there are some musical styles that require longer lengths in order to maintain the indefinite illusion. For example, slow synth pads that are held for several bars would require a longer loop to complete a multi-chord progression. Conversely, due to the repetitious nature of dance and techno styles, these loops could be much shorter. Developers may plan on specific lengths but are usually open to slightly longer or shorter loops in order to keep the musicality of the cue. Composers will ultimately determine the length of the music as part of the creative process. Nearly every video game produced today utilizes music loops. As music creation tools improve, loops have become a highly effective way to present a musical background—entertaining the player while appearing to be seamless in the process. Loops used in *DiRT, Wii Sports, Mario Golf, Midnight Club 3, Project Gotham Racing 4, Heatseeker,* and *Overlord* are musical and skillfully crafted.

Courtesy of Codemasters

Loops used in *DiRT* are musical and skillfully crafted.

Ambient Tracks

Sound designers create ambient background tracks to present an appropriate audio environment based on sound elements. Game composers are often called upon to do the same thing, only musically. Many creative factors come into play in the development process that determine the best route of these mood setting atmospheres. An organized production team will have planned early whether ambient sound effects, ambient music, or a background score will accompany the gameplay—since only one should play at a time.

Electronic Arts, Inc.

Spore makes effective use of ambient music.

Without the constriction of predictable sounds, fantasy game environments benefit greatly from the use of ambient music as a backdrop. Music's power lies in the ability to evoke strong emotions from the listener—and for video games, this technique is perfect to establish the many moods a player can encounter. Uneasiness, apprehension, mystery, menace, and fright are just a few moods an effective ambient track can induce. While it is possible to accomplish this with only sound effects in some occasions, it's not as powerful as what the right music can provide.

I especially dig the music of Richard Jacques (*Headhunter, Starship Troopers*), Ian Livingstone (*Sinbad, Mace Griffin Bounty Hunter*), and Michael Giacchino (*Medal of Honor* series). I also remember being intrigued by the sinister and yet moving cello theme in *Max Payne 2*. I think it's important to hear something new and fresh in a game soundtrack, and all of these guys have a knack of reinventing their musical style with every new game soundtrack they compose.

Henning Nugel (CEO, Nugel Bros Music)

Music created for this type of application is generally simple and very open. It is free from melodies, chord progressions, or any predictable elements—since the point is to provide the background ambience and not something the player can mentally be directed to. Flowing sounds, such as ones created using audio morphing applications, are perfect for this—typically tuned to harmonize with any accompanying music or musical sound effects and layered like any music track. If done correctly, ambient music will create the desired feeling in a musical manner and will allow sound effects and dialogue to also be clearly heard. There are many games that provide excellent ambient music examples. *Deus Ex, Myst, Uru: Ages Beyond Myst, Halo, Homeworld, Stack Attack, Spore,* and *Darwinia* make effective use of this sparse but powerful musical element. Since the music in these games has been expertly created to provide a specific and unique feeling in the player, they provide a very recognizable soundtrack that also provides a distinctive audio identity to the games they accompany.

:::

Unlike music used in film and television, video game music can serve a considerable number of diverse purposes. It is essential for the developer and composer to fully understand the specific function music will serve within each segment of a game, how it will be created, and how it will be implemented to ensure that it's effective. The days are long over when music is simply dropped into a game and left to fend for itself. Music is clearly an integral part of the overall experience—on the surface where the player hears it and deep within the programming core where it is connected to everything that happens within the game. From menu screens to the essence of gameplay, game music has reached an important milestone and has become a force all its own. Yesterday's "afterthought" has finally become an absolute necessity in the incredible experience of today's video games.

:::CHAPTER REVIEW:::

1. Play 3 games currently on the market and identify the purposes of the music in each game. How does the music set the mood, identify era and location, set the gameplay pace, or mask real-life sounds and create immersion?

2. Referring to the same 3 games you chose in Exercise 1, discuss the placement of the music in each game. Does the music appear in association with credit sequences, cinematics, menu screens, in-game background, plot advancement and cut-scenes, and finale cues? How appropriate is the music in these areas?

3. Define and describe the function of adaptive and interactive music. How is this music distinct from loops and ambient tracks? What is the purpose of and distinction between horizontal re-sequencing and vertical re-orchestration? How is adaptive and interactive music used in the games you chose in Exercise 1?

CHAPTER

6

Creating Game Music

the melding of art & technology

Key Chapter Questions

- What *technological limitations* can impact the quantity, quality, and implementation of music in a game?

- Why is *pre-production* an important element of the music composition process?

- What are the *themes* composers are often tasked to create for a game project?

- How does the selection of a *sound palette* positively or negatively affect the music composition process?

- What specific details about the music are scrutinized during the *beta testing* phase?

Music has always been a beloved form of entertainment throughout history, and it is also a very natural fit for video games. Since early game audio was so rudimentary, music in games was unfortunately cast aside and looked down upon by serious music fans. As composers began to create music for games by crafting the limited electronic resources into effective audio backdrops, a subculture of video game music fans emerged. While these early scores were quite impressive in their own way, the mainstream culture continued to overlook their significance. As technology evolved, so too did the music that accompanied games; once again, game music was back on the radar—this time with respect! Game developers and composers have an incredible responsibility—not only to the project at hand, but to the players. Today's players expect to hear fantastic audio as part of the total experience and equal to what they hear in films, television, radio, and on their MP3 players—but with the added dimension of connecting personally to it. With this in mind, let's focus on effectively creating music that complies with the goals of the game—whether enhancing the activity onscreen, or taking center stage as part of the experience.

Pre-Production

As with any element created for a game project, the requirements and constraints associated with game music need to be clearly defined and established. It's not simply a matter of slapping music on a game and hoping it works; there must be a plan, and it must be followed. The *pre-production* stage allows the development team and the composer to set appropriate boundaries and to have everything laid out and established before any work is initiated. Music creation is a highly involved process. Time must be considered, logistics must be managed, and many administrative needs must be dealt with by the composer simultaneously—while continuing to be creative. For the composer, this is often an intense effort—not only to meet the needs of the game, but to do a high-quality job. For the developers, this is a time of nail biting and crossed fingers while waiting for their vision to be translated into music. The better prepared both entities are going into the job, the better the outcome will be. Pre-production is essential.

Much like the process the developer uses when considering sound effects, music is added to the sound asset list in the early development stages. Each planned area of the game (including menu screens, game levels, and cinematics) is examined, and a determination is made about the style and format of the accompanying soundtrack. Graphic, animation, cinematic, and programming assets are also thoroughly examined and prioritized—allowing the technical sound considerations to be made and their boundaries firmly established.

Technical Considerations

In the not so distant past, music and sound effects took a back seat to the rest of the game content. The quality of graphics always seems to be the developer's first priority, and high resolutions take up massive amounts of storage and processor capability. It is extremely important to plan for the use of the game platform's capabilities; in doing so, some give and take between quality and file size is inevitable. Music has suffered greatly in these development battles and even today seems to be the first set of assets the developer degrades when faced with an obstacle.

Fortunately, today's game consoles and computer platforms have substantial capabilities—and the quality of game audio has increased significantly over time. However, resources are still limited. Managing sound effects within a game environment is simple in comparison to music that has multi-channel capability and often huge file sizes. Definite boundaries must be established to ensure that all assets are allowed to carry out their purpose unencumbered. In addition to originating suitable music for the game experience, it is essential that composers—or the audio engineers they team up with—recognize the restrictions and see to it that the music sounds its best within them.

Final Format Requirements

The file format in which the music will be delivered (or converted to by the developer) gives the composer a preview of what the music will sound like within the game. *Uncompressed* audio such as .wav or .aiff will ensure full fidelity and is the preferred method of music file creation. This format allows for crisp highs and warm lows that are fully expressed by an uncompressed format.

Compressed audio such as .mp3 or .ogg will offer significantly smaller file sizes at the expense of quality. While most of today's culture has accepted the lower sound quality of these smaller formats, game creation is all about delivering more than what the player expects—even if the compressed format works against it. While ultra high and subtle low frequencies aren't represented in the .mp3 or .ogg formats effectively, composers can work around these limitations and still make their efforts fit within the context of the game environment. Knowing about the delivered and final formats in advance will ensure the music's level of quality.

Diagram by Per Olin

Developers will often utilize both compressed and uncompressed formats, depending on the priority the music has within each segment of the game. Music that is dominant in a scene will typically be uncompressed, while music that is secondary to what is happening—such as music blaring from a boom box within a skateboarding game—will likely be heavily compressed.

Uncompressed	Compressed
.wav, .aiff	.mp3, .ogg
Larger files; higher quality	Smaller files; lower quality
Dominant music	Background music
Can be streamed directly from disc	Used when space is tight

Implementation also determines the format. Music that is to be streamed directly from the game disc will be uncompressed, since this arrangement allows for music to completely bypass the CPU and utilize the console's separate sound hardware instead. Music competing with other game assets for appropriate memory allocations will usually be in a compressed format, since its footprint is considerably smaller.

Another viable format to consider is MIDI—which, despite its reputation as an unrefined form of computer music, still maintains a purpose in games. When storage space or processor capacity is a major issue, music created in this format is a lifesaver. Ultra small MIDI files will trigger a preset sound bank, solving many problems developers face on platforms such as handhelds or cell phones. Composers will create music utilizing an internal sound set and deliver the .mid file to the developer for implementation. MIDI files differ greatly from digital audio formats both in the approach to their creation and the available sound quality—and the composer will experience a greater challenge when creating them.

Mono, Stereo, or Surround

Most music playback is represented as two-channel *stereo*, and the creation process centers around a listening field of 180 degrees. If the developer requires something different, it is good to have this revealed as early in the process as possible. It's not a difficult task to convert a stereo image to *monophonic* (or *mono*) for the occasional localized applications within a game, but creating music in multi-channel *surround* will take a bit of effort and requires advanced planning.

Diagram by Per Olin

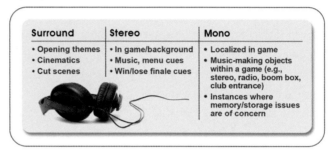

Surround	Stereo	Mono
• Opening themes • Cinematics • Cut scenes	• In game/background • Music, menu cues • Win/lose finale cues	• Localized in game • Music-making objects within a game (e.g., stereo, radio, boom box, club entrance) • Instances where memory/storage issues are of concern

Common uses for sound formats

The expected audio playback system on which the player will hear the music will occasionally influence how the composer and audio engineer utilize the stereo field. A PC game with speakers placed closely on each side of a computer monitor will benefit from an expanded spatial viewpoint. Utilizing wider panning methods will allow the music heard from the small speakers to sound larger and more encompassing. This can be as simple as panning most instruments hard left and hard right instead of attempting subtlety with only minor panning adjustments. Games that will be heard on a home theater system will naturally have wider stereo and surround fields—and there will be more options available during the creation and mixing processes. Subtle placement of instruments will be noticed and appreciated, so the extra effort will be worthwhile.

Sample Rate & Resolution

The *sample rate* and *resolution* of the final music format will determine not only the size of the audio files but also sound quality. Game composers typically record music at high sample rates and expect to convert down to the game specifications as needed. Often, 96 kHz sample rate/24-bit resolution is used during the creation phase to ensure the highest possible sound quality. While modern games don't allow for such large file sizes, they do utilize 48 kHz and 44 kHz sample rates as well as 16-bit resolution—which provide an excellent quality-to-file-size ratio. Coincidentally, 44 kHz/16-bit is the format for CD audio—and playback in a game environment using these yields outstanding results.

Diagram by Per Olin

Rate (kHz)	Description
7.418 – 8.192	Telephone (low-quality)
11.025	Voice (medium-quality)
22.05	Voice (high-quality)
32	FM standard
44.1	CD standard (digital audio devices)
44.1 – 48	DAT standard (barely distinguishable from 44.1)
44.1 – 96	DVD audio standard

Sampling rates and their common uses

Games created for next-generation consoles almost always use CD-quality audio. However, as target platforms move to PC, handheld devices, and even cell phones, lower sample rates and resolutions become the solution to smaller storage space and reduced processor capacity. Obviously, PC games are entirely dependent upon the storage capacity of the game disc and whether or not the audio can be streamed directly from it or through the sound card. Reducing sound files to 22 kHz/8-bit will enable more music to be used in a game—but at the expense of some quality. Handheld and cell phone games can go as low as 8 kHz/4-bit, but developers may opt to utilize various compression schemes in order to preserve at least some of the sound quality. These low-quality conditions invariably add audio artifacts and a significant noise floor, which make them almost unusable. However, skilled composers with advanced warning can still make their work acceptable.

A composer should always keep in mind that the usable frequency spectrum is reduced as the sample rate and resolution are decreased. Understanding the final parameters will make the available options clear—and an appropriate sound palette and instrument selection can be made wisely. Hi-hats, cymbals, percussion instruments, and the attack of a drum hit and guitars will be affected by a decrease in the available high frequency range—and their sizzle and sparkle will be noticeably diminished. At 22 kHz/16-bit, the range will increase slightly but rapidly as the sample rate and resolution are further reduced. Planning ahead for low settings will prevent wasted time and allow the composer to work around these restrictions to keep the music sounding great.

Playback Expectations

There is a huge quality disparity between cell phone music and a home theater system. Due to this, why would a composer spend countless hours massaging minor musical subtleties for a cell phone game if it will never be appreciated?

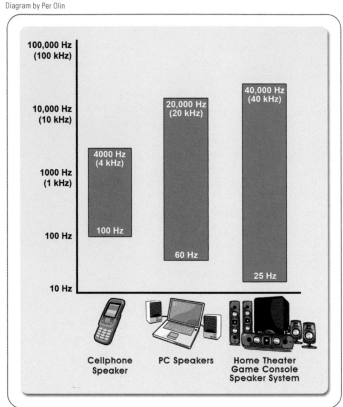

Diagram by Per Olin

Knowing what the target sound system is in advance will not only allow you to plan your time accordingly, but it will ensure a smooth creative process. Most importantly, you can create solid music specifically targeted to the capabilities of the *playback* system. Game music for earphones or tiny internal speakers is approached far differently than music for a multi-channel, subwoofer-enhanced home theater system. Music for handheld games is less complex, has minimal bass frequencies, and typically utilizes sample- or electronic-based instrumentation. This is not to say that music for smaller platforms isn't taken seriously; it's a consideration of the extra expense involved in hiring a full orchestra—which isn't justified, considering the associated platform. What *is* created should fit the game appropriately and sound great within the platform limitations.

Frequency ranges of standard game platforms, showing how the quality of the device on which the game will play influences the audio created for it.

The next-generation consoles that are normally presented through a home theater system have a greater frequency response and wider stereo/surround separation in which to fully enjoy the unique subtleties of skilled composers, musicians, and audio engineers. The music will generally be more complex, contain more instrumentation, utilize a greater frequency range (especially in the low and sub frequencies), and take advantage of the skills of live musicians on a more regular basis. Live orchestration is money well spent on these large productions—and the effort can be fully realized.

Between these two extremes lies the PC, along with its incredible unpredictability. The capabilities of computer platforms are completely out of a game developer's control, and it is impossible to know the exact configuration of each player's system. Developers will publish their minimum hardware requirements for a game and can only cross their fingers that the game runs well on the player's system.

From the sound aspect, there are many variables that can affect the quality of audio output—from the features of the sound card to the types of speakers used. A composer's best option is to target the work for standard, middle-of-the-road speaker quality and test on low-quality speakers to ensure a good overall sound. Subwoofers are not always available equipment on these systems, so a composer cannot rely on a low end playback capability as a standard. Music created for the PC typically follows the course of next-generation consoles: large productions where needed and more complex music structures.

Adaptive & Interactive Considerations

Music is normally created with a linear format in mind. The music has a beginning, middle, and end—guiding the listener on a specific, well-conceived musical journey. The composer is able to fully express an idea and create it—knowing the music will remain in the game exactly as it is composed. In a video game setting, this type of music accompanies the player in a more casual manner and might be looped—although creative programming can make it almost seem as if players are not only controlling their characters but the music as well. Regardless of how the music is implemented in this case, it is still linear.

Music composed for *adaptive* or *interactive* purposes requires additional work and planning. Enabling music to change at any moment as the player moves unpredictably through a game environment requires solid skills on the part of the composer and audio programmer. Obviously, the composer should be fully aware of the intentions of the developer, especially if interactive music is the goal—since it will entirely change how the music is created.

Due to memory and processor restrictions, it is safe to say that cell phone and small handheld game devices will not utilize adaptive or interactive music. PC, arcade, or next-generation consoles have a much higher possibility of using this advanced form of music presentation—but this ultimately depends on the needs of the game itself and whether this type of music is appropriate.

Sony Computer Entertainment America

flOw contains a well constructed interactive game score.

Metal Gear Solid series utilizes interactive techniques such as shifting the level music when the player is seen by one of the guards. *Need for Speed: Most Wanted* uses vertical re-orchestration to change the mood to accompany whether the player is winning, losing, or being pursued by a police car. *Rez*, a first-person shooter (FPS) based almost entirely on music, gradually increases the intensity of the music by both layering and cross-fading tracks as it responds to the player's actions, such as destroying bad guys. There are numerous ways to adapt music to the onscreen action, and these games only highlight a few of them. Other games, such as *BioShock*, *flOw*, *God of War II*, *The Lord of the Rings Online*, *Uncharted: Drake's Fortune* and *Halo* all contain well constructed interactive game scores worth further examination.

:::::: Combining Standard & Adaptive Music in *The Legend of Zelda: Twilight Princess*

Koji Kondo, Toru Minegishi, and Asuka Ota crafted the considerable score to *The Legend of Zelda: Twilight Princess* utilizing a mixture of standard and adaptive techniques. The opening scene, menus, and variety of seamless cinematic sequences have been created as typical linear music cues found in most game titles. Interactive music cues dominate the actual gameplay—changing and shifting to match the variety of onscreen action. This particular game has an extensive storyline encouraging considerable exploration that is often filled with tension, battles, and celebratory moments.

Nintendo

The nearly 200 music cues that accompany the gameplay are designed to change as the situation dictates. As the player explores the environment or moves forward through the story, the music is light with a simple melody. As characters appear who threaten the player, the music shifts to a slightly tense cue and then back to the exploratory cue as the danger passes. In instances in which the player unlocks a secret passage or rescues captured non-player characters (NPCs), the music changes to a brief, celebratory flourish to congratulate the player before returning to the level cue. Occasionally, to break up any potential monotony of the exploratory track, the music will become completely mute—allowing the ambient sound effects to take over. After an appropriate amount of time, the simple melody will resume until the next situation arises that requires a change of mood.

Platform

The primary *platform* for which a game is developed will determine many of the previously discussed parameters—such as final audio format, number of available channels, and expected playback systems. It will also clue the composer in to how the music will be implemented or managed by the game and the many creative options that might be available. Current generation consoles have great features and are solid improvements over the previous generation of consoles—and we can expect continued enhancements, especially in the use and implementation of sound.

Diagram by Per Olin

Design Factors	Microsoft Xbox 360	Sony PlayStation 3	Nintendo Wii
Audio channels	256	512	64
Maximum capable sample rate	48 kHz	44.1 and 48 kHz capable	44.1 and 48 kHz capable
Maximum capable resolution	16-bit	16-bit	16-bit
Sound file format	XMA (encoded from uncompressed .wav during implementation)	As dictated by developer	As dictated by developer
Playback formats	Mono, stereo, and Dolby Digital surround sound	Mono, stereo, 7.1 Dolby Digital, Dolby TrueHD, DTS surround sound	Mono, stereo, and Dolby ProLogic II surround sound
Additional console resources	320 independent decompression channels using 32-bit processing	256MB shared memory available for audio needs and playback of Super Audio CD formats	512MB shared memory available for audio needs and speaker in remote hand controller

Past systems such as the PlayStation 2 were very specific about audio formats—often requiring their own development systems to convert audio created by the composer and sound designers to what would work on the console. There were many difficulties in this process regarding file sizes, sample rates, and other issues that affected the audio outcome. While most games focus on the newest systems, there are still many opportunities to work on older platforms. If this becomes the case, you should fully investigate how the music will be implemented, along with the audio capabilities of the intended game platform and audio engine that will drive the game assets. For example, the PS2 and Xbox require a very specific number of samples in a sound file in order to loop seamlessly and to convert to the platform-specific format successfully. Current-generation consoles such as the Xbox 360 need embedded start and stop loop points in a file in order to produce a seamless loop. Minor limitations such as these can be disastrous if the audio isn't formatted correctly, but the game composer should always stay one step ahead in order to prevent such nightmares.

Tom Graczkowski on Game Platform Considerations :::::

Tom Graczkowski
(Composer/
Graphic Designer,
TDimension Studios)

After becoming a graphic designer, Tom went back to college to pursue his other passion—sound. Although he had composed electronic music for a few years, it was engineering and production that initially caught his interest. This soon changed when Tom realized the potential of sampling to create realistically sounding orchestral music. Despite his lack of experience with orchestral music, Tom drew from his music programming background and began to experiment with different methods to make his compositions sound realistic. He has received numerous awards—including the Best Audio Programming for the orchestral suite *Hocus Opus* and Outstanding Achievement presented by Studio 306 of Toronto. Tom was also recognized in *Keyboard* magazine as its Unsigned Artist of the Month. Currently, Tom is delving deep into the art of interactive scoring, and he continues to research and experiment with ways of making orchestral samples sound as real as possible. His music can be heard in a number of independent film projects—such as *Yoga at Sandy Lane, A Touch of Courage* and *Gladys and Pips.*

If you're dealing with current-gen consoles such as the Xbox 360 and PS3, you'll probably use a multi-stream system that will allow for music tracks or stems to be cross-faded between them. However, if you're composing for a portable or handheld, then you'll likely be dealing with a single-stream system. In this case, you're going to be chopping your music into small sections that the game will interchange. The challenge in dealing with handhelds is to have all the sections work well musically and seamlessly together.

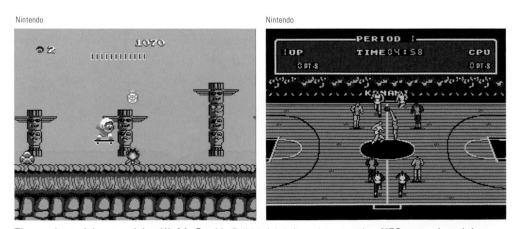

Nintendo   Nintendo

The music on *Adventure Island* (left), *Double Dribble* (right), and every other NES game shared the same sound set.

Preset Sound Banks

Most music created by game composers today is delivered to the developer in a digital audio format, but this is not the only method or the one that is always preferred. Games and the platforms they are played on can also utilize *preset sound banks*—internally stored sets of instruments and sounds that are triggered by a MIDI file to create the music. Memory and storage constraints will usually dictate this approach to provide quality music with less strain on the limited hardware assets.

The PlayStation 2 and most handheld game platforms are famous for their use of internally programmed sound sets that are either permanent to the sound hardware or exchanged on the fly by pre-loading downloadable sound fonts. Permanent sound sets allow the composer to create with a platform's standard sounds but have the downside of all games sounding similar to each other. The Nintendo Entertainment System (NES) was a good example of this; all games played on it sounded oddly similar—and instead of the individual games enjoying their own identity, it was the game system that did.

Replaceable sound sets are the most preferred method to employ when using preset sound banks. This method offers increased flexibility by giving each game its own audio identity and set of available instruments—and also even allowing a replacement of sound sets as the gameplay dictates. This method is a bit more labor intensive for the composer, but the end result is usually worth the effort. By having control over selected instruments, the music isn't limited to the 128 general MIDI sound set; the only limiting factor is the composer's imagination. In addition to creating the music, the composer will also deliver the instrument samples used in the compositions in the requested format—along with the appropriate files to trigger them.

Courtesy of Ken Ellinwood

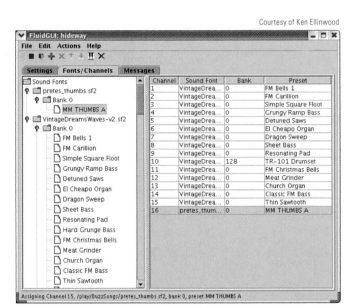

FluidGUI (www.sourceforge.net/projects/fluidgui) is a graphical front end for the FluidSynth shareware software synthesizer that can manage soundfonts.

Composer Preparations

Producing music for a video game is a commercial enterprise where compensation is exchanged for services rendered. The development studio or publisher has complete authority over every asset created for the project and will dictate what is to be done and when it will be completed. This is a work-for-hire endeavor and should be treated as such. Once the preliminary details have been sorted through, the composer can begin work. Defining the technical boundaries is essential but has nothing to do with what the music will say and what emotions it will portray. As early as possible in the development process, the composer should have discussions with the developer about the game's goals, music style, instrumentation, and preconceived ideas that may have been previously decided upon. A smart developer will solicit ideas directly from the composer, who typically has years of musical experience and is now the resident expert on the team.

From the composer's viewpoint, getting into the essence of the game can be difficult. The composer is usually hired late in the project and will have missed growing with the game like the rest of the team. In order to help jump start the creativity, composers should acquire a rough version of the game, graphics, storyboards, conceptual drawings, scripts, and anything else that will allow an inside view into the virtual world being created. By completely immersing themselves into the environments and the characters, composers will have better success creating music that is right the first time.

While information is being gathered in this pre-planning phase, it will also be a good time for the composer to do a little homework. Games based on realistic locations or time periods will typically use authentic music and instrumentation—and the composer may need to study the specific subtleties and gather appropriate instruments or instrument samples to pull it off convincingly. The composer can also use this time to experiment with rough ideas and present them to the development team to ensure that the score is on the right track. Early in the process is the best time to solicit suggestions and make sure everyone is on the same page.

Before You Compose for Games . . .

First, play a variety of video games; it is always good to know where the industry has been, where it is now, and what the newest trends are. Secondly, listen to all kinds of music; be able to pull inspiration from a large net. Finally, always try to think outside of the box; finding new ways to implement audio or adapt new musical styles can give a new depth to the game. Sometimes the most obvious path isn't always the best.

Nathan Madsen (Lead Composer/Sound Designer, NetDevil)

The composing and recording process is inherently complex—even more so when composers work outside of their personal studios. For a full orchestral score, for example, commercial studios must be researched and scheduled; musicians, copyists, arrangers, and conductors must be hired; and dozens of other logistical matters must be resolved far ahead of time—since these entities are often booked months in advance. In addition to composition duties, composers can quickly find their time stretched incredibly thin. Making a solid plan and taking care of the logistics in an organized effort early on will ensure successful recording sessions at the end of the process.

Reprinted with permission from Microsoft Corporation

Courtesy of NovaLogic, Inc.

Jack Wall, composer for *Jade Empire*, heavily researched Chinese and Asian instrumentation prior to composing in order to bring a realistic element to the musical backdrop.

Russell Brower and Ron Fish, composers for *Delta Force: Black Hawk Down*, explored African instruments and located talented musicians who could play them skillfully—resulting in a well-crafted score.

Taking Criticism: It's Not Personal!

Composers are expected to draw upon their inner spirits to create evocative and compelling musical accompaniment. However, in order to survive in the game industry, it's important to remember that criticism shouldn't be taken personally and must instead be considered as a critique of the "product" that must ultimately satisfy the needs of the game. There are developers who understand how these demands can stifle creativity and will often give composers the freedom to utilize their talents unencumbered. However, if you find yourself involved in a less than perfect situation, exercise patience and convey your needs to best serve the game's requirements.

Tom Salta & Bob Rice on Game Music Composition Challenges :::::

Tom Salta
(Composer/Producer/
Solo Artist,
Persist Music)

Tom Salta is an award-winning composer who writes and produces music for film, television, and video games. Renowned for his versatility and writing styles, Tom has composed original soundtracks for *Red Steel* (Winner of IGN's Best Original Score), *Tom Clancy's Ghost Recon: Advanced Warfighter 1* and *2* (*GRAW* nominated for "Best Video Game Score" at the 2006 MTV Video Music Awards), *Cold Fear,* and *Need for Speed Underground 2.* His orchestral music has also been featured in several motion picture trailers including *Harry Potter and the Order of the Phoenix* (Warner Bros.), *Last Mimzy* (New Line Cinema), and *Arthur & the Invisibles* TV trailers (Weinstein Co.). Recording under the artist name Atlas Plug, Tom's high-energy mix of electronica, orchestral, breakbeat, and rock grooves grace NBC's *Third Watch,* UPN's *America's Top Model,* and MTV's *Making the Video* television shows; *DOA: Dead or Alive* trailers; and *Crackdown, The Fast & the Furious: Tokyo Drift,* and *Project Gotham Racing 3* video games.

The most challenging part for me when scoring music for games is that I often don't have any final visuals to work with. I also usually find myself creating music for new franchises that I've never seen before, so it's often difficult to imagine what the locations, environments, characters, structures, props, and gameplay scenarios look like.

Bob Rice
(Founder & CEO, FBI
[Four Bars Intertainment])

Bob has been in the music business since age 15. He began as a concert promoter in Cleveland, Ohio—the birthplace of rock-n-roll—and at 16, he founded his own record label and publishing company. After 10 years as a successful entrepreneur and with several hit records to his credit, Bob moved to California to join GRT Corporation as Vice President of Sales, Marketing & Promotion. While at GRT, Bob was awarded over 30 gold and platinum record awards. In the video game industry, Bob created and executive produced the world's first rock-n-roll video game, *Journey Escape*—featuring Journey, the # 1 rock group in the world at the time. In 1992, he founded FBI—which represents award-winning "A List" game composers. Bob is on the Board of Directors of the Game Audio Network Guild (G.A.N.G.) and is a member of the International Game Developers Association (IGDA).

Even though a game is far more complicated to write for than film, game composers have gotten to a point where they are producing music equal to the quality of film scores. In film, there is one beginning, one middle, and one end—and the consumer will hear the music only once. In games, there is usually one beginning, 2-4 endings, up to 100 middles—and players will hear the music for hundreds of hours. Game music must hold up for a much longer time, while always increasing the entertainment value of the game.

Deciphering the Client's Needs

You'd be surprised how differently people interpret music. When you're asked to compose something that sounds "mysterious," this means very little—unless you've found a kindred spirit who has the same interpretation you do! Asking questions and getting examples of the "vibe" the client wants is crucial, and it will save time for both parties.

Fernando Arce (Composer/Musician, damselflymusic)

Musical Themes

As the composer moves closer to the actual composition process, the focus shifts specifically to the music. Hopefully by this point, logistical, administrative, and business matters have been resolved and efforts can concentrate solely on creating. Distractions should be minimized during the creative periods, and nothing else should matter when the creativity begins to flow. The pressures are already significant, since all eyes are on the composer to add personality to the game.

The composer must translate graphics, storyline, characters, environment, and gameplay into a cohesive and fitting musical backdrop. How this is accomplished can vary for each composer—but whatever approach is taken, the composer must be able to say with music what other elements express with pictures. This is the moment where the compositional experience, musicianship, and ability to record it successfully collide to form a solid score.

To help in the process, film scores are a great source of inspiration to generate interesting and dynamic musical accompaniment. A few techniques work very well within game scoring—such as establishing the main, level, and character themes that give a distinct audio identity to important segments of the game. By starting with these particular ideas, the process will flow much more freely and allow the composer to maintain positive momentum.

Tom Salta's score for *Tom Clancy's Ghost Recon Advanced Warfighter* was nominated for best Video Game Score at the 2006 MTV awards.

From Concept to Theme

When composing music, I normally ask for enough material to be able to develop a concept for the game soundtrack. Some time is spent on thinking about instrumentation (Would an orchestral score benefit the game? Should it be more modern and rhythm-driven? Perhaps a mixture?), structure, and form (e.g., recurring motifs for characters or events). There are many other elements to consider—such as how much music is needed and how many tracks it is possible to create within a certain budget. When the producer has agreed to the concept, it's time to start composing. I normally start on the piano, shifting around ideas for motifs. After this, I often like to create a main theme for the game by incorporating the fleshed-out motifs as far as it's suitable. This often goes along with presenting the concept so the producer can decide early on if the music is heading in the right direction. As often as possible, I like to record real instruments into the often sample-based music to give them more life.

Henning Nugel (CEO, Nugel Bros. Music)

Main Theme

The first focus is typically on the *main theme* of the game. This isn't necessarily the title theme—but it should contain elements such as a melody, chord progression, or significant use of a particular instrument that becomes the "personality" of the game. This portion of the score will serve as a reference for all other music created for the project, and the use of these common melodies and rhythms will ensure that the music is interconnected. Eventually, the title theme can be created with these established elements utilizing the appropriate dramatic flair.

Most television programs utilize this technique generously. Music that was presented in the title theme will appear throughout the rest of the program, a few notes of the melody, a familiar rhythm, a subtle instrument riff—all purposefully interwoven within the score to bring the entire production together. Even the bumper music between scenes and before or after commercial breaks remains within the familiar territory established at the beginning of the show. Game composers can successfully utilize this technique to create a consistent musical picture and keep the score focused.

A main theme that will enhance a game by setting the tone while creating a specific audio identity requires a composer who not only possesses the skills and finesse to make it happen but who also fully understands the point and purpose of the game. There are many ways to approach each game and theme; the only rule is to ensure that whatever is finally created fits the experience like a glove. Richard Jacques accomplished this for *Headhunter*; Jesper Kyd did it for *Hitman 2*; and Gerard Marino, Mike Reagan, and Cris Velasco nailed the theme to *God of War II*. Not only do these greatly enhance a game, but they can live on to define a game series—such as what Marty O'Donnell and Michael Salvatori created for *Halo*, what Michael Giacchino did for *Medal of Honor*, or what Nobuo Uematsu crafted for *Final Fantasy*.

Sony Computer Entertainment America

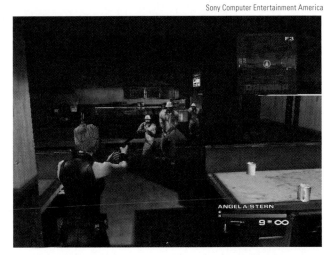

Richard Jacques' *Headhunter* theme fits the experience like a glove.

A "Top Down" Approach

I prefer a "top down" approach to writing music; that is, I feel it's important to start with a strong sense of the overall tone of the piece or project. I want to hear as much of the music in my head as possible before committing notes to paper, sequencing, recording, or playing with sounds and samples. This approach gives me the best chance of writing music with a strong thematic and melodic sense. Once I have as much music in my head as possible, I will generally put a rough sketch on paper—even if it's just an outline of the melody. After that, my process is probably similar to most. I have one PC running Cubase for recording samples and digital audio. I have three PCs running GigaStudio and one Mac running Pro Tools (which I use mostly for editing). I try to add live elements as often as I can. I play multiple woodwinds (sax, flute, clarinet, etc.) and guitar, so I often perform those instruments myself.

Billy Martin (Composer, Lunch With Picasso Music)

Level Theme

A game with multiple levels, worlds, or environments will benefit from the creation of a unique musical *level theme* for each area. Since game levels are designed to give the player a fresh perspective using a different environment, new music within them will also ensure this tactic is successful and offer some variation. Most games—from simple puzzle games with their varied colored backgrounds to major FPSs with detailed, distinctive renderings—would be perfect candidates for this type of audio treatment.

After the main theme has been established, the composer can focus on individual segments of the game—utilizing the same instrumentation. The target will be to establish a specific identity or mood for the various levels as determined by the developer. Instead of a huge production that may have been created for the opening sequence, music within game levels is less dramatic because its purpose is to serve more as background music. The occasional use of dynamic and elaborate music, as in interactive audio, will also fall within the determined level theme.

The *Legend of Zelda* series, from *Link's Awakening* on the Game Boy to *Twilight Princess* on the Wii, utilizes specific music for each area within a game. As the player wanders through villages, woods, mountains, deserts, lakes, caves, castles, dungeons, or ruins, music that was purposefully created for each section plays as the primary soundtrack for the duration. The mini-games—such as corralling the herd of goats into a barn or capturing one running down the village street in *Twilight Princess*—also have custom musical themes.

Nintendo

The Legend of Zelda: Twilight Princess uses different theme music for each level in the game.

This technique is taken even further when the player enters a shop or store; music exclusive to these places is heard and repeats upon each visit. This method allows a distinct feel and mood for each level or area of the game that often clues players into the surroundings or upcoming event without them having to actually see it—such as when a goat escapes. The players know what's happening just by the music, and not because they saw one run by.

Nintendo

Nintendo

The music's theme changes when the player reaches this new level in *The Legend of Zelda: Twilight Princess* . . .

. . . and changes again for these caves.

Most games utilizing a variety of locations, such as cityscapes and jungles, must vary the music accordingly. In *Mass Effect*, the music between the planet and space station environments is markedly different. Alexander Brandon created different level themes with distinct instrumentation for *Deus Ex* based on the area of the world the player was in—including New York City, Seattle, Egypt, or Germany. As part of the composing team on *Unreal Tournament*, Brandon also used distinct instrumentation and styles for level themes—such as those with Asian architecture. When combined with the overall electronic instrumentation and composition, these choices resulted in a unique sound specifically associated with the game.

Striking a Balance with Background

In music composition and production, it's very important to *not* let your musical ego get the better of you. Often, you just have to create background that should not distract the player but still provide sufficient atmosphere to heighten the game experience. On the other hand, background music shouldn't be lifeless and boring. The best game scores manage nearly the impossible: not commanding attention, but being a pleasing and enjoyable experience so that the player could sit back and focus on the music itself.

Henning Nugel (CEO, Nugel Bros. Music)

Character Theme

In addition to the main or level themes, composers may add another dimension to the storytelling effort by creating a unique *character theme* for each major character in the game. This technique is used widely in films to announce a main character's entrance into a scene or to subtly make only that character's presence felt. Darth Vader of *Star Wars* is one of the more famous characters who has a distinct theme—one that oozes evil and strengthens his nefarious personality. Even handheld games such as the *Advance Wars* turn-based strategy franchise utilizes looping theme music for each character who commands units during every turn. Not all games contain princesses, evil warlords, or happy cartoon creatures—but each does typically have a significant entity that could benefit from this application of music. The appearance of an important game piece, a newly awarded game feature, or a power-up are all circumstances for which a character theme could be created. The shift in music that supports the character or item will increase its significance in the mind of the player and give added emphasis to its value. It also makes the game more fun!

Ammon Jerro (*Neverwinter Nights 2*, left) and Sonic The Hedgehog (right) each have their own recognizable themes.

Masafumi Takada specifically focused on the use of the character themes in *God Hand* for the PlayStation 2. As the various boss characters return to their devil forms, the music uses the same phrasing and tone to create an interaction between itself and the player. Koji Kondo, Toru Minegishi, and Asuka Ota created themes for major characters in *The Legend of Zelda: Twilight Princess* such as Princess Zelda, the Mailman, and the many boss characters (including Zant, Stallord, Blizzeta, and Diababa). These themes appear as the player encounters each character during gameplay. Kazumi Totaka, Minako Hamano, and Kozue Ishikawa—credited as the composers on *The Legend of Zelda: Link's Awakening*—also created specific themes for Richard, Moblin, and the Fairy. Solid Snake in *Metal Gear Solid 2* has a specific music theme. Ammon in *Neverwinter Nights 2* has a theme—and so does the Emperor in *Gauntlet: Seven Sorrows*. Other well-known game characters such as Mario, Wario, Princess Peach, and Sonic The Hedgehog also have their own recognizable themes.

Lennie Moore & Matt Sayre on the Game Music Creation Process :::::

For 20 years, Lennie has been a proven force as an accomplished composer, orchestrator, and arranger of music for games, film, and television in a wide range of musical styles from jazz to symphonic orchestra. He has composed music on 10 films, over 125 commercials, and several games—including *Dirty Harry, Outcast* (2000 nominee for Best Music by AIAS [Academy of Interactive Arts and Sciences]), *Dragonshard, War of the Ring*, and additional music for *Snoopy vs. the Red Baron*. He has also orchestrated for other composers on dozens of feature films and television movies. Lennie recently completed additional music for *Prince Caspian* and is teaching game composition at UCLA Extension and the USC Thornton School of Music.

Lennie Moore
(Composer, 3l33t Music)

I'm usually called by developers to compose music for live musicians. This includes composition, MIDI sequencing, orchestration, music preparation, recording session management, conducting, editing, mixing, and occasionally consulting on implementation. Planning and time management are critical in handling large projects of this nature. My process is fairly straightforward. I compose and sequence and get approval of the work with my clients. Then I or my music prep team orchestrate and copy parts for the players, book the sessions, record, edit, mix, master, and deliver the finished work to the clients.

Matt focused on combining his two loves in life: computer games and music. He received his Master's degree from the California Institute of the Arts, studying musical issues relevant to the growing interactive entertainment medium. He has since provided music, sound, and voice for games on the PC, Xbox 360, DS, and Wii. He currently lives in Seattle and freelances for developers around the world.

Matt Sayre
(Owner,
The Game Composer)

As a one-person show, it's important to have experience with not only composition—but also recording, editing, mixing, mastering, and many other disciplines when creating music. My process begins with creating a sketch at the piano. Then I input that sketch into my notation software and begin to orchestrate the music. Once orchestrated, I begin realizing each part using a combination of samples and live instruments. Once all the parts have been captured, I begin mixing the music to make it sound more like what I was hearing in my head at the piano. The mixing can easily take up half the total time of the entire process and is sort of a black art. No two mixes are going to be the same. Mastering is the second-to-final step where I get each tune to have similar volumes and general sound so the player doesn't get jarred whenever the music changes. The final step is letting the music rest for a day and reviewing it with fresh ears, where you wear all your hats and see if anything needs to be changed—from instrumentation to EQ.

Compositional Methods

Creating game music from an artistic standpoint is essentially the same as creating any other type of music. There are rhythms, melodies, counter melodies, dynamics, key and tempo changes, fills, and other musical nuances that are imagined from thin air and fashioned into a profound arrangement of sound. A distinctive mood is generated to complement and reinforce the experience—in film, video games, radio, Internet, and other media. How music is created depends entirely on the artist.

Game composers rely on their own personal methods that have been developed over the course of their previous hobbies and careers. There are no specific rules to guarantee success other than the method that produces an individual's best results. Some composers record as they compose—preferring to hear what each instrument and layer does to the overall soundscape in real time. Others use pencil and paper, never playing a note—hearing it only in their head and later for the first time as it is performed. There are as many methods to the process as there are composers.

> There is a tendency for game composers to spend too much energy on technical aspects rather than writing a great piece of music. First, focus on writing quality material. Once you have that perfect theme, then you can figure out how to get it to "work."
>
> *Tom Graczkowski (Composer/ Graphic Artist, TDimension Studios)*

Regardless of the variety of ways available to create appropriate music, there are many shared similarities used by industry personnel that work very well for games. For new game composers, consideration for these tried and true methods will help in the process and ensure consistent, appropriate, and unique musical soundtracks for any game project.

Choosing the Best Sound Palette

One of the primary goals in the creation of audio for a given project is to provide it with a distinctive and unique sound. The selected musical style is a good first step in this endeavor, but taking it further and narrowing the selection of instruments and musical sounds will also work in the composer's favor. With an infinite amount of noises, sounds, and instruments available in the recording world, it is important to focus on only those that support and convey the intended feel of the game. This collection of selected sounds and samples is often referred to as a *sound palette*.

When the pressure is on, a composer should have as few distractions as possible. Too many choices inevitably create unwanted disruption of the creative flow, since too much time is wasted making instrument choices. By narrowing the selection to a more manageable sound set, the composer is actually forced to be more creative with the fewer sounds that are available. While the sound set is condensed, it doesn't need to constrict the composer—and if other sounds are needed, they can be added to the palette and used as necessary.

Choosing the best palette of sounds is important and may actually take a few days to put together for a large project. It's easier to assemble sound banks and instruments for some game projects than for others. Obviously, an orchestral score will require typical instrumentation—but additional elements can be added for an interesting contrast, such as electronica or rock instruments. Period-based music will require collecting instrumentation from those specific eras. Particular genres of music that have expected sounds—such as techno, heavy metal, or bluegrass—will require certain instruments as part of the sound palette. For distinctive audio needs, the composer will choose sounds that satisfy the unique style or distinguishing features of the music.

Don't Wander From the Theme

During the music composition process, you might creatively wander off to explore other musical ideas that present themselves. Frequently, these ideas will have nothing to do with the current project. Following inspiration is a natural instinct most creative people share, but it can be incredibly nerve-wracking to realize that several valuable hours have suddenly been squandered. It is very important to remain disciplined during the development cycle and stay focused on the theme of the game. A common method to help you remain centered on the current game project theme is to surround yourself with other music in the same style. By listening to similar music, you allow yourself to subconsciously tune into the nuances, subtleties, and techniques associated with the needs of the project—increasing your level of success. Movies are also a great source of inspiration and research; these large budget productions showcase top industry talent and can certainly open your mind to many possibilities. By deliberately concentrating on the required style, you will remain locked on the theme of the game and ultimately work more effectively.

::::: *Red Steel*: Working by Candlelight

During the final week of scoring *Red Steel*, the deadlines were very tight. A bad storm hit my neighborhood that knocked down a tree across my driveway—taking out all the power to my home and the entire studio. I had to deliver more cues that weekend, and the power company couldn't come for two days. I used a chainsaw to get out of my driveway and I bought a generator that was powerful enough to run my main computers and our refrigerator. I worked by candlelight, finished the score, and delivered it that weekend.

Tom Salta (Composer/Producer/Solo Artist, Persist Music)

Mark Scholl on Composing Loops & Stems ⁞⁞⁞⁞⁞

Mark Scholl
(Composer, Screaming
Tigers Music, Inc. /
International Game
Technology)

Mark owns and composes for Screaming Tigers Music, an independent scoring studio for television, video games, and commercials. He received an Emmy as part of an award-winning team of composers for his collective work on *The Guiding Light* daytime television show. Mark is an in-house composer/sound designer for IGT, the largest casino video game company in the world. His music has been placed on numerous network and cable TV shows domestically and internationally, including *The Amazing Race*, *Gene Simmons' Family Jewels*, *Access Hollywood*, and *Entertainment Tonight*. Prior to his current full-time composition career, Mark toured with pop superstar Barry Manilow for 11 years—performing for the Queen of England and President Bill Clinton. Mark has also been a featured performer with two Canadian Symphony Orchestras and has toured with Andrew Lloyd Webber's Music of the Night show. Mark lives with his wife Robbin and eight dogs on their ranch in northern Nevada.

Based on discussions with the game team and first impressions from the visual references, I will start by designing a palette of instruments into my sequencing software. I will also import any video from the gameplay into the sequence for visual reference or have screen shots open on the desktop. At that point, I will sketch out tempos and basic theme ideas. Once I arrive at themes and tempos that I feel good about, I will start developing the arrangement and orchestration for the first piece. Usually at this stage, I will also start writing out the basic melody and chords or counterpoint lines into my notation program. I have learned over time that it can be very helpful to have the basic themes written out in a chart or score form—there are often situations where it may be required to re-recorded different versions or more versions of the original concepts based on project changes, months after the project is underway. I find it much easier to simply open a chart than to transcribe and re-learn my own work later on. It is also very helpful to have a chart started, since I usually add some live instruments and need to write charts for those parts anyway.

I will usually score any cinematics first as a clear way to establish melodies, themes, and instrumentation. Cinematics follow a linear timeline (beginning, middle, and end) and are scored just like a movie—where the music enhances the emotion, accentuates visual events, and conveys the overall feeling through the game images. Music for the actual gameplay (I call this type of composition "circular writing") consists of pieces that will need to loop back to the beginning at some point, since most gameplay is indefinite in length.

The piece that you write can vary, but 2-4 minutes long is typical. Players of a game certainly don't want to be consciously aware that they are listening to the same music over and over. Writing several minutes of music for each potential level, you can change the textures, musical elements, and themes enough without feeling like you are in a loop, but maintaining some continuity within the music. It is also very important to create a seamless loop back to the beginning of the track. The easiest way to achieve this result is by matching dynamics, instrumentation, and energy toward the end of the track so that it's the same as in the beginning; this will allow for a more seamless flow. If you can get the loop transition so you can't really tell where the track ends and the repeat begins, you will have accomplished the goal. Sometimes it is also necessary to create an "intro" portion of the track that will only be played once at each level. There are two ways to do this:

1. Write a separate short piece (which may correspond with a fixed length video intro) that will lead directly into the looping piece

2. Write the intro at the front of the loop

For the second version, you will need to give the engineer implementation instructions—including the exact length of the looping piece in milliseconds and the location in the track to which the piece would loop back. It is also necessary to create at least a couple of layers (or stems). Depending on the type of game, the first layer would be a bed track for a searching non-action mode—usually just some ethereal pads or some light rhythm track; another layer might be much more energetic and may include more aggressive rhythm—often additional percussion or drums. Finally, top layers of melodic elements and additional pads of some sort might be added. These layers are really just separate mixes of the fully produced piece. The way I accomplish this is to write, orchestrate, and mix the full piece and then go back and mute elements to create separate sub-mixes/stems or layers. When these mixes are implemented into a game by the engineer, the non-action layer will be used while the other layer or two will begin at the exact same time but muted by the game engine. The engineer will set up a trigger point in the game to un-mute the action layers based on game events. The end result is that you have elevated the intensity of the music to support action in gameplay.

Immersion

When hearing a game or film score that perfectly enhances the mood and visuals, you might feel that the composer truly understands the essence of the project and is able to convey it through music. However, the talent to deliver quality workmanship in the composition and production is only a small part of the overall picture. In order to create fitting musical accompaniment, the composer must truly be *immersed* in the world being created, be a part of it, and fully understand it. This allows the composer to hit the mark and to compose the right music the first time around.

Obviously, playing a rough version of the game for 10 minutes is not going to provide the appropriate insight. If the game is available in working form, you should make every attempt to spend some time with it and become familiar with the environments, characters, and rhythm and pace of the gameplay. By becoming personally involved with the production, you will gain a unique perspective that can only be obtained by getting "inside" the game.

In addition to previewing the game in action, consider surrounding yourself in your creative space with character depictions, conceptual renderings, and any available artwork. Every time you look up from your instrument, you may find yourself subconsciously reminded of the characters and world you are supporting and remain focused on the true spirit of the game. This technique is very effective and used by many top game composers. Since it is important to work efficiently, most find this extra help invaluable.

Experimentation

Video games are cast from extreme, cutting edge technology—and the music contained within them should convey the same excitement and innovation. Obtaining a fresh soundtrack that expresses originality often requires moving beyond traditional music creation methods. *Experimentation* is a way of stepping outside of the comfort zone and encouraging the creation of unique sounds and textures that typify game development. Obviously, some games are better suited for this mindset—such as those based on the future or space, or those portraying different worlds. However, even traditional games can gain from a new approach.

Prey's soundtrack steps outside of the comfort zone of traditional creation methods.

The simple act of sending an instrument that you wouldn't normally consider through an effects processor is often enough to create an interesting sound. With an abundance of effects plug-ins, sound mangling software, and audio editors, it is fairly easy to create something unexpected that works musically within a game setting—including:

- running a synthesizer patch through a Doppler effect
- applying distortion to an orchestral string sample
- reversing a drum loop with an audio editor
- adjusting a noise gate to open late on a percussive instrument

There are an almost infinite number of processes that can be tried. As long as the process adds an element that helps give the game its own audio identity, *there are no rules* in experimentation!

Don't Follow the Formula

I try to think of things that would make people laugh. For instance, just recently I was talking to a friend about doing music for an upcoming game and the characters in the game that make this music are really snooty characters. And since we don't have a lot of budget for the music, we thought, "Wouldn't it be great if two-thirds of what you hear is those characters arguing about the music, or saying, 'That was very well played, although I prefer an arpeggio to a cadenza.'" You see, that's outside the box thinking—and that's interesting.

George "The Fat Man" Sanger (Composer/Author)

Chris Rickwood on Game Composer Guidelines :::::

Chris Rickwood
(Composer, Rickwood
Music for Media)

Chris is an award-winning composer known for creating dramatic musical scores for video games, film, and television. His work can be heard worldwide on a variety of media for clients such as Activision, THQ, Microsoft, Cartoon Network, Capcom, and Nintendo. Chris has composed over 30 scores for Cartoon Network New Media; contributed music and sound for several PC games including *Evil Dead: Hail to the King, Law & Order: Criminal Intent, Civil War: Bull Run*, and *The Apprentice: Los Angeles*; and experimented with other game platforms, such as mobile phones and video poker machines. In 2006, he was invited to the team of composers hired to produce the new *Monday Night Football* theme for ESPN. Currently, Chris is working on several projects including Hi-Rez Studio's action MMOG *Global Agenda, Kingdom Under Fire: Circle of Doom*, and other titles that will be released on the Xbox 360, PS3, and Wii. Here are just a few of Chris' guidelines for game composers:

1. *Have confidence in your abilities:* My clients often ask me to compose music in a style I have never done before. Whenever they ask me if I can handle it, my answer is always an immediate "Yes!"

2. *In the beginning, write music without judgment:* One of my favorite techniques to sketch out a cue is to fire up the sequencer and just start singing. Notes don't matter. I need to get the general idea out of my head as quickly as I imagine it. By recording my singing, I don't waste time tweaking the MIDI notes or finding the perfect patch. Sometimes I will even take my performances, *heavily* process them, and use them in the final track.

3. *Challenge yourself daily:* My trumpet instructor in college followed this mantra: "Practice the things you can't do." I get most excited about projects where I am really uncomfortable and not quite sure if I will be able to pull it off or not. That way, I know that I am stepping outside of my comfort zone and challenging myself. By then end of the project, I will have learned something new and will be able to challenge myself even more on the next project.

Recording Methods

Game composers work in various ways to translate their compositions into what the player eventually hears. With powerful and flexible technology literally at a composer's fingertips, there are a wide variety of options available to create the final musical product. Music can be composed, recorded, and mixed on a simple multitrack audio program on a laptop or in a high-end, multi-million dollar, state-of-the-art recording studio. The game's budget, abilities of the composer, and needs of the music will dictate which route is taken.

As the quality of game audio increases within the industry, the player expects each new game to sound better than the last one. This phenomenon is generally forcing game composers and developers to increase their standards in order to keep up. This means continuous upgrades of equipment and software in their personal recording spaces and a more frequent use of commercial studios as the needs arise. Large game companies see the value of equipping their in-house teams with professionally designed studios and high grade gear—something that the independent composer can't always afford.

Commercial Recording Studios

Developers with large audio budgets tend to lean either toward using their own in-house spaces or commercial recording studios to capture appropriate performances. For an independent composer, there are many times when the size of the project and the number of musicians that will be recorded won't fit in a personal studio, and they look to other resources to assist in their needs. Recording a full orchestra, for example, requires a large space and team of experts who can produce a successful recording—typically something way beyond the composer's capabilities.

The advantages to contracting a *commercial studio* are many. Acoustically treated recording spaces, top of the line equipment, a team of experienced engineers and assistants, and the ability to focus solely on the job at hand instead of being bothered by maintenance issues, lease payments, employees, and insurance are just a few of the reasons why it is often worth the expense.

Ron Jones conducting in a commercial studio

As with any complex endeavor, there are also a few disadvantages as well. Renting a studio always means keeping one eye on the clock with other sessions booked and occasionally disrupting an already tight schedule, setting up and tearing down around those other sessions, and the expense that sometimes can eat into your budget. As with anything worth doing, there are always pros and cons to consider as you carefully weigh the quality and the expense.

Personal Project Studios

A composer's comfort zone is usually within the personal base of operations, and most create and record in their own studios. Whether it's simply in a spare bedroom, a dedicated recording space on their property, or in a rented office building, game composers establish a comfortable working space that encourages the free flow of creativity whenever their muse appears. Patterned specifically to their working style, the space is fully customized with favorite equipment placed where it is most ergonomic.

Home studios (such as that of author Aaron Marks) are a common part of today's game audio world.

A *project studio* can make all the difference in the quality of a composer's work. Except for a looming milestone, composers have full control over when and how they operate and can work when they are at their best. On top of that, there are none of the disadvantages that plague a rented commercial space. Composers with project studios can come and go as they please, with everything remaining just the way they left it. They don't have to agonize over monetary issues and rush because of limited funds or expiring session time. They can compose at a more leisurely pace and record as they go instead of trying to cram everything in during a single, expensive recording session.

> Don't go overboard with the track count. Unless you're composing an orchestral score, 8-10 tracks of nicely recorded or high-quality sampled instruments can be *plenty*.
>
> *Jamie Lendino (Composer/Sound Designer, Sound For Games Interactive)*

There are a few disadvantages that come with being the composer, engineer, musician, and technician, but—except for occasional equipment or software failures—these are minimal. The expense of equipment isn't much of a drawback, since most game composers put their previous hobby and gear to good use—and any new acquisitions are made from recent profits. Being in business as a composer allows for generous tax benefits in the form of write-offs for purchases of any equipment required to do the job. A personal studio space can be used to lessen the composer's tax burden as well.

Other Music Creation Methods

Any form of music can be used in today's video games—from acoustic instruments featuring live players to distorted electronic sounds generated randomly by computer software. Due to the limitless possibilities, there are many valid approaches to recording and producing—several often blending together on the same project. The type of music and the talents of the composer will determine the best course of action.

Courtesy of Sony Creative Software Inc.

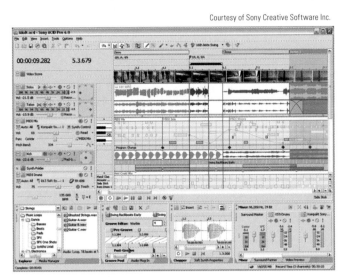

ACID Pro 6 is a one of many good non-traditional tools.

Traditional recording methods include capturing live instruments utilizing analog mixing consoles, multitrack tape recorder combinations, digital mixers, and hard-disk-based recording systems. Creating music with these tried and true methods allows years of experience to guide the process unencumbered by the complexity of newer technologies. These systems have been in use for most of our modern times and have become second nature to many composers—permitting them to concentrate on the music without being distracted by the mechanics of the process.

Newer recording methods and technologies also have a place in the creation of music for games. Progressive techniques through the use of loop-based software, MIDI sequencing, virtual instruments, samplers, plug-in effects processing, multitrack software, and audio editing programs produce unique musical soundscapes using sophisticated tools. As music production becomes more computer-based, the new audio textures and instrumentation that are discovered in the creative process merge with traditional instrumentation and recording techniques to create cutting edge audio. These progressive methods directly influence the creativity of composers and their music.

High-pass filters (HPFs) are essential for clean sound, particularly when mixing lots of tracks. HPFs take the load off the outputs and let you carve up your mixes with greater precision.

Jamie Lendino
(Composer/Sound Designer, Sound For Games Interactive)

Incorporating Live Instruments

When I write and record, I will almost always use some live instruments. . . . Even though we now have such great sound libraries of realistic orchestral instrument samples and a huge variety of articulations as well as good rhythm instruments, adding one or more real instruments can bring some life into a piece that may lack dimension otherwise. I have written percussive drum tracks for numerous projects. I will often write with samples such as Taiko drum and anvils—and then I will add several performances on different live toms and/or snare drums and mix them all together to get a huge powerful sound. For a groove-oriented piece, I will often play live drums and hand drums on top of drum loops. The mix of the live and sampled percussion can often be more effective then just one without the other. I will also use this same concept with other instruments such as brass; adding one or two live horns (trumpet or trombone) on top of horn samples really breathes life into a track that may otherwise lack dynamics and emotion. From my perspective, it is also important to have at least an understanding of orchestration and composing for live instruments. Even with the great samples that are available, composers still need to have a basic understanding about how each instrument is performed and articulated to create the most effective version of their compositions.

Mark Scholl (Composer, Screaming Tigers Music, Inc. / International Game Technology)

Editing & Mastering

Once the composition, recording, and mixing phases have been completed for each music cue, they will be saved or imported as digital audio files for fine tuning. These two-channel files will require specific editing to clean them up, perform minor adjustments, and prepare them for delivery to the developer. *Editing* is done in a similar manner to sound effects editing—except the files are much larger and require more processing power to handle them this time around.

The first step with a rough sound file is to trim any silence from the beginning and ending of the file and apply an appropriate fade in or fade out as necessary. This ensures that the music begins to play immediately upon triggering and that there are no "pops" associated with the sound file being cut off prematurely. Before any further adjustments are made, the music should be given a critical listen to determine what, if any, other actions should be performed. Minor equalization or overall volume corrections are common procedures to make certain the overall sound of the piece is consistent with the vision of the composer. A visual inspection of the file to determine any critical peaks, and proper alterations to tame them, will round out the process. The newly edited file can be saved and set aside for the final step.

After the entire body of music is completed for a game, a highly recommended phase is *mastering*. The purpose of this process is to add the final polish to the music, ensure consistency of equalization and volume between each cue, and apply minor compression and general enhancement. Professional mastering studios are occasionally enlisted for this step—with composers often paying for it out of their personal budget to ensure that the audio sounds its best. The expense is generally minor compared to the privilege of an experienced mastering engineer employing high grade electronic circuitry to really make the music shine. The other alternative is for composers themselves to conservatively use mastering software to apply appropriate enhancements. No matter how it is accomplished, this critical phase focuses on the sound quality of the music and ensures that all of the music for the project is consistent.

Courtesy of IK Multimedia   Courtesy of Adobe

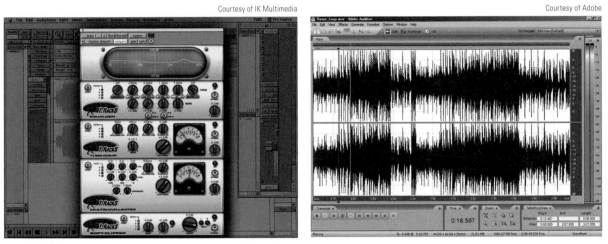

T-RackS Plug-In (left) and Audition (right) are both effective editing and mastering tools.

The Challenge of Implementation

With players always expecting more, it's important to create audio that is not only on par with today's Hollywood blockbusters but also works seamlessly in an interactive medium. Games are not linear; a fight scene lasting two minutes in a movie may last 10 minutes or longer in a video game. The music has to be created in such a way that it does not distract or bore the player. When the fighting finally concludes, the music must transition seamlessly; this may happen after five minutes, 10 minutes, or who knows!

Tom Graczkowski (Composer/Graphic Designer, TDimension Studios)

In-Game Format

The final step in music creation for games is to convert the audio files to their final *in-game format*. Early in the process, the developer will have specified the exact parameters the game will utilize—and by having the files delivered in the appropriate format, they can be immediately dropped into the game for implementation. Typical specifications include the sample rate, resolution, number of output channels, and the file format (such as 44.1 kHz, 16-bit, stereo, .wav). Since the music is usually created in the highest sample rate and resolution available, this will be a fairly simple process of converting down to the required rates. Saving to the final digital file type is also a straightforward task—unless a platform-specific format is required, in which the developer will usually perform this function.

Additionally, specific file naming conventions will need to be adhered to in order to keep the large number of music files and their purposes organized. A composer caught up in the heat of the musical moment isn't usually concerned with something as trivial as the name of the file and will label them practically anything when they are saved. However, the developer will expect the composer to complete this seemingly minor but very important step as a condition of the contract. Care and attention to detail is important, since the file name must exactly match the tag placed within the programming code. With file names such as **music_background_level_01_battle_sequence_a.wav**, troubleshooting might quickly become a nightmare easily prevented by the composer.

Reprinted with permission from Microsoft Corporation

GameAudioDevelopmentRocks! - Microsoft Cross-Platform Audio Creation Tool (XACT) v2.0 (Xbox 360)

File Edit View Wave Banks Sound Banks Global Settings Audition Window Help

Tree:
- Interface
- Music
- Player
- Pod_0000_Denebola
- Pod_0001_Ember
- Pod_0002_Kepler
- Pod_0003_Eden
- Pod_0004_Spore
- Pod_0005_Ice9
- Pod_0006_Titanium
- Pod_0007_Tranquil
- Pod_0008_FarmersMarket
- Pod_0009_Brainstorm
- Pod_0010_SuperCreamGoodness
- Pod_0011_CircusStackus
- Pod_0012_RockIsland
- Pod_0013_Championship

Bowl_0000_Denebola (Wave Bank)

Name	Size	PC Format	PC Co...	PC Ratio	Xb Format	Quality	Xb	Xb Ratio	Loop	Rate	Bits	C.	Path
DamageState_01	308,224	ADPCM	80,171	26%	XMA	60	??	??	N	44100	16	2	Raw\
DamageState_02	248,832	ADPCM	64,974	26%	XMA	60	??	??	N	44100	16	2	Raw\
DamageState_03	294,912	ADPCM	75,456	26%	XMA	60	??	??	N	44100	16	2	Raw\
DamageState_04	292,864	ADPCM	74,932	26%	XMA	60	??	??	N	44100	16	2	Raw\
DamageState_05	511,792	ADPCM	132,046	26%	XMA	60	??	??	N	44100	16	2	Raw\
Destruction	794,868	ADPCM	204,359	26%	XMA	60	??	??	N	44100	16	2	Raw\
HitByLaserFire	267,188	ADPCM	69,167	26%	XMA	60	??	??	N	44100	16	2	Raw\
RollOnPlatform_Var1	88,200	ADPCM	22,532	26%	XMA	60	??	??	N	44100	16	1	Raw\
RollOnPlatform_Var2	88,200	ADPCM	22,532	26%	XMA	60	??	??	N	44100	16	1	Raw\
RollOnPlatform_Var3	88,200	ADPCM	22,532	26%	XMA	60	??	??	N	44100	16	1	Raw\
RollOnPlatform_Var4	88,200	ADPCM	22,532	26%	XMA	60	??	??	N	44100	16	1	Raw\
RollOnPlatform_Var5	88,200	ADPCM	22,532	26%	XMA	60	??	??	N	44100	16	1	Raw\

12 Waves (0 unused)

Pod_0000_Denebola (Wave Bank)

Name	Size	PC Format	PC Co...	PC Ratio	Xb Format	Quality	Xb C.	Xb Ratio	Loop	N...	Rate	Bits	Chann
AttachToBowl	157,160	ADPCM	41,394	26%	XMA	60	??	??	N		44100	16	2
AttachToPod_Var1	91,272	ADPCM	24,627	27%	XMA	60	??	??	N		44100	16	2
AttachToPod_Var2	133,904	ADPCM	35,107	26%	XMA	60	??	??	N		44100	16	2
AttachToPod_Var3	88,064	ADPCM	22,532	26%	XMA	60	??	??	N		44100	16	2
AttachToPod_Var4	91,392	ADPCM	24,627	27%	XMA	60	??	??	N		44100	16	2
AttachToPod_Var5	89,088	ADPCM	24,102	27%	XMA	60	??	??	N		44100	16	2
Destruction	200,240	ADPCM	52,399	26%	XMA	60	??	??	N		44100	16	2
FighterCrashInto	88,200	ADPCM	22,532	26%	XMA	60	??	??	N		44100	16	1
HitByLaserFire	267,188	ADPCM	69,167	26%	XMA	60	??	??	N		44100	16	2
HitGoalFanBody	51,108	ADPCM	13,100	26%	XMA	60	??	??	N		44100	16	1
HitPlatform	88,200	ADPCM	22,532	26%	XMA	60	??	??	N		44100	16	1
HurlingThroughAir	180,060	ADPCM	46,112	26%	XMA	60	??	??	N		44100	16	1

12 Waves (0 unused)

General
Name: Pod_0000_Denebola
Notes:
Type: In Memory / Streaming   Size: 0
[ ] Friendly Names   [x] Sync In-Game Data
Compression Preset: Sample Compression
Paths
Header Path:
Xbox 360 Build Path: Xbox\Pod_0000_Denebola.xwb
Windows Build Path: Win\Pod_0000_Denebola.xwb

Ready

XACT is Microsoft's proprietary formatting tool for Xbox audio.

After the final conversions and formatting are accomplished, it is important to give each music cue a final listen before delivering the files to the developer. Conversions to a lower sample rate, resolution, and compressed file formats will often introduce noticeable audio artifacts that may need attention—usually in the form of quantization noise, frequency attenuation, lost sound data, or sound degradation that, depending on the signal to noise ratio, may be unacceptable. Additional adjustments will need to be performed to minimize these results from the conversion or formatting processes; this must be done before delivery.

Beta Testing

As game assets come together in the final stages of a project, it is important that they all work as advertised. The most effective way to do this is to put them in the game and see what happens. *Beta testing* is typically a highly involved process with professional game testers identifying glitches, anomalies, or "bugs." While testers are running through their carefully scripted routines, they will also listen to the music and flag any glaring problems for de-bugging. Other sets of ears are appreciated, but the best beta tester for the music is always the composer.

A professional composer and musician with many years of experience to draw upon will have the perfect insight and sensibilities when it comes to recognizing any music issues. While the triggering of cues within the game code is important, the composer's focus is more on the entire soundscape and how the music interacts with the sound effects and dialogue. If bass-heavy sound effects are playing over bass-heavy music tracks, the competition for the lower frequencies can cause unwanted distortion and muddiness. By recognizing this, the producer can decide which audio has the most priority in that particular section and have the appropriate bass frequencies reduced to alleviate the overlap. The composer can apply appropriate equalization if needed and take advantage of this final chance to ensure that all of the audio sounds great and works together well.

Composers may also be called upon to lend their expertise to implementation issues. Typically, the audio programmer will be responsible for these assets—but it is always in the best interest of the composer and for the overall sound of the game to have that extra set of trained ears available if needed. When a cue is triggered on or off, are pops or glitches evident? Do programmed crossfades, fade ins, or fades outs sound musical? If scripting is used, is it working as planned? These are the types of questions that will be considered—and the composer, if available, is always the best evaluator.

Producing music for any medium requires talent, creativity, and the skill set to bring it to life. On top of these more standard attributes, game composers need to be proficient in many additional abilities to ensure that the music is not only of the highest quality but specifically serves to enhance the game. Understanding the technical boundaries and having the dexterity to skillfully work within them are complex but important aspects that directly affect the longevity of a game composer's career. The ability to organize, stay creative under pressure, and get the job done on time and on budget will equally ensure success. Music in games is an important emotional expression—and with the right person doing the right job, the potential for incredible results is enormous. With the application of music growing progressively more involved, the game composer's contributions are becoming increasingly focused and more difficult to perform. Now more than ever, a solid understanding of the work involved is paramount and will set the stage for the incredible audio yet to come.

:::CHAPTER REVIEW:::

1. Define and differentiate between compressed and uncompressed audio—discussing at least 4 features of each. How do the platform and gameplay affect which form of audio is used? In what situations would you utilize the MIDI format?

2. Play 3 games currently on the market and describe the main theme, at least 3 level themes, and at least 3 character themes in each game. Differentiate between each with regard to style/genre, instrumentation, mood, and tempo.

3. Create a sound palette for an original game idea. After deciding on a premise, theme, environment, 3 levels, and 3 primary characters, choose a primary style/genre and instrumentation that reflects the overall mood of the game. Create a main theme, 3 level themes associated with the levels, and 3 character themes associated with the characters.

Game Voiceovers
adding personality to the characters

Key Chapter Questions

- Where voiceovers frequently *placed* in a game?

- What are the *categories* associated with voiceovers?

- What specific *characteristics* are considered when choosing voice actors?

- What are the goals of a *voice session*, and what is the workflow needed to ensure its success?

- What are some *editing* considerations when preparing voice files for implementation?

The general perception of game audio often naively entails only music and sound effects, but a third and equally important audio entity also exists: voiceovers. In the early years of video games, the best character voices were only distorted synthesized sounds that weren't actually recognizable as voices at all. Today, the game industry uses professional voice actors and well-known celebrities to bring game characters to life. While the visual depictions of these characters are still far from being lifelike, the audio to go along with them couldn't be any better unless the renderings were speaking themselves! In the early years, the composer and sound designer were one and the same—and when recorded voices became a new game feature, the development team simply looked to the person who was holding the microphone. Almost 30 years later, the developer still often employs the composer or sound designer to accomplish this task. Granted, there are many similarities between sound, music, and dialogue assets—especially when the digitized voice files are edited and implemented—but as this area of game audio grows more complex, distinct experts are emerging who specialize in the intricacies that result in effective voiceovers.

Voiceover Challenges

The responsibilities associated with a scriptwriter, casting director, session director, recordist, voiceover artist, and audio editor are separate areas of expertise that are quickly dividing into a variety of sub-specialties in the game industry. Large budget game projects will typically employ the many distinct individuals needed to accomplish dialogue-heavy ventures with thousands of individual "lines." However, despite the trend of these larger projects, most small- to mid-sized game developers will still hire one or two audio professionals to do it all: music, sound design, and voiceovers.

With quality scripts in hand and the sound person or team ready to go to work, the real focus is on how to find the right actors and to coax worthy performances out of them. Theater, film, or television actors have a noticeable advantage because they are able to use facial expressions and body language in addition to their voices to make their characters believable. Unfortunately for games, a physical actor portrayal isn't possible; instead, the entire effort relies solely and quite heavily on quality voice acting to bring the character to life.

From the auditioning process to directing actors in the recording session, it is sometimes a little more labor intensive to work with voice actors. Understanding and anticipating an actor's needs and mindset during a session can mean the difference between a great performance and a total waste of time for everyone. Being prepared and ready for anything will make all the difference.

::::: Cortana the "Conscience" in *Halo 3*

Reprinted with permission from Microsoft Corporation

The *Halo* series is a prime example of a character narrative that helps propel the story forward and provides feedback to the player's performance. The artificial intelligence character, Cortana, is essentially the "conscience" of the Master Chief character—providing appropriate backstory and tactical advice as needed. Whenever the player needs the next clue or when a new story element is unveiled, Cortana is triggered—acting much like an automated instruction manual.

Purpose of Game Voiceovers

The spoken word is an extremely powerful form of communication. Nothing is more vital to the survival of our species than effective interaction. In the world of video games where every component is make believe, the use of voiceovers—whether dialogue or narration—is essential to communicate what is happening within the virtual environment. In the past, the only way a game could convey specific information was to have the player read it on screen as part of the game. Although classic adventure and turn-based strategy games could tolerate the interruption of text, the pace of gameplay and the immersive effect were broken in the process. As technology improved enough to allow multiple simultaneous audio tracks, voiceovers have replaced the scripted text and keep the player in the game.

Today, the use of vocal elements serves many distinct purposes—including:

- Allowing players to interact directly with the characters
- Giving players the feeling that they're part of the story
- Immersing players in the game experience
- Telling the game's story and expressing its dramatic elements
- Delivering important clues to the player (such as game objectives, player health, and other stats)

The numerous cut-scenes within *Grand Theft Auto III* utilize a first-person camera perspective as a way to involve the player in the scene. The opening sequence to each new mission level in the *Medal of Honor* series does the same thing in an effective manner, making the player an integral part of the story. In these instances, the player characters don't speak but are directly spoken to as if they themselves were standing there. A well-crafted script and effective voice acting make all the difference.

Types of Voiceovers

When voice actors are hired to play particular roles, talent determines where they will be used in the game. Are they strong character actors? Do they have engaging warmth that would make great narrators? Sometimes the same actor can satisfy many of the voice needs of a game, and sometimes a new individual must be hired for different requirements. Multi-talented actors who can be great narrators, play several character roles, and make unique vocal sounds (such as creature or alien characterizations) are highly sought after. Game voiceovers can be extremely creative, and actors can really help push the overall audio of a game over the top.

Consider the war-themed, first-person shooter (FPS) *Medal of Honor*—which has multiple voice uses. As the game loads, an announcer engages players in the history of the conflict they are about to join. Upon entering the game, the player is met by a character who is yelling something about having to graduate from boot camp before being allowed to fight. Muttering from other members of the newly formed platoon is heard as players begin training. Moving through the obstacle course, players hear grunts and groans as other team members negotiate difficult obstacles while racing to the finish. Only 10 minutes into the game experience, several types of voice elements have already been used: narrators, characters, and vocal sound effects.

Understanding the needs and objectives of each type of dialogue will increase the chances that the chosen actors are correct for the part, the session director has a clear objective to achieve, and the techniques used to obtain the performances are right for the task at hand.

Character Dialogue

The most common and obvious use of game voiceovers is in *character dialogue*. Whether the in-game character is depicted in full animated glory or simply as a voice heard in the background during a scene, the talents of a voice actor will literally breathe much needed life into it. Game characters can appear in any portion of a game but are seen most often in cinematics and gameplay. These types of character performances are important storytelling tools, providing both background information and a method of moving the game forward. Strong examples of character dialogue can be found in *The Simpsons Game, 24, Tomb Raider: Legend, Final Fantasy, Primal, StarCraft II,* and *Prince of Persia: The Sands of Time.* Character voices

The character dialogue in *Prince of Persia: The Sands of Time* is an important storytelling tool.

implemented for background or off-screen situations will not require any special consideration outside of capturing and delivering a solid performance from the actor. Dialogue created specifically for animated characters will be significantly more labor-intensive, either for the actor and recording team or for the animator. It is important for the audio content provider to find out which methods will be used before starting work.

Sony Computer Entertainment America

I personally love games that have great stories to tell. *Heavenly Sword* not only has a great story but is filled with realistic character models capable of displaying real emotion as the story progresses. Above all, it's the amazing voice acting that makes this emotion really come through.

Tom Graczkowski (Composer/Graphic Designer, TDimension Studios)

Voice Followed by Animation

It is most common to record character voices first and create the associated animation afterward. After the best performances are identified, the near final audio files are delivered to the animator as a template. Rendered mouth movements must be coordinated with the vocal performance—either manually in an arduous frame-by-frame effort or with the assistance of specialty software and the use of *phonemes*, where pre-programmed mouth shapes are used with corresponding vocal sounds.

Voice & Animation Together

While voice followed by animation is the preferred creation order, a reduced development schedule may force animation and vocal assets to be created concurrently with the hope they magically synchronize together—or obligate the audio editor to make difficult adjustments after the fact.

Animation Followed by Voice

Rendering an animation first and recording the dialogue to it afterward is another technique that may be used if necessary—although not without consequence. Voice acting is difficult to begin with, but forcing an actor to attempt a good performance to a pre-rendered animation can make it even tougher. Inflections, pauses, stumbles, emphasis, or any number of other voicing nuances that may be natural to the actor are often lost on the animators or rendered by them in the wrong places. While there may be situations in which an animation is pre-rendered for specific artistic purposes, the best method is to let the voice actor perform freely and create the animation to the performance. Using animation followed by voice sparingly for game applications is acceptable—but in order to facilitate a good performance, it should not be used as the primary method.

Recording dialogue after rendering animation is very similar to *automatic dialogue replacement (ADR)*—a technique used in film, where it is also known as *dubbing* or *looping*—and is approached in a nearly identical fashion. ADR has more success in film because the performance has already been shot, and the actor simply replaces the dialogue due to noise or other issues.

Depending on the situation, character dialogue can be recorded as individual sentences, paragraphs, or as an extended monologue. Multiple intermingling characters may be recorded separately and later edited together as a complete conversation— or they may be recorded collectively, with the actors interacting as they perform. The method used will depend entirely on the implementation process and how the voice files will be triggered within the programming.

Story Narrative

Storytelling that isn't associated with a specific character depiction is considered to be *story narrative*. These background vocal performances play the role of narrator during a cinematic or in various places within the gameplay to establish or continue the story, provide specific clues for further progress, or support the environment and its theme. They can also appear at the beginning or end of a game level or in specific areas within the game to prompt players to take a prescribed action, familiarize them with the environment, or to act as a tie-in between game levels. Games such as *Enclave*, *Myst*, the intro movie to *Asheron's Call*, and the cutscenes in *Sly 3: Honor Among Thieves* are all good examples of story narratives utilized in various parts of a game. In addition to fulfilling their technical objectives, narratives are also creatively designed to support the mood at a particular moment of gameplay. Fast and energetic, slow and deliberate, or anywhere in between, the vocal quality and performance all help sell the emotional atmosphere of the scene. The use of character portrayals or accents in the narrative role can further immerse the player into the theme of the game world.

The narrative in *Myst* is an important element, providing specific clues for progress.

Unlike the considerations required for character dialogue, narratives will not follow any critical mouth movements and will be less labor intensive as far as timing is concerned. However, the performance will still need to fit within a specific amount of space to synchronize with the length of a scene or accompanying onscreen text. Scripts will normally be written either to pre-existing visuals or in conjunction with them, where timing is estimated in advance of an actor's performance. The actor will have to speak at an appropriate pace to match, but the process isn't as confining as attempting to synchronize to mouth movements. The combined visual and audio playback can be tightened as needed by correcting the timing of the visuals in code or utilizing minor time compression or expansion tools for the audio.

> *H*alf-Life 2 is an excellent example of successful use of dialogue. Everything from the civilians on the street to the propaganda videos playing around City 17 is completely immersive and tells an excellent story without the use of cut-scenes.
>
> *Robert Burns (Lead Sound Designer, High Moon Studios)*

Narratives can be recorded as full sentences, paragraphs, or extended monologue—depending on the requirements of the game. These will be treated as single character portrayals, with no other character interaction to consider—allowing the actor and director to focus on a performance that can stand on its own. It is important that the narrative be strong and convincing, since players will be focusing much of their attention on it. This is definitely not the time to cut corners with an amateur performance.

::::: Adjusting the Script in
Clive Barker's Undying

Electronic Arts, Inc.

While gameplay is still the most important element affecting audio, the script is what makes or breaks the dialogue—the last hair of the tail that wags the dog. There are so many games with excellent soundtracks and music that it's difficult to narrow it to a handful. When I had the chance to rewrite the main script to *Clive Barker's Undying*, we received rave reviews about the voice acting. Although we adjust scripts for the spoken word and to suit accents and character descriptions, the credit or criticism starts at the writing. As a good director/actor myself, I am able to add subtle emotes to a dry line or suggest them to other actors. This helps make dialogue flow and not distract from gameplay.

Lani Minella (Master Creator, AudioGodz)

Vocal Sound Effects

While they might imply the use of voice to create sound effects within a game, *vocal sound effects* are actually used to indicate specific character-related sounds. As part of the total immersive effect, games such as FPSs benefit greatly from the addition of vocal sounds to make the gameplay more compelling. During complex gameplay, there are a variety of sounds that match action taking place either onscreen or just out of view. Gunshots, explosions, and footsteps are typical sound effects that will be heard during these moments—but in multi-character situations, screaming, yelling, or appropriate comments will complement the soundscape and make it that much richer.

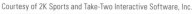

Even when the player can't hear each character clearly speaking, *BioShock's* vocal sound effects convey important clues.

Vocal sound effects will also be used to provide feedback to the players, indicating death or injury of their in-game personas. These vocalizations can provide important clues to their characters' health status and help them decide whether to join the fight or to seek cover to heal. The use of these effects also adds a degree of realism that is generally missing in a virtual experience. By utilizing other senses, the player does not have to rely solely on visual cues to provide the needed information.

Vocal sound effects tend to be brief and, as such, are recorded and edited as sound effects. Grunts, groans, yelps, gasps, and cries are examples of normal usage—but these can also include short sentences or comments, long screams, or steady breathing. Any human or creature sound that may be used in this capacity will be treated as a sound effect. Typical usage of these vocal sound effects are heard in games such as *God of War II*, *BioShock*, *Medal of Honor*, *Call of Duty*, and *Jade Empire*.

Game Interface

The voiceover associated with the *game interface* acts as an unseen character that accompanies the player through most of the game. It is often used in situations as the player's alter ego or as an intelligent computer system that provides appropriate clues and a much needed conscience. This voice can relay messages such as the next objective, feedback for specific actions performed, appropriate clues, and a detailed health condition of the player.

> *M*ass Effect contains great dialogue —with an intuitive interface that allows the player to interact in a variety of ways with the world.
>
> *Jed Smith (Lead Producer, betafish music)*

The interface voiceover may also reveal specific emotions the player should be feeling as part of the ongoing storyline. Games such as *MechWarrior 4: Mercenaries*, *StarCraft*, *WarCraft III*, *I of the Enemy*, and *Halo* effectively utilize a talking interface. The interface voiceover may be recorded as a narrative or sound effect, depending on how it will be implemented and used within the game. Since the purpose might vary or take the place of the narrative, it can be as simple as a short statement such as "Health critical!" or a lengthy monologue—edited with the final use in mind. Audio associated with the game interface is typically tagged as high-priority and will usually have minimal timing issues when recording due to its high precedence. Gameplay will normally pause while the interface speaks, or the character will continue to move in a limited capacity as the voice is heard. The audio will play as long as needed, and the rest of the game will generally work around it as required.

Reprinted with permission from Microsoft Corporation

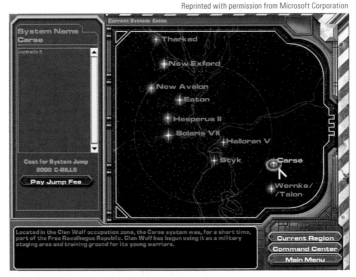

The interface voiceover in *MechWarrior 4: Mercenaries* helps teach the player while maintaining the game's ambience.

From the session director's perspective, the actor will perform game interface voiceovers in character—more so than what may be heard in the narrative role. This particular character will have a definitive human personality but might be robotic or computer-like—either through acting or applied through effects processing in post-production. The game interface is typically the most important voiceover role of a production and should be first-rate.

Choosing Voice Actors

The most crucial task when creating voiceovers and other vocal elements for games is the selection of voice actors. Not only do these individuals need to be outstanding at their trade, but they must be the right voice for the character or narration. Games with extensive voice work can live or die based on the quality of the actors, who must be able to sound so convincing and fit the part so well that the player believes them completely. While the temptation and convenience may be great, asking friends to speak with an accent or funny voice while a mic is held in front of them shouldn't be an option. There is a huge responsibility to the game and the players to ensure that these voices are created professionally.

Voiceovers from actors such as Jon Jones (left) and Lani Minella (right) help perfect the audio quality of a game.

Choosing appropriate character actors can be handled in many ways. During the scriptwriting process, the writer may already have a specific actor in mind—or the game developer may have already retained the services of one. In these cases, the audio provider would record the actors, edit the voice files, and make delivery. These situations make the task of providing the voice content much easier and are more common on large projects from large development houses—especially when the use of celebrity voices is a marketing highlight of the game. Typically, there will be more work involved outside of recording and editing.

Except for the script and some initial ideas provided by the developer, the content provider is left managing a wide array of details. This means that the game composer and sound designer may be tasked to cast the actors, conduct auditions, schedule appointments, direct and record sessions, edit voice files, and convert files to final, in-game format. While there are more companies appearing that specialize in full voiceover production, small- to mid-sized game developers will regularly look to their composer or sound designer for this often enormous undertaking.

Resist the Temptation

There's always the temptation to let that clever assistant producer (AP) write some of the dialogue, or to have the woman from customer service with the great voice be the narrator. The AP is clever and the woman has a wonderful voice, but neither of them can match world class specialists.

Don Daglow (President & CEO, Stormfront Studios)

Before considering voice talent, the developer and sound team should determine the following:

- characters needing to be voiced
- gender
- age
- accent
- vocal qualities (speed, pitch, tone, inflection, and unusual tics or errors)
- other creative details that may help make the choice for an appropriate voice actor less complicated

Despite advanced and often diligent planning, choosing the right actor sometimes comes down to intuition. For voice actors, most game audio specialists draw from their own talent pool or networks. Since each game project can be a new challenge, other research may be necessary to not only find the right actor but one who has the time to do the job. Auditioning actors can be tedious, but local talent agencies and web sites specializing in showcasing voice talent are all great resources that will make the process less stressful. Reviewing demo reels, conducting phone interviews or holding a "cattle call" with a talent agency's assistance will allow candidates to audition for specific roles within the production and give the development team an opportunity to provide input on the selection process.

During the actual audition, it is important not to be persuaded by the actor's charisma, resume, or animated performance. Maintaining complete focus on the voice, attitude, and talent actors can bring to the characters is absolutely critical. It's very easy to get caught up in an audition only to discover later that the chosen voice doesn't work. To avoid being influenced by the wrong attributes, it is sometimes preferable to never see the actors but only hear them in front of a microphone from another room. If the actor can't embody the character with just their vocal chords, it may be better to try someone else.

Keythe Farley & Lani Minella on Voice Casting & Directing :::::

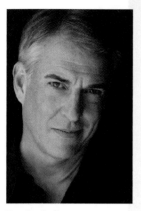

Keythe Farley
(Casting/Voice Director)

Keythe is a voice director for animation and video games. From 1997 to 2002, he was an in-house voice director for Klasky/Csupo Inc.—where he directed the hugely popular *Rugrats* and *As Told By Ginger* cartoons. Keythe continues to cast and direct video game titles; his most recent credits include *God of War, Marvel: Ultimate Alliance 2, Transformers,* and *Resistance: Rise of the Chimera.* As a voice actor, Keythe has appeared in *Rugrats, Aaahh!!! Real Monsters,* and *God of War II*—and his commercial clients include Toyota, IBM, Caesar's Palace, and National Geographic. Keythe is a graduate of the UCLA department of theatre, film, and television.

The job of the casting/voice director is two parts storyteller, one part manager, and one part diplomat. Story, people, and management skills are all put to use in this career. It is my job to find performers whose voices are right to portray the characters in a video game, and to direct the performances of these actors so that they are believable in the world of the game. I receive a list of character "breakdowns" from the client that usually contain character concept art, background/history, and a few sample lines of dialogue from the game. From this document, I create an even more simplified breakdown that I send to agents who represent performers specializing in voice acting. The agents send me submissions from clients that they believe would be right for the roles; I listen to the demo reels and whittle the hundreds of submissions down to five or six prospective performers for each role. Many casting directors would then submit these demos to the clients for final casting, but I have the opportunity to bring the actors into the studio and work with them as I would in the final session. This gives me the opportunity to further narrow the field of prospective performers down by actually working with them on material from the game. I get a feel for their unique take on the role, how they respond to direction, and the rapport that develops (or doesn't) between the actor and me. I send my final choices to the client, who decides which actors are ultimately cast in the roles.

Before recording begins, I receive a script from the client—and we usually have a conference about the story and what the client is looking for from the performances. On the day of recording, I am always in the studio with the writer(s) and producer(s) when the actor comes in to record the dialogue. Actors are recorded individually—so it is my job to fill them in on all relevant information pertaining to the scene we are recording and often to read opposite them so that we get the feeling of an actual conversation taking place. Frequently, producers or writers will have ideas about how they want a specific line to sound. They express their intentions to me, and I interpret them for the performer. Generally, producers, writers, and directors are more results-oriented, while actors are more process-driven—so my job is almost that of a translator with most direction being of the "faster-slower-louder-softer" variety. Here's a typical exchange:

Writer (to director): This scene takes place in a zombie factory that's been run by the government since 1963. The character has just discovered that her father is working for the secret society that set up the factory, and that he is covertly using her to get to her college friends so that he can turn them into zombies. But her father knows that she knows, so he has set a trap for her. When she says "Get your hands off me!" it's because 15 zombies have come out of nowhere to grab her.

Director (to actor): You need to be a little more startled when you say "Get your hands off me!" And you could be a little louder, too.

Lani has voiced more than 450 computer and video games, as well as several television and anime series. She is famous for her role as Rouge the Bat (in *Sonic The Hedgehog* games). She has also had roles in the following games: *Baldur's Gate, Clive Barker's Undying, Diablo, Diablo II, Duke Nukem 3D, EverQuest: The Legacy of Ykesha, Half-Life, Leisure Suit Larry: Magna Cum Laude, Sonic Adventure 2, Sonic Heroes, Sonic Battle, SoulCalibur III, StarCraft, Unreal, Unreal Tournament 2003/2004, WarCraft III: Reign of Chaos/The Frozen Throne, World of WarCraft,* and the *Nancy Drew* series. Since 1992, her company, AudioGodz, has provided voice acting, directing, casting, and writing for games. As a one-stop shop, AudioGodz also utilizes sound designers and composers to provide all things audio.

Lani Minella
(Master Creator,
AudioGodz)

With voice acting, we ask for an estimated line count and love to see the script if possible. I offer to sweeten or do scriptwriting if it seems like it would help. We get character descriptions and hope for pictures to help us cast the right people. Most of my talent pool consists of actors who can do multiple roles and sound completely different. This helps budgets—and it's necessary, since most games have a small number of lines but a lot of characters. Then, I direct auditions using only the finalists whom I think would be best suited for each role. We submit the choices, or the developer allows me to cast without auditions. All parties are then coordinated for the recording session, which is done in a swift but effective manner—saving the throat damaging emotes until the last. Most of the time we then cut up the files and name them (editing)—and if there is processing needed, we provide the files both dry and processed. If there are full motion videos or cutscenes that are already completed and need ADR or looping, we watch the videos, lay down the voice, slip and slide the audio, and redo until the animations fit perfectly. Then we deliver the entire video file mixed, as well as the dry audio files. I do the casting, directing, writing, and many of the voices if I'm chosen. I also do the scheduling, payroll, and project management. We sometimes roll film to capture the "making of" or to help animators with gestures and facial motion capture. Foley is very fun when we customize sound effects by recording everything originally and compositing things to create creatures, weapons, etc. This can also be added to library sounds to make things sound much more unique.

Online Voiceover Resources

Here are just a few online resources for aspiring voice actors:

- Voiceover & Agency Database (www.voicebank.net)

- Tongue Twisters (www.geocities.com/Athens/8136/tonguetwisters.html)

- Dialects (web.ku.edu/idea/)

- Demos (www.compostproductions.com/demos.html)

- Job Listings (www.entertainmentcareers.net)

- Sample Sides & Scripts (www.showfax.com)

We also suggest that you read Janet Wilcox's *Voiceovers: Techniques & Tactics for Success*, which contains the above and many other resources.

Voiceover Sessions

A four-hour block of time is the standard session for which both union and non-union voice talent expect to be paid. This may change slightly depending on variables such as the intensity that might be required for a role or the number of character voices that one actor will be expected to perform. Yelling and death sounds have a tendency to shorten vocal endurance and affect the length of the recording session—and union contracts generally limit the number of unique characters to three per "session." Due to these factors, it may be preferable to plan for extra sessions.

The amount of work to be performed by the actor will determine the number of required sessions, making advanced planning essential. During the audition process, it should be obvious which actors have a natural fit to a character and which will need to spend extra effort to correctly voice the characters. These factors will help decide the number of sessions needed for each character and allow for a workable schedule for everyone involved.

Advice for Budding Voice Actors

Take a lot of improvisation classes where you get to create many different characters and physicalize them. The more you explore your characters, the truer the voice will sound—which will eventually translate in a recording. Keep logs or record unique accents, character traits, and mannerisms—and explore different levels and pitches to your own voice.

Hope Levy (Voice Actor)

To ensure consistency of the performance and recordings, each character should be fully recorded on the same day—within one or two sessions, if possible. Various issues crop up by having an actor return a week or two later that will cause noticeable differences—including mic placement, mixer and recording settings, the actor's health, and even the weather. Most importantly, the voice or accent in use by the actor will invariably be different enough to render the previous session unusable. Players are very perceptive to begin with, so any steps that can avoid distracting them from the game should be taken in order to ensure a good final product.

Despite the chaos and countless other elements that require attention during a session, the needs of the actor should always be the primary focus; this simple rule will do more to ensure a successful session than anything else. To help ensure that the actor feels comfortable, uninhibited, and free to be creative, consider these requirements:

- Visitors should be kept to a minimum
- Climate and energy during the session should be suitable and positive
- Drinks and snacks should be abundant
- Throat spray, lozenges, or lemons should be close by
- A comfortable stool, music stand to hold the script, and appropriate lighting should be available

Identify any other special needs and ensure that these reasonable requests are granted in order to have the full attention and best work of the actor. When possible, encourage talent to arrive early to allow them time to acclimate to the team and the surroundings. If this isn't possible, expect the first 30-45 minutes to be spent building a working rapport. It is possible to take advantage of this time by allowing the actor to view a working version of the game, character renderings, cinematics, or any other visual cue from the overall project. Establish the background of the character they are playing and discuss any ideas or expectations before the recording starts. Give actors adequate information to enable them to fully understand their particular roles in the production.

With the final script as reference, perform a dry run with a few lines of actual dialogue. Audition any ideas the actor may have and zero in on the specific character voice to be used before recording begins. It is essential to have an established reference and allow the actor time to get into "character." While they are assuming their target personas, have the actors review the script and make any notes that might help during the session. Clarify pronunciation of odd words or consider any minor script changes if needed. Once the talent is fully prepared, it's time to record.

Regardless of the talent and experience of the script writer, there are occasions in which it only becomes obvious that a word or line in the script isn't working when the actor performs it. This can be as simple as a single word that the actor cannot say to other issues such as a line that can't be pronounced at the needed intensity while simultaneously staying in character. You must deal with this issue immediately—either by having a representative from the developer present during the recording session or by a developer granting the session director rewrite authority. In order to utilize actors to their fullest while they are present, and to prevent scheduling another session, an on-the-spot rewrite can save the day.

At some point, either before the session begins or at its conclusion, ensure that the actors have signed a contract or talent release for their performance. It is imperative that the audio content provider, who in this capacity is acting as a representative of the developer, not only delivers quality voice files but is able to guarantee that all rights to the performances have been released and transferred to the developer for their exclusive use. Concentration on the session can distract from other important responsibilities, but this one significant legal matter should be a top priority.

There are two principal responsibilities that must be managed during a voiceover session: capturing and recording the performance (engineering), and monitoring the efforts of the voice actor (directing). Both of these tasks occasionally fall to the same person—but when the situation permits, it is recommended that at least two persons are involved. While the recording engineer is in fact "listening," attention focuses mainly on:

- the mechanics of the process
- the sound of each voice
- input levels
- equalization
- effects processing
- headphone volume
- other needs associated with the physical recording

In contrast, a dedicated session director will be free to concentrate specifically on:

- the actor's performance
- how each line is spoken
- vocal inflections
- ability of the actor to remain in character
- energy and consistency
- motivation
- other performance-related issues

The director will also determine the flow of the session and determine which lines are good and which may need to be re-recorded or modified. Having a separate individual devoted to the actors' performances will increase the chances of a successful session.

Jon Jones & Hope Levy on Game Voiceover Rewards & Challenges:::::

As a musician and composer, Jon's work appears in several games—including *ESPN MLS Extra Time*, *Stack Attack*, and *I of the Enemy*. His voice has been heard in over 30 game titles—including *DiRT*, *I of the Enemy*, and various casino games. Jon has also voiced several game trailers for Codemasters—including *Overlord*, *Heatseeker*, *DiRT*, and *Operation FlashPoint 2: Dragon Rising*. He is also a master metal crafts-man and carpenter whose creative energies are applied to graphic arts, sculpting, and computer aided drafting and design (CADD). Jon resides in Oceanside, California with his wife and son.

Jonathan D. Jones
(Voice Actor/Composer/
Musician, Jam Design/
On Your Mark Music)

It's rewarding to be entrusted with the responsibility to create a believ-able and entertaining personality for the characters—to dig deep down and bring each of them to life. Voice work can also be challenging. Not only are you taking it all in from the producer or creative director, but you're also trying to bring something unique to each character that distinguishes it. I've had sessions where the clock is ticking, and the director realizes that there wasn't enough time or money budgeted for the session. Staying in character when the reality sets in that you only have a half hour to get the last two pages of scripts perfect can be nerve-wracking—but holding it together enough to finish the perfor-mance is appreciated by all involved. Some sessions can be very grueling, and those are probably the most challenging as a performer.

Hope is a Los Angeles-based actress who has voiced such games as *The Matrix: Path of Neo, Resistance: Rise of the Chimera, Bratz 1-4, Ape Escape 3, Polar Express, EverQuest II, Jumpstart, Vampire: The Masquerade – Bloodlines,* and *Resident Evil: Biohazard.* In the animation world, Hope can be heard as various voices in *Howl's Moving Castle, Brother Bear, Madagascar, Kung Fu Panda, Quantum Quest: A Cassini Space Odyssey,* and HBO's *The Life & Times of Tim.* Hope lives with writer Tom Lavagnino and their toddler, Sam Anthony.

Hope Levy
(Voice Actor)

My role is to breathe as much life into a character as possible—even if it looks, speaks, moves, and acts completely differently from me! In game voiceover work, it's challenging to keep the lines fresh, alive, and new even after saying them for the 100th time when only one word has been changed—such as "You sure look great wearing that outfit," "You look great wearing that outfit," "You look great in that outfit," and "Look at that great outfit"! The fun thing about recording work is not having to worry about looking ridiculous! You sometimes have to make the strangest looking faces and body language to get a unique sound out of yourself. You can't be self conscious of how you look if you are creating a character that lives under a rock and never has seen daylight!

Directing Voiceover Sessions

There are several individuals who might be qualified to be session directors. In addition to a professional voiceover session director, the game producer (who has the overall picture of the game) or a trusted associate producer would be best suited to fill this role. The session director will oversee each session and ensure that the actors are fulfilling the game's overall vision. However, not every situation is the same—and others may be appointed to this role. The scriptwriter, audio lead, or one of the other experienced members of the audio team might be called upon. Regardless of who is selected, the session director will have the specific purpose of drawing great performances from the hired talent.

iStockphoto

An effective session director is acting coach, diplomat, and drill sergeant.

An effective session director is a combination of an acting coach, diplomat, and Marine drill sergeant—each personality having a particular purpose during a voiceover session. Good actors will already have the talent and the discipline to perform as needed—but, even then, guidance is often necessary to create a character voice that does the job. How the session director chooses to elicit the appropriate response from the actor is the key.

Demonstration

The easiest way for an actor to understand what a director wants is for the director to show the actor. The acting coach method gives the talent something to emulate—a specific way to deliver a word or a line. Assuming the director is communicating effectively, the actor simply repeats the director's example until a good take is obtained. This is probably the most commonly used directing technique.

Information

Another method is to give actors all of the information and background associated with their characters—allowing them search through their own talents and experience to find the best voice. This diplomatic approach is very effective and includes the actors in the creative process, letting them add their own style and character to the voices. Creative individuals such as voice actors enjoy lending their knowledge to a project—and by including them in this process, they feel good and produce better performances.

Motivation

Humans respond to certain stimuli—and an incredibly effective way to increase the energy of a performance is to give the actor a verbal boost. The intention is not to berate actors but to give them a shot of adrenaline by pleasantly expressing the needs of the session in a raised voice. If done with a smile, this can have a tremendous effect. The other use is helpful for actors who may feel inhibited due to the surroundings and number of people watching them. By loudly showing a "crazy side," directors can help loosen up the actors and let them know that it's okay to be wild. The free flow of new energy from the actor will make for a great performance.

Recording Voiceover Sessions

The main goal of the recording engineer during any voiceover session is to capture the performance as cleanly as possible. While this means the focus will be on issues such as noise, input levels, and over-modulation, these technicalities (for the actor's sake) should be transparent and not impede creative efforts while performing, The engineer should set up the gear and initiate and test the appropriate programs before the talent ever steps foot in the studio. Nothing brings the momentum of a session to a grinding halt faster than having to wait for the engineer.

While the actor is getting comfortable in front of the microphone and obtaining a final briefing from the session director, the engineer should be preparing tracks and setting recording levels. As actors prepare for their performances, they will often warm up in character—giving the engineer a chance to preview the material and the intensity of delivery. Taking advantage of these moments to make adjustments will minimize the prep time and allow actors to flow right into the session when they are ready. Making the session as seamless as possible to the actor is important in obtaining a great performance.

iStockphoto

The engineer must remain fully conscious of the intensity of the actor's performance and the recording levels during a session.

It is extremely important that the engineer remains fully conscious of the intensity of the actor's performance and the recording levels at all times during a session. Takes that are too loud and over-modulated will be useless. Takes that are too soft, where the noise floor is as loud as the speech, will create other headaches. The worse time to find out about these issues is after the talent has left the studio. Remaining mindful of the levels at all times will ensure solid, consistent recordings of material that can later be edited to work within the game setting. Tools such as limiters or compressors in the recording chain will help keep the unpredictability of a performance under control.

As the session begins, the director is in charge. It is important that the actors have someone designated to work creatively with them and don't receive multiple, sometimes conflicting, instructions from various people. The director will be the actors' primary focus, but there may be acceptable instances in which the engineer must interject for technical reasons—such as the positioning of the actors in front of the mics, errant levels or glitches that require additional takes, or unacceptable background noises.

Materials from a vocal session will require extensive editing and adjustments to make them work within the context of a game. Occasionally, unplanned situations will require creative editing, replacement of certain dialogue, or use of a different inflection. To ensure that the editor has numerous options to choose from and that "adaptive dialogue" can be achieved when needed for gameplay purposes, it is recommended that actors repeat each line of dialogue several times. The director will encourage the actors to utilize different vocal inflections or emphasize certain words, which not only increases the material for the editor to use but also helps the actors perfect their performances. For longer phrases or narratives, this technique isn't as necessary—since the tempo of the narrative is important and should flow naturally. Allowing the actor to read these a few times and immediately repeat any sentences or words that may be stumbling blocks will help the editors and give them enough to work with should a word or line need to be replaced later. Recording several takes will often save the time of having to recall the actor for another session.

Juggling Vocal Qualities

In what was perhaps the most challenging voiceover job I have ever done, the producers decided that the character should have a "gravely" vocal texture, speak with an authentic Tennessee accent, and be able to sing on key. I really had to concentrate and stay focused to maintain these vocal qualities and to avoid drifting out of character. I sing in a cover band on a regular basis, so singing on key was not an issue—but keeping the gravely texture in my voice while doing it was tricky. It's this kind of voice acting that makes my job interesting and challenging!

Jon St. John (Owner, Jon St. John Productions)

Non-Human Voices

Occasional jobs call for a non-human voice. Unless the actor is contributing a unique talent that allows for a direct recording, effects processing will be required. The performance can either be recorded dry, without effects processing, or with the effects processing active in its final form. Recording dry allows the editor to apply appropriate effects during the editing process, permitting experimentation and adjustments without affecting the actual voice recording. Determining the correct settings can be time consuming, but this method gives the audio team a chance to find the right voice for the creature without having an actor waiting around. Recording with active effects processing gives the director a chance to hear what the final voice will sound like; it also lets actors take advantage of the processing and manipulate their performances to match. This technique is used most often for creature, alien, or animal sound creation—but it can force a new session if the voices don't work in the game, since they cannot be changed after the fact.

Multiple Actors

Multiple actor scenarios can be a challenge for both the director and the recordist. Performance-wise, it is always preferable to allow actors to perform together as they play out a scene—taking cues from each other while they interact. The recordist will set up a microphone for each actor and assign a separate channel within a multitrack application. This session will either be delivered for editing as a mix of the entire scene or as individual tracks as needed. However, on occasions where not all actors can be present, recording each actor individually can be accomplished with equal success. Someone on the team can read with the actor, or the actor may choose to perform alone—playing out the scene mentally.

Adaptive Dialogue

A "theatrical" model in which multiple actors record performances in context can be quite beneficial to game dialogue and can result in much better performances from the actors. Ultimately, only snippets of the performances need to be used—especially if you are capturing *adaptive dialogue* that corresponds to non-linear gameplay scenarios. Game writers and designers often write character dialogue in flowchart format to map onto a variety of player choices and "pathing." Multiple performers can act out several possible scenarios, and dialogue can be captured from each of these performances; the dialogue will appear in the same area of the game but will be triggered by distinct player actions. For example, let's say that the player character is lost and has a chance encounter with a group of non-player characters (NPCs), played by our voice actors. Scenario A might be triggered by the player engaging the NPCs in combat; Scenario B might be triggered by the player asking the NPCs for assistance; and Scenario C might be triggered by the player fleeing the scene. Each scenario will yield a different line of dialogue and vocal sound effects. More detail might be required if there are many possible variations within any given scenario.

Editing

Once the recordings are completed, the next phase is to edit them for the game. How this is accomplished will depend on the developer's requirements, so it is extremely important that the content provider understand what they are prior to beginning the process. Voice files are often handled identically to sound effects files and are triggered as needed by the game coding. However, there are other instances in which the dialogue might be lengthy or will be synchronized to animation sequences or cinematics; these files will require a different editing approach.

Whenever possible, the sound editor should acquire pre-rendered cinematics or animation files to assist in the synchronization and editing process. Due to chaotic development cycles, production of each game asset is more often than not created simultaneously. Even though the best-case scenario is to create the voice files and then render the animation directly to them, all is not lost if an animation was done first. In this case, having access to the animation will give the editor something to work with and save time by editing directly to the visuals. Even if the animation was created to the voice file, the editor would more than likely have to re-edit—so a step is saved by doing it this way.

Voice Files

Character dialogue and the game interface voice are primary examples of voice files that will be edited for unique applications within the game. There is a wide variety of uses for these types of vocal performances; cinematics, animation, and gameplay will all utilize character speech as part of the experience. How the audio files are edited and implemented depends on their use within each of these areas.

	Direction	Speech	Context Within Game	Cross Reference to Original Word Documents
3	These are actors' directions for use in the recording studio. Unless specified otherwise, the tone is neutral and professional.	This is the actual speech to be recorded.	This field contains a short description of the context for the speech to help the actor.	
52	Distort, a little angrily	You are too far from the rest of your squad!	Avoiding PLA troops by scuttling along behind a wall.	Stay low
53	Distort, a little angrily	You are too far from the rest of your fireteam!		Stay low
54	Distort, angrily	You have left the engagement area!	Creeping around the back streets.	Where to?
55			Creeping around the back streets.	Where to?
56	Mandarin, distort, command	Clear the area!	Creeping around the back streets.	Where to?
57	Mandarin, distort, command	Secure the objective!		
58	Mandarin, distort, command	Move on to the next waypoint.	Using a low barrier as cover.	Crawl
59	Mandarin, distort, command	Move on to the next objective.	Using a low barrier as cover.	Crawl
60	Mandarin, distort, command	Attack!	Using a low barrier as cover.	Crawl
61	Mandarin, distort, command	Retreat!		
62	Mandarin, distort, command	Withdraw to the assigned waypoint.	On the outskirts of town in a fairly safe place	Head for helo
63	Mandarin, distort, command	Wait.	On the outskirts of town in a fairly safe place	Head for helo
64	Mandarin, distort, informative	Objective completed.	On the outskirts of town in a fairly safe place	Head for helo
65	Mandarin, distort, slightly up	Mission completed!	On the outskirts of town in a fairly safe place	Head for helo
66	Mandarin, distort, grim	Objective failed.	On the outskirts of town in a fairly safe place	Head for helo
67	Mandarin, distort, grim	The mission is a failure!	On the outskirts of town in a fairly safe place	Head for helo
68	Mandarin, distort, grim	Abort the mission.		
69	Mandarin, distort, authoritative	Air assets are available.	Finding an abandoned vehicle outside town	Take a vehicle?
70	Mandarin, distort, authoritative	Fire missions are available.	Finding an abandoned vehicle outside town	Take a vehicle?
71	Mandarin, distort, warning	Incoming!	Finding an abandoned vehicle outside town	Take a vehicle?
72	Mandarin, distort, command	Defend the objective!		

A vocal asset list helps to maintain a consistent system of file organization.

In most cases, character dialogue will play out as an entire scene and will require careful editing to ensure a natural rhythm to the performance. A normal approach would be to select the best take of each line, splice them together, and save them as a mix of the entire scene. However, a professional voice actor will say much more than simply the scripted dialogue. The inflection, pauses, and tone of each word can communicate volumes—and an editor must be conscious of the timing and flow of the performance as much as the clarity of the words. For longer dialogue, it's best to leave these takes intact and only edit the misspoken words or stumbles.

Character dialogue, when recorded as a single character, will be edited within an audio editor—and sentences, lines, or longer monologues will be saved as individual lines as needed. The game interface speech may be treated either as short narratives or sound effects for editing purposes and will be delivered as requested by the developer. These files will be transferred to the developer for creation of the cinematics or animations, if needed, in order to develop the artwork around the voice. File labeling will depend on the developer's pre-selected naming conventions for deliverables— and for further work to be performed by the editor, the files will be given intuitive names and later added to cinematics or some other mix.

Vocal Sound Effects Files

Sounds associated with injury or death, one-liners, or player taunts are examples of voice files that are treated as sound effects for both editing and implementation purposes. These vocal sounds are typically short in duration, play back without delay when triggered, and are the easiest of all voice file types to record and edit. Since these sounds don't repeat very often during gameplay, the editor will simply select the best take from the rough recordings—or several of them if other variations of the same line are needed—and deliver them as appropriate. An experienced session director will have ensured that several takes were recorded to give the editor plenty to choose from.

Generally, the editor will create the voice file so that play begins immediately after triggering by deleting any silence at the front of the file. There are occasions in which a short delay may be required; if it can't be solved within the programming, the editor will create silence within the file to accommodate. Timing to an animation or a scene change is usually easier for the audio editor than the programmer to adjust.

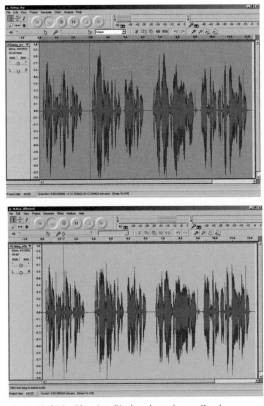

A rough ("dry") voice file (top), and an edited ("effected") version (bottom). Note the difference in thickness and height of the waveform associated with the effected version.

Long Narratives

Voice files associated with long narratives are generally treated as long sound effects similar to the creation and editing of an ambience track. These longer performances can be delivered as a single file, or they may be divided into several files if critical timing or programming issues are present. Single files can also be adjusted to hit specific timing marks by adding silence in the appropriate locations. This is made easier by either having a rough version of the game or animation for reference or being provided with the exact time points in minutes and seconds and then ensuring that the lines of dialogue start at the correct spots. As with character dialogue, care should be taken to ensure that each word is clearly understood, mistakes are corrected with appropriate replacement editing, and actor performances remain intact. Longer monologues performed by a talented actor have a particular ebb and flow of emotion that will make the dialogue interesting and keep the player listening. A large amount of significant information will be relayed to the player in these narratives, and it is important that the details are clearly understood. Missing any of this information can lead to later frustration as a player attempts to navigate a particular area.

Courtesy of Sony Creative Software

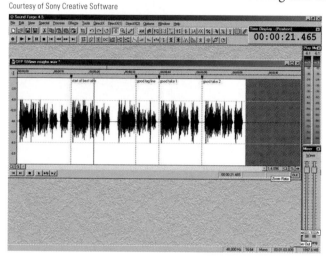

Markers flag the start of each section in this Sound Forge voice file.

Multiple Characters

The most challenging voiceover editing occurs when multiple characters are engaged in conversation. The timing, rhythm, and pace of the exchange must be well thought out and edited to sound as natural as possible. Typically, a single actor will record dialogue separately—and other actors will be brought in later for their own individual sessions. This method is much more difficult to piece together as a faithful conversation and requires much attention to detail—not only on the technical aspects of the editing, but to the performance as well. The advantage of this technique is that the editor may make corrections to one character without affecting the performance of the other characters. The editor can piece together solid dialogue among the several takes and make the scene work.

Working with material from a multitrack session with actors present and recorded simultaneously presents its own advantages and disadvantages. While this recording method may have created a more natural performance, it gives the editor less material to work with—and editing can sometimes be more difficult. If the session director and recordist were paying attention, any mistakes will have been caught and re-recorded—allowing the editor to substitute them appropriately. If not, the editor will be facing a big challenge.

Courtesy of Steinberg Media Technologies GmbH

Files from three different actors have been pieced together to create a conversation using Nuendo.

As always, the implementation of the voice files will dictate how they are edited and delivered. When individual files of character dialogue are required, they will typically be edited and saved from the point at which the first character begins speaking to the point at which the next character begins. Each of the other characters will be treated in the same way—saved as an individual file until being interrupted by the next character. There will be no overlap of character voices within the delivered files; if needed, the programmer can implement with appropriate overlap—assuming the capabilities of the audio engine and other issues allow for this application. For timing purposes, each line of dialogue will play back immediately upon triggering the file, and any predefined pauses that occur between the characters will be edited in as silence at the end of the file. This is one specific time where silence will remain in the file, since it has the purpose of simulating a real conversation.

Multiple actors recorded together, each on their own separate track, are usually edited and delivered as a single voice file. This will include dialogue overlaps, interruptions, and other nuances that cannot be duplicated by individual voice files. Cinematics or other similar applications may require delivery in this form so that the file can be simply dropped into them or rendered by the artists based on their timing. However, if the editor is also doing post-production to the cinematic, individual voice files may be used and mixed within a multitrack program instead.

Game Voiceovers: adding personality to the characters   chapter 7

::::: Believable Character Interaction in
Grand Theft Auto

Courtesy of Rockstar Games and
Take-Two Interactive Software, Inc.

Grand Theft Auto IV

For dialogue, I've really been impressed by the *Grand Theft Auto* series, primarily due to the vocal performances and the fact that the characters really seem to be interacting with each other. I find that often you'll have dialogue that really sounds like it was recorded in a vocal booth, with actors giving their performances a few days apart—and this takes me completely out of the immersive experience. We all know that this is often how game dialogue is recorded—but either through good voice direction, editing, or a combination of the two, some games are more successful at making me believe that the characters exist in the world onscreen and are really communicating with each other.

Jeff Tymoschuk (Composer, GreenWire Music & Audio)

In-Game Format

As with sound effects and music, the developer or publisher will specify the file format of the voice files. Not only does this refer to the type of file (such as .wav or .mp3), but it will also specify the sample rate, resolution, and number of output channels that are expected. Most of the time, voice files will be delivered as monophonic unless there is a specific stereo or surround effect related to the character. Their precedence within the soundscape will further dictate the quality; high priority dialogue will use 44 kHz/16-bit, while less important voices may use 22 kHz or a compressed format. It is not unusual for the developer to want a variety of formats for the same game project.

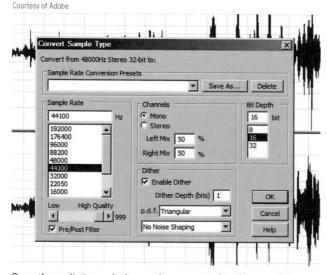

Courtesy of Adobe

Once the audio is ready, it must be converted to the game's format (Audition, shown).

The voice files will have been recorded and created in the highest possible quality, which may require down-sampling and conversions to meet the needed parameters. As with any step that reduces the quality, it is important for the editor to give another critical listen to each file after the formatting is complete and make any adjustments prior to delivery. Speech relies on midrange and higher frequencies to be understood—and within a busy game environment, it is even more important that the dialogue is heard. Down-sampling below 22 kHz or conversion to the .mp3 or .ogg formats will affect the frequencies—allowing the dialogue to cut through the rest of the audio. The adjustments may only be minor, but it is something to be mindful of during this process.

Beta Testing

Testing the voice files within the game is essential. Once all of the audio assets are added to the soundscape, it will quickly become obvious whether or not everything is working together and what will require adjustment. Unless the developer has a final quality assurance review of the game, the beta version will be the last official testing phase prior to the game's release. This is the segment of the development cycle where the developer will strive for a nearly complete version of the game, and it is the perfect chance for the audio team to evaluate its efforts.

There are specific questions that must be answered with regard to dialogue, narrative, and vocal effects:

- Do the voices fit the characters?
- Is the editing acceptable?
- Are the voice files consistent in quality, volume, and equalization?
- Are the vocals synchronized appropriately to their respective animations?
- Can the dialogue be clearly understood in segments that are important to successful game completion?
- Are the right voice files triggered at the right times?

Beta testing is designed to bring out any problems before a game is shipped—and all of the sounds should be reviewed meticulously. Any issues that arise will need to be dealt with quickly and efficiently to ensure shipment of a quality product.

Courtesy of Sony Creative Software

Are the vocals synchronized to their respective animations (Vegas Video, shown)?

Voice in today's video games is an essential ingredient used to fully engage the player in a complete and entertaining experience. The ability to communicate is a basic human need that is even more important within a game's virtual world. Characters speaking directly to players make them feel included and build a valuable relationship that adds another dimension to gameplay. The information delivered within the dialogue guides players to a successful end and keeps them out of the instruction manual; this absorbs them with an extra touch of reality instead of making it seem like an impersonal software program. The process of getting voiceovers into a game can be time-consuming and sometimes frustrating—but at the same time, it can be one of the most enjoyable and rewarding efforts in game audio. From the lone game voice actor performing his or her heart out in front of a microphone, to a room full of professional actors making injury or death sounds, opportunities to laugh out loud are plentiful. All of the fun experienced by the audio team will translate directly into dazzling performances that will greatly increase the entertainment value of the game.

:::CHAPTER REVIEW:::

1. Play 3 games currently on the market and identify the purposes of the voiceovers in each game. How do the voiceovers allow you to interact directly with the game's characters, give you the feeling that you're part of the story, immerse you further in the game experience, express the game's story and dramatic elements, or deliver important clues?

2. Referring to the same 3 games you chose in Exercise 1, discuss the types of voiceover elements in each game—and where each type is used. Do the voiceovers appear as character dialogue, story narrative, vocal sound effects, or a talking interface?

3. Experiment with capturing and editing dialogue, narrative, and vocal sound effects for an original game idea. You can work with pre-existing material or create it yourself from scratch. How will your methods differ based on the type of voiceover material you're capturing or editing? Where will you place the material in the game? How will you account for "adaptive dialogue" connected to triggered events and pathing?

Part III: Finishing Touches

CHAPTER

8

Creating the Total Soundscape

the successful blend of audio elements

Key Chapter Questions

- What is the primary importance of audio *mastering* in the development process?

- What are the factors that determine the priority given to *playback* of music, sound effects, and dialogue?

- What role does *technology* ultimately play in the final quality of individual game sounds?

- Which *implementation* factor has the most influence over game sound, and why?

- What specific audio issues are considered when conducting final *beta* and *playtesting*?

As the assets of a game come crashing together in the final stages of development, the creative and technical teams cross their fingers—hoping for the best. Graphics, animation, cinematics, programming, and audio are assembled to complete months (if not years) of planning and effort. The audio team is especially concerned with the quality of its audio assets and how they will blend together into the overall *soundscape*. The balance of music, sound effects, and dialogue is as important to a game as the mix of each instrument—such as guitars, bass, drums, and vocals— are to a well produced song. The soundscape must be given every consideration and created with intent.

Post-Production

Game companies can spend hundreds of thousands of dollars on music production by hiring the best composer, recording studio, and orchestra. The investment in sound effects can be enormous, since months of effort and many thousands of dollars are put into them. A project is made even more expensive when Hollywood celebrities lend their voices to it. There is a tremendous amount of time, effort, and money that can go into the creation of game sound—but all of this will mean absolutely nothing if each audio element has to battle for the same sonic real estate. Skillful blending of these assets is essential.

Post-production should be considered the most important, since it will ultimately have the most impact on the audio landscape. The assets will have been created with this stage in mind in an effort to minimize any extra time spent this late in the development cycle. The producer, composer, and sound designer will have discussed their contributions to the project and will have anticipated each others' needs—coming to an understanding and planning their creation strategies around each other.

Reprinted with permission from Microsoft Corporation

Electronic Arts, Inc.

Halo 3 (left) and *Medal of Honor: Airborne* (right) can easily fill the entire frequency spectrum with a myriad of audio elements.

Games with an ambitious use of music, sound effects, and dialogue are ideal cases for an overall audio mix. First-person shooters (FPSs) such as the *Medal of Honor, Call of Duty*, and *Halo* franchises are examples of games that can easily fill the entire frequency spectrum with a myriad of audio elements. By their nature, loud gunshots and explosions take center stage—leaving little sonic room for anything else. Knowing this ahead of time, the composer will tread lightly with heavy drums or any other low-frequency instruments during these segments of the game. However, the audio priorities for a racing game will be almost the opposite, since the sound effects take a back seat to the bass-driven, drum-laden music tracks. The sound designer will tune the car sounds and crash effects so that they aren't competing with the score.

Despite pre-planning efforts, audio assets will inevitably interfere with each other. More games are being pre-mixed without any menu controls for volume modifications—and for these cases, some of the interference might be controlled by simple volume adjustments within the programming and sound engine. However, some instances will require a bit more effort in order for all of the audio to fit better within the mix.

If explosions or gunshots can't be heard over the music, the composer may equalize the bottom end of the music—taking out the bass frequencies that are getting in the way. Perhaps the ambience track is too busy and the foley sounds are buried. The sound designer might pull out some of the mid to higher frequencies of the ambience or add a little to the footsteps to remedy this. If the dialogue is obscured by the music or sound effects, the mid frequencies could either be reduced in the effects or increased in the vocal playback. There are many modifications that may be made to create appropriate holes in the soundscape so that everything is heard.

The cooperation of the audio team is only part of the crusade to create an effective sound blend. Technical considerations such as how the assets are implemented by the programmer, how the sounds are affected by the game's sound engine, and whether scripting will be in use will play just as much of a role in the overall mix—and they must either be anticipated or dealt with prior to the game's release. In the old days of game development, this was almost as simple as throwing sound triggers in the programming and adding the audio to the sound file directory—but today, it's a whole new ball game!

Audio Asset Assembly

With the huge amount of assets needed to create a respectable game, efficient organization is necessary to see that everything has been created, delivered, and implemented as planned. The sound asset list is constantly revised as music and sound effects files are added or removed, delivered, and implemented—with everything checked off and fully accounted for. This file is typically in Microsoft Excel format and is easily accessible by anyone within the game company from a central server, which will also be used to assemble sound assets as they are completed; each file is added to the appropriate subfolder so that the game code knows where to find it when the sound is accessed. Other departments will also use a similar system for their assets as well, adding their portions to the game until it is finished. For an in-house audio team, this is standard practice.

Independent contractors working outside of the developer's office will operate a bit differently. The point of contact for the outside composer or sound designer will assume the duties of organizing and tracking the audio assets, which can often be from several different contractors. They will not only collect the sounds but will ensure that the quality of the work is consistent and completed in a timely fashion. Large game companies will utilize their audio directors, who are usually accomplished composers and sound designers in their own right, as points of contact for the contractors. Due to their backgrounds and authority within the game company, audio directors can provide appropriate guidance and assistance to the outside audio creators as necessary.

Smaller game developers, without the luxury of an audio director on staff, will utilize the game producer as their point of contact. While game producers may have a reasonable handle on the creation of the game, their audio knowledge may not be as extensive—and they will rely more on the contractor to provide the appropriate guidance and deliver quality audio within the timeframe allotted. The producer will ensure that the milestones are met and that all assets are completed and implemented as needed.

Will Davis & Simon Pressey on the Role of Audio Director:::::

Will Davis
(Audio Director,
Codemasters)

With over 23 years composing and creating sound effects for video games, Will has amassed sound credits on almost 500 video game projects such as *Race Driver: GRID, Overlord, DiRT, Driver, Alien vs. Predator, Battlemorph,* and *Nightmare Creatures 2.* His current multi-platform expertise includes audio for PlayStation 2 and 3, Xbox and Xbox 360, Wii and GameCube, PC, Nintendo DS, Sony PSP, and all wireless handhelds. In addition to his love for game audio, Will is also an award-winning martial arts instructor, rock climbing instructor, commercial rescue diver, stunt and fight choreographer—and he has film and video editing credits as well. Will and his wife, son, and daughter hail from England.

As Audio Director for a fast-growing publisher, it's my job to ensure that any audio released meets the quality allowed by the budget and timescales. Needless to say, I spend a lot of time fighting for larger budgets and more time. In addition to internally developed titles such as the award-winning *DiRT*, there are also externally developed titles to keep an eye on—not to mention brand and marketing movies, presentations, and web sites! It's a busy place to be. The current team consists of eight sound designers, four game audio programmers, and three audio tools and technology programmers. Part of my job is to hire composers, sound designers, and other audio specialists for various projects.

The biggest tip I can pass on is to make your information easy to access—and avoid waffling. Be professional and to the point. For show reels, include context: Why is the sound design or music the way it is? Everything is about context. Is the audio doing what it needs to do? This is especially true for music. All music has a place, and great music isn't really about how good the tune is. It's about how well it's used and how well it fits. Good audio used badly is just ugly audio. The other questions I have to ask myself are: Can someone deliver on time? Can they really do what they say they will? How easy are they to work with? For someone new, that's a hard thing to get across.

Simon has been an audio engineer/producer for more than 20 years. He spent 10 years as Chief Engineer at Le Studio Morin Heights, working with a diverse variety of popular music artists. At UbiSoft Entertainment Inc. in Montreal, he spent seven years as Audio Director—contributing to many popular video games such as *Assassin's Creed, Tom Clancy's Rainbow Six, Ghost Recon,* and *Splinter Cell* series, *Prince of Persia: The Sands of Time Trilogy,* and *Myst IV: Revelation.* In 2007, Simon joined BioWare—the creators of *Mass Effect.* In his role at BioWare, he is responsible for the audio quality of all the company's titles.

Simon Pressey
(Audio Director,
BioWare ULC,
a division of
Electronic Arts)

My role currently involves primarily guidance and unbiased feedback—and the development and maintenance of the project's focus. I don't teach by doing; I drive people to exceed their expectations and mine. Sometimes they thank me for it. With the increased complexity and sophistication of games, it has become more important that audio accurately reflects the key focus of the game design. I put a lot of effort into helping define what the audio focus should be and make sure that that is maintained across the long development cycles.

Asset delivery depends entirely on the developer's needs and capabilities. Outside contractors may be given access to the developer's FTP site and are instructed to upload their work to a specific location. This will either be the same server the company is using to gather the rest of the game assets or one on a protected network that will be transferred after the files are reviewed and accepted by the audio director or producer. DVDs and CDs with the completed audio files may be hand-delivered or sent overnight by a courier service as well. This process continues for each milestone until the game is completed.

	Character	Direction	Speech	Context Within Game
2				
3	Some characters have specific actors assigned to them while others use one of the ten generics.	These are actors' directions for use in the recording studio. Unless specified otherwise, the tone is neutral and professional.	This is the actual speech to be recorded.	This field contains a short description of the context for the speech to help the actor.
6	Control Voice #1	Distort, command	Secure the objective!	The US Consulate is under attack. Hunter is in a guard hut in the line of fire.
7	Control Voice #1	Distort, command	Move on to the next waypoint.	The US Consulate is under attack. Hunter is in a guard hut in the line of fire.
8	Control Voice #1	Distort, command	Move on to the next objective.	
9	Control Voice #1	Distort, command	Attack!	Speaking to the sergeant in the main building.
10	Control Voice #1	Distort, command	Retreat!	Speaking to the sergeant in the main building.
11	Control Voice #1	Distort, command	Withdraw to the assigned waypoint.	Speaking to the sergeant in the main building.
12	Control Voice #1	Distort, command	Wait.	
13	Control Voice #1	Distort, informative	Objective completed.	Sergeant gives out tasks in the consulate.
14	Control Voice #1	Distort, slightly up	Mission completed!	Sergeant gives out tasks in the consulate.
15	Control Voice #1	Distort, grim	Objective failed.	Sergeant gives out tasks in the consulate.
16	Control Voice #1	Distort, grim	The mission is a failure!	Sergeant gives out tasks in the consulate.
17	Control Voice #1	Distort, grim	Abort the mission.	Sergeant gives out tasks in the consulate.

A small portion of an asset list

Sony Computer Entertainment America

The most challenging experience I've faced as a video game sound designer had actually very little to do with designing sound. It was the task of taking the existing sound effects bank from *flOw* for the PS3 and squeezing it onto the handheld PSP. In *flOw,* you're an ocean-dwelling organism that swims around and eats other creatures—allowing you to grow and evolve. The gameplay is somewhat minimal; the real draw is the beautiful trancelike state that the graphics and sound can induce. Austin Wintory, the composer and sound designer, did a phenomenal job of making very expressive, delicate, and downright gorgeous sounds. Paul Fox was the senior sound designer at Sony who took Austin's sounds, incorporated them into a sound bank with our proprietary sound tool called SCREAM, and took them about 10 steps further by scripting complex organic sound events that used Austin's sounds as building blocks. It really is remarkable what they pulled off, and it was my goal to make the portable experience a seemingly identical one. Unfortunately, as I got close to my budgeted RAM, I started to realize there were some unexpected problems:

First, there was the issue of the PSP hardware. With it, you can listen through either the PSP's speakers—or through headphones, which could be of any type. I had assumed that I'd need to find a balance. I began to realize that if I tried to balance it so that everything was being heard on speakers, I was in fact throwing the mix off considerably—since those speakers could barely push out anything below 500 Hz (which is very common in *flOw*). If I tuned it like that and then listened on headphones, all of the low and low-mid sounds I had boosted were deafening. I eventually realized that this is an audiophile's game, and no audiophile is going to be listening on speakers.

Listening loudly with no ambient noise, I started getting freaked out by a second problem—what I'll call "the microscopic effect": When people listen on headphones, I think they tend to play music and games a bit louder than they would on their living room televisions. If you're on a plane or somewhere noisy, it's easy to keep cranking the volume louder and louder. When you do, you'll hear all kinds of detail buried in the mix—good and bad.

I started really zeroing in on the flaws and began to realize that no matter how much I up-sampled most sounds, I could not get rid of some of the artifacts that seemed to be present in the ADPCM codec that the game was using. It was the same codec as the PS3 version, and the artifacts had always been there due to the nature of the sounds themselves—but in the PS3 version, with subtle levels, those artifacts would never be heard unless the game was being really blasted in a home theater (and *flOw* just isn't that type of game). Fortunately, Jim Sproul of our audio tools and tech group helped me track down an old Japanese utility that had even better algorithms. I went through and re-encoded every sound file in the bank offline and swapped them in for what was there. Not only did the sound bank become a fraction of its original PS3 size, but every sound in the bank was significantly cleaner as well!

The third major issue was a nail-biter until the very end. The complex scripts in the original sound bank were too much for the little PSP to handle. The sound was clean, and I had fit it all into my memory budget—but there were occasionally sharp clicks, pops, and crackles that no one could explain. Fortunately, this problem also got resolved: First, the audio tools and tech department came up with a custom version of the audio runtime engine that helped some of the major issues—and they worked closely with Supervillain, the developer who handled the port, to implement it into the game later in the development cycle than is normally safe. Kudos to Keith Charley and Alan Gerrard at Sony—and to Steve Martin at Supervillain! Second, some of the pops that were attributed to voices getting maxed out got fixed with some careful trickery in the bank. It became a difficult situation to thin them down because so many of the signature sounds in *flOw* were due to complex scripts that might have as much as ten sound files playing at once for a single sound event. Combining the elements offline into a single sound file seemed plausible, but I realized that the elements that make up that sound event were shared by a bunch of other sound events throughout the bank. In the end, the clicks, pops, and crackles got fixed due to a very careful and selective approach to thinning down the voices in the bank so that the original game's sonic character wasn't lost.

My most challenging audio-related experience thus far also proved to be my most rewarding. When the reviews came in, every one that I read made a special note of *flOw* PSP's sound. I'm a sound designer—it's what I do and love—but successfully porting *flOw*'s existing sound effects has been one of my proudest accomplishments. As you can see, sound creation is only half the battle; sound implementation makes up the rest.

Steve Johnson (Sound Designer, Sony Computer Entertainment America)

Creating the Total Soundscape: the successful blend of audio elements   chapter 8

Audio Mastering

Audio mastering is an important but often overlooked process in game music and sound effects creation. This step is standard in the music industry, and it utilizes the very best equipment to add the final bit of polish to the audio prior to duplication. Not only do the record companies take advantage of the incredibly expensive electronics, but the mastering rooms are finely tuned to reveal every nuance to the expert mastering engineer who will ensure that the music sounds its best when it hits the streets. Due to scheduling, time constraints, or additional expenditures of this step, game developers unfortunately disregard this process and miss out on what it can do for the audio.

Courtesy of IK Multimedia   Sony Creative Software

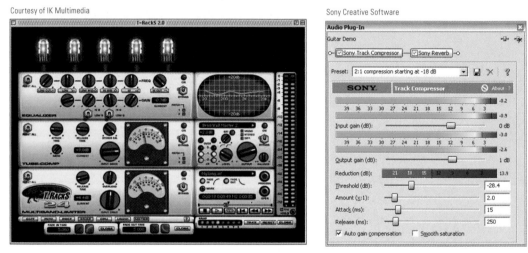

T-RackS 24 (left) and CD Architect 5 (right) are two effective audio mastering tools.

Mastering, on a simpler level, may still be accomplished by the composer or sound designer prior to final delivery of their respective assets or by the audio director as needed. This step is most important when multiple composers and sound designers are involved, and the process will ensure that the music and effects sound like a cohesive collection of audio. While they will most likely bypass the professional mastering facility, their final touches can be considered "mastering" as well.

Music and sound effects are typically created over the course of many months and sometimes even years. Even if the audio was recorded in the same studio with the same equipment, there will always be a noticeable difference in the first and last music or sound effects that are created. The intent of the simple mastering process is to resolve volume and equalization mismatches among the audio to bring consistency to the entire production. The idea is that the music or sound effects heard from start to finish will have similar audio characteristics throughout the game, nothing will stand out as being different, and the player won't be distracted by audio that seems out of place. Once a baseline is established, all music can be adjusted in volume and equalization to sound similar. Sound effects and dialogue can be adjusted separately, according to their own baseline characteristics.

Self-Funded Mastering

Many game composers spend their own money on mastering to ensure that their music has the highest quality, whether the developer is involved or not. Since the game is part of a composer or sound designer's resumé, this can be a good idea!

Mastering the entire body of work before a game is published is not always convenient, especially in a milestone-driven production cycle. An alternative method would be to complete the mastering for each specific game level to ensure that the audio within each level is at least consistent. Transitions between levels will hopefully distract players enough to where they may not notice that the next level sounds slightly different.

Courtesy of Jrod2 (Wikipedia Commons)

A fully equipped mastering studio is always handy to have available.

The non-linear structure of most games, along with the player's unpredictable actions and frequent menu accesses, make it tough to achieve this consistency—but it's possible with a little pre-planning. AAA games with large budgets almost always go the extra mile to make the audio sound its best—and with good reason. Their success and payoff comes from an outstanding product, and skimping is not an option. A game production at any level can benefit from the audio mastering process.

Halo has it all. Everyone knows the music to this superb game—and the sound design and dialogue are exceptional. What makes the music so great is the fact that even upon first listen, you already feel like the hero and can't wait to play.

Mike Brassell (Composer, Brassell Entertainment, Inc.)

chapter 8 Creating the Total Soundscape: the successful blend of audio elements

::::: Finding the Balance in *Tom Clancy's Splinter Cell: Double Agent*

When I worked with Mike McCann on the *Splinter Cell: Double Agent* soundtrack, the challenge for me was not only just a musical one, but one of defining my role within an existing structure. I was brought into the project very late in the process to arrange and flesh out the fight music for the Xbox and PC versions. Mike had tracks that were very saturated and not long enough for substantial loops. So I was to tweak, cut, paste, arrange, sweeten, add, subtract, and multiply his already very cool music. The challenge was finding my voice creatively and my place within a machine that was already in motion. From a creative standpoint, you have to walk a thin line between being proactive in your suggestions and respecting the existing music. You have to be ready to criticize the tracks and defend your critique logically and aesthetically—and you have to be able to take criticism of your own work and suggestions. It's a give and take process—and at the end of the day, it comes down to how cool you are to work with. If your work is great, but everyone hates you by the end of the project, to me, as a professional, that's not a successful outcome.

Tim Rideout (Executive Hit Writer & Groupie Herder, Tim Rideout dot com)

Audio Asset Priority

There is a fine line between reality and the simulated realism that is attempted in most video games. During intense real-life situations, sounds are happening everywhere and can be incredibly chaotic. The human mind contains a subconscious mechanism that filters out unimportant background noise—allowing only the significant and life-impacting audio cues to be heard. Intense video games can be equally confusing—but instead of being entertaining, they cause discomfort to the player who would rather turn the volume off than filter through the noise internally. To keep a third of the game experience from being cast aside, the sounds for each occasion are prioritized to relay important information and maintain a certain level of entertainment:

The *God of War* series has been very strong overall. The voice acting is full of emotion and helps push the narrative forward. The music is intense and dramatic—and it complements the Greek mythology setting perfectly. A high level of audio work has been evident in each title, which is very impressive.

Nathan Madsen (Lead Composer & Sound Designer, NetDevil)

Diagram by Per Olin

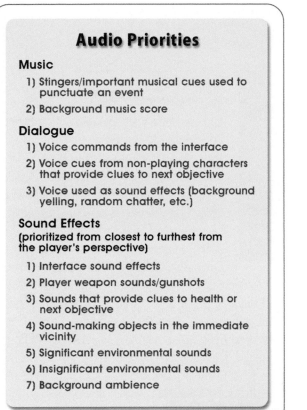

Audio Priorities

Music
1) Stingers/important musical cues used to punctuate an event
2) Background music score

Dialogue
1) Voice commands from the interface
2) Voice cues from non-playing characters that provide clues to next objective
3) Voice used as sound effects (background yelling, random chatter, etc.)

Sound Effects
(prioritized from closest to furthest from the player's perspective)
1) Interface sound effects
2) Player weapon sounds/gunshots
3) Sounds that provide clues to health or next objective
4) Sound-making objects in the immediate vicinity
5) Significant environmental sounds
6) Insignificant environmental sounds
7) Background ambience

The producer and sound team will decide in advance which sounds will have the most importance and assist the audio programmer in the execution of the plan. Whether the music, certain sound effects, or dialogue will always be heard is a matter of creative choice and depends on the goals and needs of each game. Important clues—whether in the form of dialogue or sound effects, health indications, or status of the player—and any sounds that provide the bulk of the entertainment comprise the main focus of sound prioritization.

Electronic Arts, Inc.

The audio assets in *Medal of Honor* were prioritized effectively.

Jed Smith on Avoiding Game Audio Misunderstandings :::::

Jed Smith
(Lead Producer,
betafish music)

Jed heads up betafish, a Los Angeles-based music composition company. Out of Jed's studio in Santa Monica emerges music incorporating classical, world, lounge, soul, and electronic elements into both traditional and non-traditional settings—including film, television, web, CD production, and interactive installation sound. Jed has worked for and with notable cinematic and musical talents and companies as diverse as Lionsgate, New Line, Dimension, Macy Gray, Carmen Rizzo, Paul Oakenfold, BT, Dido, Ladytron, Comedy Central, Chiat-Day, Six Degrees Records, Amp Fiddler, Electronic Arts, High Voltage, JunkieXL, Cirque du Soleil, Wim Wenders, David Arquette, and Wes Craven. His work has been in Hollywood films such as *The Bank Job, The Mist, The Tripper, Harold and Kumar 2, Pledge This!, Cursed, Thirteen*, and *Tomb Raider: The Cradle of Life*—and on television series such as *The OC, Grey's Anatomy, Windfall, Commander in Chief*, and *Reno 911!* Jed's music has also been featured in films screened at the Sundance and Cannes Film Festivals—as well as in other domestic, European, and Korean film festivals. His sound design and short subject compositions have been featured in ads for Mercedes, Target, Samsung, AT&T, Bacardi, and HP. Jed's award-winning custom-made instruments and performance sound installations have been featured at Soundwalk, the 2nd City Council art gallery, and Redcat—the performing arts space for the Disney Concert Hall.

The most challenging part of an audio professional's job is reading the minds of the clients. It is a rare treat to come across a job where the musical or sound design concepts are fully formed and clearly conveyed in technical language. This means that there is an element of translation involved most of the time. Misunderstandings stemming from inappropriate musical or technical lingo inevitably fall at your feet—so it is advisable to be as clear, concise, and politic as possible in professional correspondence.

Music will almost always play in one form or another, having been designed to sit well in the setting—and only its volume will have to be set. Background music is just that, and the mood it creates will always have priority. Most dialogue and narrative will also have a high priority in the soundscape due to their importance to the experience. Sound effects will undergo the most scrutiny when prioritizing is in effect, since the potential to have dozens of sounds playing simultaneously can really affect the nature of what is coming out of the speakers.

First-person shooter (FPS) and real-time strategy (RTS) games typically contain dense soundscapes. Music, dialogue from other players, voice commands from the interface, background ambience, environmental sounds, explosions, gunshots, and several other sound effects will all be fighting for attention during gameplay. There is usually so much sonic activity that it would be very easy to miss specific clues, health status, and much more if something isn't done about this cacophony.

The audio programmer, or the audio team via scripting, will tag specific sounds that will always play and those that will be muted as more sounds enter the picture. The approach is fairly simple: Start from the back of the soundscape and work forward. Consider a fierce battle as an example. Explosions, falling debris, machine guns, yelling, tanks rolling by, distant artillery, aircraft flybys, footsteps, wind, dogs, birds, and insects are all sounds the player would expect to hear on the battlefield. However, all of these sounds being triggered at once would be pure madness. By clearing out the less significant sounds from the background, especially those that have no real relevance to the immediate situation, there is less confusion—and the sounds that remain are heard more clearly. Prioritizing what will be heard will definitely create a better sounding game: Each sound won't necessarily be noticed, but the overall experience will be satisfying for the player.

> *M*ass Effect has a wonderful dialogue engine—and though the sound design of the environments is minimal (due to the dialogue footprint), everything you do hear sounds rich and lush with nice reverbs. The music is synthy and cool—reminding me a bit of the film *Sunshine*.
>
> *Rodney Gates (Lead Sound Designer, High Moon Studios)*

Technology

Video games are far different than any other type of entertainment medium. Integrating music, sound effects, and dialogue is much more involved than simply creating a linear mix in a film. At the beginning of the production cycle, the developer and publisher establish the target platform of the initial game release. Multiple platforms may be targeted—but even in these cases, one main game console will be set as the objective. Pre-planning will only get the developer so far when the various assets are concerned, and further adjustments are inevitable. The audio content provider must keep a close eye out for technical modifications as the production progresses.

Developers working on a PC game designed for release on a single CD-ROM with a physical storage capacity of 650-700 MB will be very conscious of the size of the assets. Toward the end of the development cycle, there is always give and take between the large real estate graphic, animation, and audio assets. Since developers always seem to give priority to the "look" of their game, the graphics (while they can be converted to lower resolution to save space) are usually left untouched. The cinematics are also deemed important to the production, which leaves audio as the unfortunate recipient of size reduction.

By re-sampling 44 kHz audio to 22 kHz, the developer will decrease the size of the file by half and usually solve the storage issue in one fell swoop. There is some consequence to this option, since the audio quality is degraded—but it's a decision that is often made. Fortunately for the player, other options are available involving decent compression algorithms that offer less impact on quality while still allowing enough of a size reduction. Re-sampling and format changes create their own issues—but being prepared for them will lessen their impact to the composer, sound designer, and player.

Courtesy of Atari Interactive, Inc.

Nintendo

How much room will there be for audio? Will you have a disc (*Neverwinter Nights 2*, left) or a cartridge (*The Legend of Zelda: A Link to the Past*, right)?

In addition to creating an evocative score, the composer may be responsible for other technical duties. The use of an internal sound bank or sound fonts will add a level of difficulty to an already complex process. The PlayStation 2 platform, for instance, can store 2 MB of instrument samples in its memory. In this case, the composer would deliver cues as MIDI files, along with the triggered instrument files. The sounds will be adapted to the internal 2MB audio chip, reformatted, and converted in order to fit within the constraints. Developers can be highly creative when implementing and triggering audio assets, and the content creators have to be ready for practically anything. A developer often asks the composer and sound designer to deliver files in one format, intending to complete conversions and reformatting itself as needed for the game. Audio creators don't always have access to development kits, which are closely guarded and controlled by the console manufacturer, so they often have no control over the final quality. The potential for unwanted audio artifacts created by this final process is enough to have the composer or sound designer close by for one last listen to ensure that the audio quality remains acceptable.

Charlie Cleveland on the Role of Game Director :::::

Charlie has worked as a software engineer and/or game designer on *Grand Prix Legends, MindRover, Empire Earth, Natural Selection* and *Zen of Sudoku*. At Unknown Worlds, he is working on *Natural Selection 2* for online distribution. Charlie has contributed articles to *Game Developer Magazine* and *Game Design Perspectives,* and has spoken at Casuality and the Game Developers Conference.

Charlie Cleveland (President & Game Director, Unknown Worlds Entertainment)

I oversee the game as a whole, which means I'm responsible for the game audio as well. I decide on the mood, write dialogue, and guide creation of all audio assets. For sound effects, this primarily involves choosing the right talent, making a spreadsheet of all the sound effects, and then writing up at least a few adjectives for each one if possible ("metallic undertone," "2.3 seconds long," "evil," "sad," etc.). For voice talent, this usually means a few hours of talking about the game world and developing a unique tone or accent. I also integrate the sounds into the game and write tools (such as one that creates ambient natural soundscapes without requiring a programmer) to help the sound designers do their jobs without relying on me.

Implementation

The *implementation* phase is where the rubber meets the road, so to speak—since the music, sound effects, and dialogue are all painstakingly integrated into the game. A developer has spent thousands of dollars creating the audio assets and understandably places a high priority on ensuring that they work in the game correctly. This means that all audio volumes are set appropriately, triggers are activated at the right time, and other technical aspects are considered.

The impact the audio programmer may have on the success of the final audio implementation is immense. While the programmer may be highly skilled at the mechanics of the programming process, there is always a risk that the quality of the audio presentation might be affected negatively. Music, sound effects, and dialogue are creatively produced and are far more about art than science. However, since technology can sometimes cloud artistic judgment, it is always a good idea to have the trained ears of the composer or sound designer available to assist the audio programmer. Composers and sound designers can relate their overall soundscape concept and listen for implementation issues that disrupt the important subtleties of the audio mix. If integrated incorrectly, quiet, almost insignificant sounds such as footsteps or wind can ruin the entire feel of the game and sound amateurish.

There are numerous issues to consider during implementation that go far beyond sound placement, triggers, and volume. Games are incredibly complex technological feats and, as expected, the integration and use of audio is no different. The pursuit of realism through incredible imagination may often lead to much more than creating audio for the content provider. It can also lead to inventing entirely new ways to show it off.

Game Audio Engine

Deep within a game's programming code lies another program that manages the audio assets. The *game audio engine* is designed to control how music, sound effects, and dialogue are played back throughout each segment of gameplay. If the schedule and budget allow, most developers prefer to create the audio engine from scratch and program in unique features specific to the project's needs. Audio implementation tools are often created in conjunction with the engine to allow the audio team access to its features. This, however, is time consuming and requires specific expertise that isn't always readily available. In these cases, audio engines may be licensed from other game or *middleware* software developers as necessary. The upside to licensing is that a working audio engine is immediately available—but the tools that allow the audio team to make full use of the engine may not be.

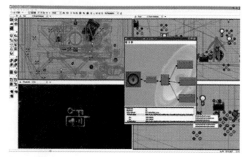

Unreal Editor includes one of several effective game audio engines.

For composers and sound designers, it is important to understand how the audio engine works and ultimately affects the sound. This tool will impact the volume, panning, surround, effects processing, and many other parameters—and knowing a little about how the engine processes and plays back the audio will ensure that the chain of quality isn't broken. For example, an audio engine that simulates an environment such as a large room or tunnel will introduce a significant amount of reverb and will drastically change the characteristics of the sound. Knowing ahead of time that the engine will be adding this effect, composers or sound designers can keep their use of reverb to a minimum. If positional audio is in use by the audio engine, the sound designer will automatically know to deliver certain files as monophonic. This audio will remain fixed as players turn within the game, allowing them to maintain a sense of direction by the position of the noisemaking object. The audio engine will selectively determine where in the listening field the sound will be placed and which speaker will play which audio channel. There are many instances in which the effect of the audio engine will impact the creative process and how the final files are delivered. Changes with the audio engine can send a ripple through the entire audio development process and must be considered carefully—especially if it is late in the cycle.

Pre-packaged game audio engines are abundant, and developers enjoy these robust applications that ultimately make the production of a game easier and more streamlined. If a game company decides against in-house audio engine development, it still has a variety of options, feature sets, and licensing fees to choose from. While it is impossible to be familiar with all of these options, there are some that are more popular than others.

RAD Game Tools Miles Sound System is perhaps the most used commercial audio engine on the market. It provides MIDI, XMIDI, Redbook, MP3, and DLS support—including a software synth and integrated support for numerous compression schemes. Other features include multiple Dolby and 3D-compatible surround formats, Ogg Vogis and MPEG-3 (mp3) decompression support, DSP Digital Audio Filtering, and support for most current game platforms.

Courtesy of RAD Game Tools, Inc.

Miles Sound System is perhaps the most widely used commercial audio engine on the market.

Firelight Technology's FMOD Ex is touted as a revolutionary audio engine for game developers, multimedia developers, sound designers, musicians, and audio engineers. This new API is based on the previous product, FMOD—but it aims high to push the boundaries of audio implementation, while using minimal resources and being fully scalable. This new engine is written from the ground up and involves years of experience and feedback from FMOD users to create the most feature-filled and easy-to-use product possible. FMOD Ex supports Windows, Macintosh, Linux, Sony PS2/PS3/PSP, Microsoft Xbox/Xbox 360, and Nintendo GameCube/Wii.

Courtesy of Firelight Technologies

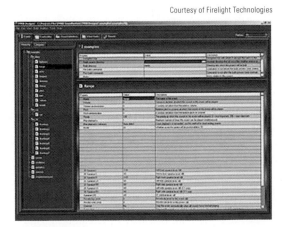

FMOD Ex is touted as a revolutionary audio engine for game developers.

Microsoft DirectMusic (DM) is a powerful computer music development tool, using DLS as its primary delivery method for sounds and MIDI as its control. The DirectMusic SDK is available free with the current DirectX SDK—along with DirectMusic Producer, the editor for DirectMusic. Its main features include the use of DLS level 1, imported MIDI files, and expanded interactivity through use of variations, chord maps, real-time reverb, and chorus.

Reprinted with permission from Microsoft Corporation

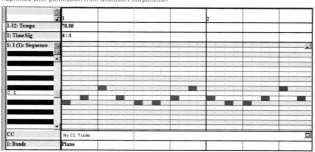

DirectMusic is a powerful computer music development tool.

Audiokinetic Wwise (WaveWorks Interactive Sound Engine) is marketed as a complete audio pipeline solution—from an extensive implementation tool to a fully developed cross-platform sound engine. The advantage of this application is the graphical interface that streamlines the audio creation workflow and allows users to build audio structures, define audio behaviors, edit and mix in real time, manage sound integration, and implement "on the fly" audio authoring directly in the game. All sounds can be created, auditioned, and adjusted without the programmer's assistance. The complete application also includes a real-time game simulator, architecture for source, and effect and source control plug-ins.

Courtesy of Audiokinetic

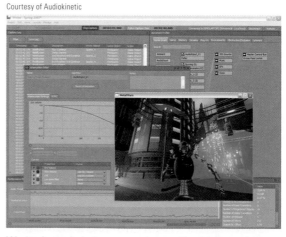

Wwise is marketed as a complete audio pipeline solution.

Microsoft's XACT (Xbox Audio Creation Tool) and its companion Audio Authoring Tool are limited to audio formatting and implementation on the Xbox and PC running Windows Vista. These applications allow audio to be optimized for use on these specific platforms—organizing sound assets into *wave banks* and instructions into *sound banks*. Audio creators are given the ability to script volume and pitch levels that may then be implemented into the game by the developer using the same tool. Key features include the ability to save to different audio file formats, support stereo and 5.1 channel arrangements, organize and bundle sound assets, and audition and adjust sounds under gameplay conditions.

Reprinted with permission from Microsoft Corporation

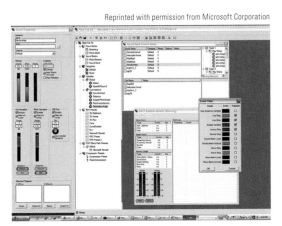

XACT provides audio formatting and implementation functions on the Xbox and PC running Vista.

Sensaura GameCODA, Creative Labs ISACT, and the Unreal 3 engine are also worthwhile audio middleware applications that include very similar feature sets as the others listed in this section. The primary differences are the available budget for licensing fees and how the features integrate with other assets and tools in the development process.

Audio Triggers, Hooks & Callouts

Segments of programming that tell the audio engine when and how to play a sound are referred to by various terms such as *audio triggers, hooks*, and *callouts*. Each sound asset will have at least one trigger and multiple instances depending on its usage within the game. During the course of development, programmers will have predicted where sounds are required and will have coded the proper callouts and added placeholder sounds in the appropriate directory to test them. By the time the composer or sound designer enters the picture, most of the programming logistics will have been taken care of and are ready for the new audio to be dropped in as it's created. However, not all of the sounds and music uses can be anticipated—and the audio content creator often comes in with great ideas that will be implemented further into the cycle. In these cases, the audio team will work directly with the audio programmer to ensure that new triggers are placed as needed.

An example of a simple sound trigger that would play the designated sound as Button A is pressed by the player might be expressed as:

```
If button_a = depress, then play button_sound_01.wav
```

A line of code similar to the above would appear whenever Button A was active within a game but would change to activate a variety of different sounds as the purpose of the button changes. Controller buttons, for example, not only activate certain menu functions and player selections as expected but could also activate or reload weapons, drop mines, or change the view. Triggering a different sound is as easy as changing the name of the file within the code. There are more complex methods of coding sound, but even this basic example shows how implementation can become a challenge. More complicated programming will involve designating the correct file to play, along with many other parameters that affect playback. The volume setting of the sound can be programmed to vary under specific conditions or to be muted if higher priority sounds are triggered. Real-time effects processing accomplished by the audio engine, such as adding reverb to an engine sound as a vehicle drives through a tunnel, will also be established. The car's engine is not only triggered to play but is set to vary as other conditions apply.

Diagram by Per Olin

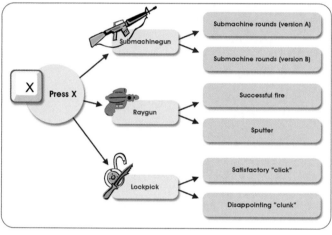

Machine gunshots are interesting examples of creative triggering and coded effects processing. In the real world, each shot will sound slightly different in volume, pitch, and rate of fire. The old days of triggering a single shot file have been immensely improved by the addition of real-time effects processing in the programming. As the weapon is activated by the player, the audio engine will be told to make minor volume, pitch, and timing changes in real time so that the overall succession of shots will have a more natural sound. Another approach to the same issue would be to have the sound designer deliver several individual shot variations that would be triggered at random by the programming. This produces good results as well, but there is yet another method that could be employed: The sound designer could also deliver the recording of one long machine gun burst with markers set before each shot within the file. The programmer would then code random starting points for each trigger pull, which would continuously loop as the trigger button is held. This method is the most realistic, and it works great as long as memory and storage space aren't prevailing issues.

Audio Scripting

It is generally acknowledged that those who create audio professionally have a unique ability to hear at an entirely different level than those who do not. Concentrating intently on a game's audio will naturally result in an overall big picture of how a game should sound and the uses of audio that will complement it. The industry has finally accepted the expertise of the composer and sound designer—and it has realized that by placing more power and control of the audio assets in their hands, the overall audio presentation greatly benefits. *Audio scripting* is an application that has quickly become prevalent in the industry—especially in large, complex game projects. It's highly unique to have scripting capacity as a composer or sound designer—and because it is virtually unheard of in any other form of entertainment, it sets game audio creators apart from any other audio specialty.

Courtesy of Audiokinetic

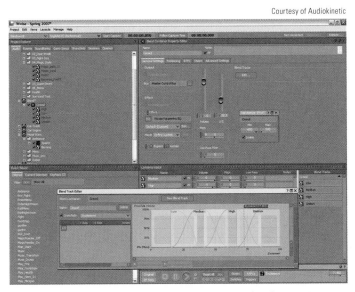

Wwise is an effective application program interface (API) for audio scripting.

Scripting, in a nutshell, is the equivalent to the programmer's version of implementation. Instead of a programmer writing the lines of code, the composer or sound designer delivers script files that specify which sound files to play, when to start and stop them, volume, panning, effects processing, and any other instruction appropriate to the situation. The programmer will then drop these completed scripts into the code, and the job is essentially done. This in effect leaves all of the creative decisions to the audio provider and allows the programmer to focus on the technical aspects of seeing the vision through. This does require a little more effort on the part of the composer and sound designer, but the development tools in use today help make the process very user-friendly.

Scripting is always used in interactive and adaptive music applications, where the complexities of the actual music creation can be better managed through the control of playback aspects. A typical scenario involves music that is designed to shift as the game changes in difficulty, such as when the number of bad guys increases or decreases. This can be achieved by selecting and deselecting various stems of a single multitrack piece of music that might begin as a simple orchestral string track for the exploration mode. As the tension builds with the appearance of unfriendly characters, a booming percussion track, grinding bass track, and poignant counter melody may be triggered in line with the original string track. The composer would deliver the script, which sets the parameters of these additional tracks.

A more complex option that benefits from composers utilizing scripting instead of having to translate their visions for a programmer is when seamless transitioning is required between various cues of adaptive music. Unlike the previous example, which mutes and unmutes tracks within a piece of music, this method utilizes separate music files that are designed to crossfade smoothly as required. A sample script for this type of application could work something like this:

```
If bad guys = 1, then play music_01a.wav

If bad guys = 5, then play music_01b.wav

If bad guys = 10, then play music_01c.wav
```

In this particular scenario, the music is designed to change to something more intense and up-tempo to influence the emotional state of players while they are engaged in battle. Sound designers might also use similar scripting to alter ambience tracks, environmental sounds, and dialogue to fit the same situation.

Diagram by Per Olin

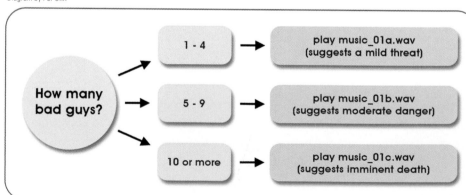

Occlusion & Obstruction

As games strive to deliver realistic audio environments, acoustic interaction of sounds within their surroundings are being simulated with much greater accuracy. In FPSs such as *Half-Life 2, Doom 3, Operation Flashpoint,* and *World War II Online,* credible aural depictions are critical to maintaining the sense of immersion—and having the ability to direct or affect sound waves within the game environment is the key.

Diagram by Per Olin

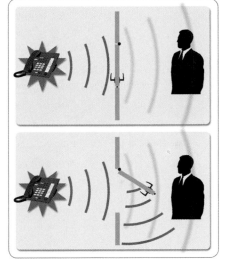

Sounds are not always heard directly from their source, and they instead may be muffled by a wall or blocked by other objects. A full or partial obstruction determines the parameters that will be adjusted. A sound is *occluded* when it is heard emanating from another room through a wall or closed door. The sound source is fully enclosed within another environment and causes the sound waves to be severely muffled and reduced in volume—with the doors and walls acting as filters. To simulate this phenomenon, audio engines are set to apply real-time frequency adjustments—utilizing a low pass filter or equalization settings that reduce the mid to upper frequencies and cut the volume if needed. Turn a radio or television on and listen outside the room with the door closed to experience this effect.

Sound heard through a complete barrier (top) is *occluded*. Sound heard through a partial barrier (bottom) is *obstructed*.

A sound is *obstructed* when an object blocks the direct path from its source to the listener but does not enclose it. Consider the previous example of a sound heard from another room through a closed door. If the door is opened and the listener stands out of the direct line of sight of the object, just outside the door, the audible sound waves either diffract as they bounce off walls and objects within the environment, or pass through the obstacle separating the two. In a game application, the sound engine will be set to vary sound reflections and decay times utilizing complex mathematical algorithms to reproduce this with believability.

Used by permission from id Software, Inc.   Courtesy of Codemasters

In *Doom 3* (left), the sound of combat behind closed doors is occluded, while crouching next to a tank in *Operation Flashpoint 2* (right) obstructs some of the battle sounds.

Panning

Panning is the physical placement of sound within the stereo or surround listening field. Games use directional sound to provide aural clues to players to help maintain their sense of direction and provide useable feedback when something requires their attention. Most third-person RTS titles have a fixed player perspective but can take advantage of panning to direct the player to an important situation off screen. The programmer will include specific real-time functioning that determines the location of the sound source and the screen position of the player—and then direct the sound to the appropriate speaker. Through this use of sound, the player has the correct information to quickly highlight the appropriate area of the playing field.

Firaxis Games Inc.

The direction of a sound cue in *Sid Meier's Civilization IV* prompts the player to look in its direction for more information.

Games such as *Sid Meier's Civilization IV*, *The Settlers II: The Next Generation (10ᵗʰ Anniversary)*, *Command & Conquer: Generals*, *Homeworld 2*, and *WarCraft* are outstanding examples of the importance and need for panning in this genre of games. Since there are so many layers to this brand of gameplay and not all of the action can be contained on a single screen, directional audio provides important feedback to the player during critical moments.

FPS titles rely on panning for the same purposes, but it is accomplished in a more complex fashion due to the player's continuously changing perspective. Sounds are often attached to specific objects and move only as players maneuver within the environment. This type of panning is more dynamic, since constant evaluation within the programming is made to determine the objects' positions in relation to the view of the character. While this is not "panning" in the simple musical terms of left and right, it is something that must be considered as sounds are implemented. *Half Life 2*, *Operation Flashpoint 2: Dragon Rising*, *Medal of Honor*, *Call of Duty*, *Halo 3*, and *Doom 3* all exemplify an attempt at audio realism.

Reprinted with permission from Microsoft Corporation

Accurate sound cues in *Halo 3* alert the player to danger.

The positioning of audio within the environment is incredibly important—and when done correctly, it is instrumental to achieving a believable virtual world. Typically, noisemaking objects within the setting—such as a diesel generator, crackling fireplace, buzzing light, radio-emitting static, and moving vehicle—have the sounds "attached" to them and will be heard by the player depending on their location and directional orientation. The panning of the sound to the appropriate audio output channel will give the player a directional clue for the object.

The Lord of the Rings: The Battle For Middle-earth II has wonderful sound for an RTS. I especially love the sense of the army's size as the player commands them to attack, and the dialogue callouts that resound well in the environment; the developers really nailed the sense of outdoor ambient distance and reflection. The original *LotR* score fits perfectly without getting in the way.

Rodney Gates (Lead Sound Designer, High Moon Studios)

Volume & Player Distance

In conjunction with other audio programming challenges, the *volume* of an object in relation to the *distance* of the player from it must also be considered. In an effort to create a believable soundscape in a game, acoustic principles relating to this phenomenon may be applied that decrease the volume and diffuse the sound as the distance is increased from the sound source. Conversely, the sound becomes more focused and louder as the noisemaking object moves closer.

As players move around an environment, objects will be constantly scrutinized by the game code; their sounds will also be adjusted in loudness and (in more advanced games) in diffusion, utilizing reverb or obstruction algorithms. Some games will actually be able to achieve this effect by simple manipulation of a sound's volume, depending on what other sonic activity may be happening.

As a soundscape becomes more involved and chaotic with an increase of action, the established priority of sounds will take precedence over distance-related concerns. Sound sources farthest from the player's position are disabled first, as the closer, more relevant sounds are played. However, during exploratory phases of the game, the use of distance can be very powerful. For example, let's say a player is wandering through the landscape looking for a waterfall for a clue. When the player has reached a predetermined distance from the waterfall, the sound associated with the waterfall may be enabled at a low volume to let the player know that the goal is somewhere nearby. However, since the sound is diffused, the direction is purposely vague and won't fully reveal its secret until the player chooses correctly and moves closer to it. This can be a significant storytelling device by providing foreshadowing and building anticipation of the reward. FPSs typically make the most use of volume and player distance as another method to pull the player into the audio landscape. *Unreal Tournament*, *Red Steel*, *Warmonger – Operation: Downtown Destruction*, *Thief: The Dark Project*, and *Deus Ex* are worthy examples.

© 2007 NetDevil, Ltd.

Warmonger – Operation: Downtown Destruction makes effective use of volume cues.

Similar to the issue of panning, volume in relation to the player is an important clue to the distance from a noisemaking object. Gunshots, explosions, and non-player character (NPC) dialogue, for example, warn the player of possible danger nearby. Other audio-producing objects could indicate clues to finding the level objective or other intermediate goals.

Surround Format

Identifying music and sound effects that will be played in a surround format such as Dolby ProLogic II, Dolby Digital, or DTS is another major consideration when implementing audio. For 5.1 surround, these assets will be delivered as six separate mono files, three stereo stem files (left/right front, center/LFE, and left/right rear channels), or complete encoded stereo files—depending on the platform and how they will be implemented. The Xbox 360, for example, has a built-in encoder within the development kit hardware—and the separate stem files are encoded as part of the integration process.

Courtesy of Apple Inc.

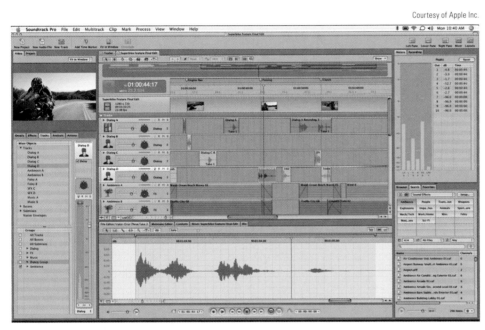

Soundtrack Pro 2 helps the sound engineer encode and implement surround sound tracks.

Surround sound in games requires double effort—encoding and implementing the sounds correctly on the front side, and tagging these files for decoding for playback by the audio engine on the other. It is important that the files are clearly identified prior to implementation to ensure a smooth procedure. While surround applications are generally targeted for game consoles connected to home theater systems or high-end PC surround systems, it is equally important that the audio is tested somewhere along the line on stereo speakers to make certain it is acceptable.

*H*alo and *Star Wars: Knights of the Old Republic* contain excellent music and dialogue, respectively. The main reason for both is immersion. For music, the key is to have pieces that you want to listen to even when you are not playing the game. With dialogue, the system for introducing it must be elegant and unobtrusive—and *KotOR* makes you feel like *you* are actually doing the talking.

Mark A. Temple (Founder, Enemy Technology)

Final Beta & Playtesting

Testing is usually conducted as the game is assembled, after each milestone and as major audio assets are implemented. The *final beta testing* phase, as far as audio is concerned, isn't usually a huge undertaking, since the audio has had close scrutiny all along. Most issues will have already been identified, and corrective actions will have been taken by this point of the development cycle—but with the game now fully assembled and all assets in place, one last look will allow the team to hear what the consumer will experience. This final beta testing phase allows the game designers to take a step back and see the project as a whole instead of being intently focused on the smaller details.

Playtesting is the phase of development that allows the game developers a chance to see if all of their efforts have paid off. The overall process includes examining graphics, animations, cinematics, programming, music, sound effects, and dialogue—and to see if everything is working together as planned. Publishers and some developers have in-house playtesters—trained individuals who have not been involved with the development who will put the game through its paces. Other companies will contract this phase to outside testing services that will perform the task. The best case scenario is to have a group of well-trained, professional playtesters examining the game. These folks will approach the task in an unbiased fashion and closely evaluate each element of the game, including the audio. After living with various music and sound effects over the course of the development, it's good to have other ears assessing its effectiveness.

With fresh ears and impartial judgment, game testers use the same criteria composers and sound designers did when creating the audio:

- Does the audio work in the game?
- Is the overall volume and equalization good?
- Is the music effective?
- Are the sound effects appropriate?
- Do the sound effects play when they are supposed to?
- Are there any sounds that have been duplicated or omitted?
- Is the timing of triggered sounds correct?
- Are the character voices believable or do they distract from the gameplay?
- Is the timing of the characters' mouth movements synched correctly?
- Are there any annoying sounds?
- Is any sound element monotonous?
- What adjustments should be made?

After the testing team makes an evaluation, determines specific trends, and puts together a report, the developer will meet with department heads to discuss what should or can be done in the remaining time. Not everything has to be fixed, and sometimes the lack of time prohibits anything but major defects to be addressed. Tasks are prioritized, a firm plan is established, and "crunch time" begins.

From the logistical standpoint and despite the extreme effort at organization and asset tracking, some bugs will appear due to content that is missing, mislabeled, or incorrectly formatted. Large game projects can get incredibly chaotic, and it is understandable that some things can get overlooked. These will be the easy fixes. Unfortunately, not everything can be redone or fixed. It's next to impossible to get studio time and assemble musicians and the support crew to re-record an orchestral piece at the last minute. The sound designer won't have the time to jet off to some remote corner of the globe to grab a new sound. The voiceover artist might be shooting a movie and is unavailable. Any reworks have to be done on a smaller scale.

For music, instruments that have been determined to be annoying or interfere with other game elements can be individually replaced or adjusted within a cue. A multi-track audio program has the advantage of being able to replace or adjust those specific instruments within the piece. You can also adjust the length of the cues, fade-ins/outs, volume, and equalization (EQ). Re-recording entirely new music is out of the question at this late stage. Sound effects may need to be modified to match animation or character movements. Sounds that are found to be too grating or monotonous may be replaced or modified appropriately.

This is the absolute final opportunity to hear how the audio elements work together as a whole and to gauge the effectiveness of the overall soundscape. There is little time to completely redo any major number of assets, and concerns that present themselves at this stage will have to be massaged appropriately to fit. EQ, volume, and synchronization changes will be made quickly to meet the final deadline as the game is rushed out the door for duplication. This phase typically means late nights and long hours as the race to completion is made, but this final phase prior to "gold" is an invaluable chance to catch what has been missed and fix it. Shipping a quality product is the number one priority, and every effort will be focused on that endeavor.

> *Call of Duty 4* blends great sound effects, music, and dialogue in a seamless and cinematic way. The implementation of the sound effects with tasteful use of smart panning and variation—along with the AI-driven dialogue of other soldiers shouting at the player and great music kicking in at climactic events—conveys a powerful sense of drama and excitement.
>
> *Robert Burns (Lead Sound Designer, High Moon Studios)*

A professional sounding game is what every audio team strives to deliver—but the overall soundscape is only as good as the sum of its parts, regardless of the quality of each ingredient. It's tempting to create single elements that sound incredible by themselves; however, the mix of music, sound effects, and dialogue must be carefully crafted to sound good together—or the efforts of the other content providers will have been wasted and the game will suffer. Mixing down a piece of music can be very involved as a recording engineer adjusts volume, equalization, and placement of each instrument within the listening field—skillfully maneuvering and interweaving each element so that the overall mix will sound its best. Soloing each instrument will often bring a surprise to the inexperienced who might make the discovery that the guitar, piano, vocals, and other instruments sound thin or weak by themselves. However, adjusting them to sound acceptable by themselves will end up destroying the delicate balance and the overall sound quality. Creating an agreeable soundscape is very similar in mindset to mixing a piece of music. Looking at a game from this larger perspective greatly increases the chance that it will sound fantastic. There will be appropriate times where all the stops are pulled out for a single element—such as the opening title music or a special sound effect indicating victory. However, when the player is knee deep in the fray—amid bullets flying, screaming, gunfire, tanks, aircraft, and explosions only feet away—all of the elements must work together or the player will reach for the volume control and turn it off. If the player ever does this, it would be a miserable failure for every member of the audio team.

:::CHAPTER REVIEW:::

1. Play 3 FPS or RTS games currently on the market and identify the different sounds you hear at any one time during gameplay containing a high level of action. Consider music, character dialogue, narration, vocal effects, sound effects from objects, interface sound or voice commands, background ambience, and environmental sounds. How are these sounds distinct from one another without resulting in cacophony? Note the relative volume, texture, quality, pitch, complexity, and tone of each sound.

2. Referring to the games you played in Exercise 1, note specifically which sounds are triggered based on certain events—such as the player character's or NPC's actions and movements or a change in the environment. Create a flowchart that maps each event to a particular sound. Indicate when one event triggers distinct sounds or different variations of the same sound—and note their context.

3. What is the distinction between occlusion and obstruction? Find examples of both in the soundscapes associated with the games you played in Exercise 1 and describe the specific context in which they appear. Close your eyes and see if you can detect how the sound design alone successfully conveys the occlusion or obstruction of an object.

CHAPTER

9

Future of Game Audio Development

the best is yet to come

Key Chapter Questions

- What are the main factors that drive the continued *evolution* of game audio?

- Which methods used to present *new ideas* to the game community are most effective, and why?

- What are the major *organizations* that participate in the debate and exchange of ideas in the game industry?

- What are some options and paths associated with a *career* in game audio?

- What are some *future* trends and improvements expected in game audio development?

Video games have made tremendous strides in just the past decade, and it is inevitable that they will continue to do so at an exponential rate. The industry is driven by both technology and creativity—at the mercy of both hardware and software advancements, and the unbridled imaginations of those who create these recreational diversions. As the industry continues to evolve, developers and console manufacturers will exploit any new advantage for the sake of a better game experience, resulting in continued improvements as game creators invent better ways to present their work. The prospect of unlimited potential makes it a great time to be a part of the industry. Game audio is a respected element of the entertainment experience—and much is expected from it. Entertainment, realism, and immersion are incredibly lofty objectives for sound effects, music, dialogue, and voiceovers— and extraordinary skill sets and talents are required to create them successfully. The purpose of this book has been to provide a solid foundation to help prepare the game audio professionals of tomorrow to continue the march forward and champion their own game audio causes.

Game Audio Trends

It doesn't take a crystal ball to see the future of game audio. Predictable improvements are based on years of previous benchmarks that have already been met. It is certain that the quality of music and sound effects will continue to increase. As storage space and faster processors are developed, the size of audio that can be stored and the speed with which it will be processed will always improve. Only a few short years ago, it seemed like an unreachable goal that a 44 kHz sample rate and 16-bit resolution would ever be obtainable. Now these are the standards. Some games have bumped the sample rate to 48 kHz successfully, with 88 kHz and 96 kHz now in the crosshairs—and 24-bit resolution is also the next fully obtainable milestone. These improvements are significant for audiophiles—but for a generation that accepts the reduced quality of compressed MP3 files, this unfortunately could take a back seat to other game improvements. Only time will tell.

Surround sound usage has become commonplace and is foreseen to be an accepted standard in the near future. As home theater and surround systems become less expensive and easier to install and maintain, the abundance of this hardware will encourage developers to make wider use of the standard. The 5.1 or Dolby ProLogic II will be the first achievable target—but with 7.1 and 9.1 gaining momentum, games will eventually incorporate these formats into a truly mind-blowing audio experience. The ability to immerse players inside the game is becoming increasingly important, and the usage of surround is helping developers realize this successfully.

Several years ago, interactive and adaptive audio were mere ideas. In the 1970s, *Space Invaders* and *Asteroids* subtly offered the potential of an interactive soundtrack—and today, they have risen from elaborate concepts to possibly the entire future of game audio. Games such as *Halo 3*, *Guitar Hero*, *BioShock*, *flOw*, *God of War II*, *The Lord of the Rings Online: Shadows of Angmar*, and *Uncharted: Drake's Fortune* have taken adaptive audio and have made their own advancements to it. These interesting little ideas have the potential to drive the creation and implementation processes far beyond anything even imaginable today. Adaptive audio elements alleviate the curse of monotony and repetition—making the interaction increasingly more stimulating. The good news is that this significant method of audio implementation is only in its infancy—with the best yet to come!

Big Stock Photo

Surround sound is helping developers immerse players in the game.

As interactive and adaptive audio become more commonplace, additional enhancements to streamline these elements in both creation and implementation will follow suit. Not only will the appropriate tools be created by the developers themselves, but middleware and console manufacturers will join forces to assist in the integration of these complex issues. Scripting—performed by the composer, the sound designer, or a designated audio scripting specialist—will become widely accepted and used on a regular basis. As the complexities of music and sound effects increase, audio experts will personally ensure that their intricate visions are conveyed correctly—taking audio programmers out of that process and allowing them to focus on their technical assignments.

Courtesy of RedOctane

Space Invaders (left) hinted at the possibilities of interactive audio; *Guitar Hero III: Legends of Rock* (right) is beginning to fulfill that potential.

The increase of storage space and processor capabilities has led game developers to unintentionally discover the value of more music and sound effects variations in their games, and the creative implementation of these assets. What was once accomplished by a single individual has grown to a more specialized and segmented production process that now requires an entire team of specialists to accommodate this significant increase in complexity of tasks. Larger game development houses require fully staffed audio departments with an energetic workforce—including composers, sound designers, engineers, mixers, audio editors, field recordists, and voiceover specialists. The need for individuals to concentrate on the many small details associated with audio creation and implementation is growing rapidly.

Future of Game Audio Development: the best is yet to come   **chapter 9**

Game vs. Film Audio

The game you play and the DVD you buy both play through the same speakers. At its best, game audio can do what the audio does in a great movie. What if you watched the D-Day scene from *Saving Private Ryan* with the sound off? There's very little dialogue in that scene; most of the action is shown through images and audio. Without the audio, the scene loses much of its power. Go back and watch a classic old movie such as *High Noon*—where by today's standards the audio technology is primitive. Yet the music and sound effects in that film were critical to winning several Academy Awards. That same potential exists for music and sounds in games. It's a very exciting time for our industry!

Don Daglow (President & CEO, Stormfront Studios)

Game audio is becoming indistinguishable from soundtrack audio development in the movies. Just as the first silent films and talkies appear amateurish to us today without a movie soundtrack, so will today's games appear amateurish compared to the games created in the next decade.

Bill Louden (Founder, Genie / Professor, Austin Community College)

Game audio has finally caught up to movie audio. In many ways, it has surpassed the film industry. Sound for games is much more complex to create. We aren't simply working in a linear timeline. We have to plan for every possible use in the game. If a gun fires, we can't just create that one perfect gunshot; we have to make 30 perfect variations of that gunshot.

Chad W. Mossholder (Sound Designer/Composer, Sony Online Entertainment)

My hope is that more producers and designers think of audio as an integral aspect of the game rather than as an afterthought. There's so much left to explore in game audio, and I hope developers realize this. I also hope game composing gets out from under the shadow of film composing. They're entirely different. I don't think saying a game has a "film-quality soundtrack" is necessarily a compliment.

Matt Sayre (Owner, The Game Composer)

Sound Effects

The biggest weakness in game sound has always been the monotony of repetition. The same sound played over and over again has the tendency to promote an agony similar to the constant drip, drip, drip of a water torture machine. Sound effects will achieve major advancements in the years to come as the move toward realism, subtlety, and more directional sound cues continues to advance. New ideas in the creation and implementation of these important assets are in constant development and have the potential to change the way game sound designers do business altogether.

Watson Wu records a skate board scratch from Charlie Canham (left), and immortalizes a flamingo (right).

On the creation front, an increase in field recording is likely as game audio professionals pursue their own audio identities, reaching less for stock sound libraries. Most sound production for films utilizes extensive field recording on location, during filming, or separately in order to capture fresh and unique sounds. Larger game productions rely heavily on this method not only for new sounds but to record sounds suited to their needs. For example, to create usable engine loops for a racing game, the sound design team will strap microphones to a professional race car and record a steady rpm for the length of time needed. Since stock libraries are limited in these types of sounds, it is necessary that they are captured specifically for the application. The increasing complexities of implementation guarantee that more customized recording will be needed.

New tools are also on the horizon to battle repetitive sounds and simplify the creation process. There is currently experimentation underway to generate sound effects on the fly in real time instead of triggering pre-recorded ones. The dynamics of environmental physics and acoustic modeling are colliding to provide another perspective to sound implementation. As an example, multiple shell casings ejected from a weapon currently trigger one of several pre-recorded sound files as they hit the ground. The new idea is to generate the sound of each single shell casing in real time as it is ejected, hits the ground, bounces, rolls, hits other shell casings or objects, and settles.

As the in-game character moves to a different surface and around other objects, the shell casings will react and make appropriate sounds based on these changing parameters—all generated by the audio engine and not from a pre-recorded sound. The possibilities are endless, since this technique guarantees non-repetitive audio and ensures that the player will never hear the same sound twice.

Sound effects generation is also closely tied to the development of real-time mixing within the game environment. The dynamics of sounds would depend on many factors such as the object, surface, or obstructions encountered. Real-time effects processing, such as reverb or delay, and simulated acoustic modeling of the game environment will also be used and greatly improved upon as elements fall into place.

Technology Factors

Storage capacity continues to increase, and game platforms will soon begin to include chip-based sample libraries that are equivalent in size, scope, and quality to the Vienna Orchestra and have real-time tools similar to Absynth included in the hardware. This will allow for the flexibility that MIDI and other paramatized tools have, while maintaining realistic high-quality sounds.

Kemal Amarasingham (Audio Director, dSonic Inc.)

We're already running real-time plug-ins, mix automation, multitrack sounds, and as many as 256 voices. With console hardware providing more DSP time and memory, it will soon get to the point where there's basically a Pro Tools HD system running under the hood of your favorite game console.

Robert Burns (Lead Sound Designer, High Moon Studios)

I want to work on the AI of mixing audio that brings together the player/game input and the sound designer's desire to mix the game, with all of the detail and focus that is currently the norm in film. I want run-time speech recognition and synthesis / run-time granular and physical synthesis of sound that is tied in directly to animation and physics systems so that sound for movement collision and machinery is automatically created by the engine. I expect all of this inside of my career in games. On the shorter term, I want to see the wider adoption of audio tools such as Wwise so that I can better leverage the wealth of talent that is the wider audio community—and see that the toolset and the knowledge on how to leverage it grow, rather than the in-house proprietary systems that (while highly optimized) don't feed on the wider expertise and creativity of the whole audio community.

Simon Pressey (Audio Director, BioWare—a division of Electronic Arts)

Music

The future of game music appears to be heading in two distinct directions. One path seems to be tending toward live orchestras, musicians, and large audio production budgets to accommodate them. Composers will become highly proficient at scoring a game much like film composers are, but their focus will be on adaptive music that can change at any moment to follow the ever unpredictable onscreen action. Game composers will no longer be writing music to simply fit a mood, but also for the innumerable possibilities encountered by the player.

Photo: Derek Askem

Richard Jacques conducts the London Session Orchestra at Studio One, Abbey Road Studios, London for *Headhunter*—the first game score recorded in world famous Studio One where The Beatles, *The Lord of the Rings*, and *Star Wars* were recorded.

While some developers seem to be following the pre-recorded music path for the sake of a more cinematic experience, others are beginning to revisit an older technology found in the MIDI format. The power of current next-generation consoles has revealed the possibility to substantially increase the interactivity of game music through the use of this basically off-the-shelf music tool. Just as a composer would select specific instrument samples and trigger them via MIDI messages, today's console technology can create interactive music cues in the same fashion—but in real time within the game. MIDI files are small, and instrument samples are easily stored and recalled—allowing games to load more quickly. While essentially the same as "chip music," the superior sound quality of today's samples, the ease with which MIDI can be manipulated, and the ability to create an almost unlimited amount of music on the fly changes the rules entirely and is a giant step forward for the interactivity of future games.

The Importance of Composition & Originality

I'd like to see a continued commitment to raising the bar in composition and orchestration excellence. Mixes are sounding better all the time—but it's continuing to develop the craft of composition that gets me out of bed in the morning.

Lennie Moore (Composer, 3l33t Music)

I hope composers and sound designers will continue to push the envelope with regard to originality. In the "early days," there were no rules—and experimentation was a huge part of finding your voice as a composer. At the time, there were many more hurdles and barriers in the process of creating music and sound effects for games, due to limited resources (e.g., available memory, disk seek time, MIDI vs. "real" audio). Sometimes those limitations forced us to be more inventive with our scores. I hope that current game composers aren't compelled to write for a 90-piece symphony orchestra simply because . . . they can!

Spencer Nilsen (President & Creative Director, Ex'pression College for Digital Arts)

Voiceovers

Voiceovers have the potential to take an interesting turn in the near future. Work is currently underway to perfect voice synthesis and automate the synchronization of animation and speech. The possibilities would be limitless, since fully functional actors who can do or say anything could interact realistically with the player and other characters encountered within the game. While voice synthesis is relatively crude, the potential is too great to ignore.

Reprinted with permission from Microsoft Corporation

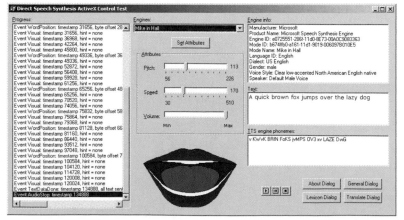

Microsoft's DirectTextToSpeech speech synthesis tool, part of its Direct Speech SAPI

Perhaps the Linker will have speech created with voice synthesis in a future update of *Tabula Rasa*.

It will take many years to perfect voice synthesis—but it would be particularly effective in computer interfaces, radio transmissions, or alien creatures. As the subtleties of acting are integrated and this new form of voice creation is refined, a very powerful application will ensure some interesting player experiences.

Voice Acting Advancements

I would like to see more effort going into dialogue and voiceover. Voice acting is arguably the most human element in a game and must be handled correctly. Hearing the exact same dialogue line over and over can kill the magic in a game. Several slightly different voice takes of the same line can make a huge impact.

Ben Long (Composer, Noise Buffet)

I hope more attention is paid to script development and actual voice acting—letting the characters be more unique instead of stereotypical, and not coming up with the same celebrity soundalike wish list from Vin Deisel to James Earl Jones. Producers need to realize that just because they liked Uma Thurman's quiet, menacing performance in *Kill Bill*, it doesn't mean this performance is right for a dragon or something!

Lani Minella (Master Creator, AudioGodz)

Michael McCann, Jeff Tymoschuk & Mark Temple on the Future of Game Audio Development :::::

Michael McCann
(Composer/Music Producer,
Behavior Music Inc.)

Michael is an award-winning composer, producer, and sound designer for film, television, and video games. His broadcast and client resumé includes some of the biggest companies in entertainment and advertising—including MTV, NBC, Ubisoft, Deutsch Inc. L.A., Fox, Ogilvy & Mather, and Alliance Atlantis. Michael's credits include *Tom Clancy's Splinter Cell: Double Agent, ReGenesis, It's All Gone Pete Tong,* and *FUBAR.*

In film and other visual arts, there is a long and consistent relationship between composers and other team members. In games, it seems that there is a ton of technical and creative people that work on a game but rarely stay together from project to project—building on creative ideas throughout their careers. In film, there are lifelong collaborations (e.g., Bernard Hermann/Alfred Hitchcock, Walter Murch/Francis Ford Coppola, and Angelo Badalamenti/David Lynch). Even for mainstream work (Williams/Spielberg/Kaminski/Rydstrom), it seems people do their best work when growing together—with similar interests and styles. (It also helps that many film directors have a strong interest in audio—with directors such as Coppola, Scorsese, and Hitchcock who have written crucial analyses of film audio and its importance.)

With games, a great team spends over two years making a great game and then the team members all split off. I've done this in other fields, and it really feels like you're starting all over again. If you find a group that really comes together, there's a chance that it will never happen again. There are exceptions in franchises—but beyond these, it's pretty rare. In other fields, where you have these long-standing crews, there's a lot of risk-taking, evolution, and consistency. More importantly, you develop strong styles and characteristics—and every individual becomes indispensable in creating that style. For audio, this is important. Film audio has grown to become a very powerful art form in itself. There are definite styles and schools of thought. There is a strong language of communication that has been built over the last three or four decades—helped a great deal by the support of directors, editors, etc. It's possible to listen to just the sound design (no music or dialogue) in a Michael Mann film—and know who the director was and even what the film looks like.

In games, audio feels more fragmented—more like a utility, where a lot of the audio is interchangeable from game to game. Technically, game audio is hugely complex. Artistically, in my opinion, it has a long way to go—and it will take interest from all fields to move it forward.

Jeff is an award-winning game composer based in Vancouver, British Columbia. He has written music for the James Bond franchise of games from Electronic Arts (*James Bond: Nightfire* and additional music on *James Bond: Everything or Nothing*, supplementing *24* composer Sean Callery's score) and *The Simpsons Hit & Run* for Radical Entertainment/Vivendi Universal Games. Jeff has completed work for Richard Jacques Studios on the score to *Pursuit Force: Extreme Justice*, and he most recently wrote the score to the Hothead Games release *Penny Arcade Adventures: On the Rainslick Precipice of Darkness*.

Jeff Tymoschuk
(Composer, GreenWire
Music & Audio)

What's starting to happen with the degree of interactivity in games is really exciting. It's going to expand even further as people get more experienced writing in this style and as the technology gives us even more options. I also think that as game audio has grown as an industry, people are starting to give it a little more respect than they gave it in the earlier days. Hopefully, this will lead to composers being brought in earlier, having access to more game assets, and being given the time and budget needed to give them every opportunity to craft something exceptional.

Mark has worked as a programmer and project lead with various companies on several games and real-time programming projects. He currently works for Northrop Grumman on the X-47B unmanned fighter project. Mark is a reserve officer in the United States Marine Corps who founded independent game developer Enemy Technology with his brother Bill in 1996. Their first project, *I of the Enemy*, was released in late 2004. Their latest game in the series, *I of the Enemy: Into Infinity* is scheduled for release in 2009.

Mark A. Temple
(Founder,
Enemy Technology)

As a developer, I am more concerned with the future of *independent* game development. Within this context, I see the audio professional taking on more of the audio creation process. This includes an ability to take a game design including voiceover scripts, and design and implement a complete sound plan—leaving only the technical integration to the programmer.

::::: Asset Management: Presenting New Ideas to the Industry

Many worthwhile ideas that have evolved into standard game features have been presented to the industry over the years. In the early days, pre-recorded music and sound effects were proposed to improve upon the computer generated bleeps. Later, the idea of creating a movie-like experience with a full orchestral soundtrack was suggested. Interactivity, surround sound, and audio scripting were all ideas that took root and flourished. There are many talented individuals and teams who are always moving toward game audio improvements.

Multiple game platforms have caused composers and sound designers to work around a wide variety of audio formats. Confusion reigns when working on a game title that will be ported to many platforms—causing the creator to focus more on technical issues instead of creative ones. Efforts to standardize file formats that support cross-platform interchange of advanced interactive audio soundtracks have been spearheaded by influential game audio personalities and organizations. Formats such as iXMF (Interactive eXtensible Music Format) promise to help establish a public standard that is non-proprietary, programming-neutral, and royalty-free. If a standard such as this can be agreed to and widely used, many of the difficult technical issues dealing with multiple platforms could practically disappear overnight. This particular idea is gaining solid support within the industry, and it's only a matter of time before it sees widespread use.

Reprinted with permission from Microsoft Corporation

Microsoft's XACT is a multi-platform tool that helps audio professionals create, implement, and manage assets.

In the meantime, other efforts are in motion to develop cross-platform and multi-platform tools to create, implement, and manage audio assets. Audio teams dealing with sound creation for many titles across several platforms may solve many issues with the ability to utilize a single tool instead of having to be highly proficient on several. Many game audio advocates are also making the push for tools that will minimize the repetitive, manual tasks faced by the sound team—especially for large projects. The biggest weakness in the movement for better game audio involves tools that are currently available. While many large game developers are accomplishing much within their own sphere of influence, there is much these types of tools can do for the industry as a whole. The release of Microsoft's XACT (Cross-Platform Audio Creation Tool) and Sony's SCREAM (Scriptable Engine for Audio Manipulation) to the public, for instance, marks a great beginning—and it may encourage others to follow suit.

Ask audio directors at any large game developer, and they will tell you the same thing: asset management is absolutely critical to the success of their games. As the complexity of game audio intensifies, the number of audio assets required to fulfill the needs of the game will continue to increase exponentially. Managing this work is a full-time job as assets are created, implemented, tested, replaced, and finalized over the course of the development cycle. Tools to oversee this incredible undertaking are being considered and developed in-house—and hopefully will be released to the community at some point in the near future.

The one obvious initiative for the future of game audio is the gain of significant improvements in audio creation and playback. How this will actually come about is a question currently being posed through a variety of venues. The systems used for playback will drive the rest of the process, as the quality baseline is established. Game audio experts have become involved with hardware manufacturers on many levels—including participation in speaker design, enhanced sound card capabilities, and improved game console resources. As the potential of these systems is realized, the composers and sound designers will adapt their techniques and capabilities to take advantage of them. A general plan is forming that will map out the process and focus appropriate attention on specific issues that can make the most difference. Many ideas have been presented to the industry over the years, some with incredible potential. The player and the technologies available will ultimately decide which will come to light—but it is certain that whatever is to come will be remarkable.

Game Audio as a Career

The field of game audio has progressed into an exciting profession that allows those with passion for audio and games to turn this enthusiasm into lifelong careers. Whether the intention is to bring home a decent paycheck or to seek the prestige of a Grammy award, the audio corner of the industry has much to offer those who fervently pursue it. With 48,000 game developers in the United States alone (according to Jill Duffy in *Game Developer Magazine*, August 2007), the chance of meeting the right people and getting your foot in the door is pretty high.

With the growing complexities of creating and implementing sound effects, music, and voiceovers, there is an even better chance of finding rewarding work as the number of sub-specialties increase. The days of a single person creating all of the audio for even a mid-sized game are quickly fading; game audio professionals are finally able to master specific tasks instead of remaining generalists. With a variety of job titles to choose from—such as composer, sound designer, audio director, audio manager, audio programmer, audio editor, dialogue specialist, casting director, and voiceover artist—the industry is evolving to meet the demand for quality work.

There are many routes that can lead to a career in game audio. Colleges and universities offering game development curricula will teach you about the mechanics of game development by providing hands-on exercises to gain practical experience and job placement to graduates.

Those with sufficient music composition or sound effects creation backgrounds but little game experience might offer their services to garage developers or student game projects as a way to learn the trade. As experience grows, targeting small development houses will bring a small paycheck but more invaluable practical experience that will eventually lead to the big developers and the bigger incomes. Those with extensive experience in the music or film industries have the unique position of being on top of the creative game but lacking in the technical aspects. These folks,

Tom Graczkowski (Composer, TDimension Studios) records a drum beat.

based on the quality of their work, can often walk into mid-to-large-sized developers and be successful. However, regardless of the path leading to the game industry, there is a definite place for anyone who makes the effort.

Game audio can be a tremendously gratifying career that offers many kinds of challenges and the sense of accomplishment that comes with overcoming them. In-house audio specialists have the opportunity to work with other highly creative minds, as a team and on epic projects.

They enjoy a steady paycheck, good benefits, camaraderie, and a company that shoulders the expense for all that great audio gear. Independent contractors get to be their own boss, work on a larger variety of interesting projects, and accept only the projects they want to work on—all with a greater income potential than the in-house crowd. No matter which course is chosen, both have their own distinct advantages and rewards.

Gene Semel (Senior Manager, Sound Group, SCEA) engineers audio for a new game.

Educate Yourself

Don't get tunnel vision. Take it all in—all of it. Get an education if you can. The old "knowledge is power" adage holds true. It won't get you every gig you want, but it will allow you to create a higher quality product in the end.

Fernando Arce (Composer/Musician, damselflymusic)

Make sure you understand music. Good audio should be transparent—nobody notices audio unless it is really good ("Hey, what a *cool* explosion sound!") or really bad ("What did the character say? I couldn't hear it!") Make sure your audio fits the former description. To do this, you need to understand EQ, panning, distortion, volume level balancing—and most importantly, timing. You should also develop a discerning ear; differences in audio can be as subtle as visual differences in graphics. Train your ear to hear them.

Russell Burt (Composer; Instructor, Art Institute of California—Los Angeles)

Choose the direction that interests you the most, whether it involves being a music composer or a sound designer, and work hard on perfecting your craft. Look into schools that have game audio in their curricula, do research on the net, and read books just like this one. Learn as much as you possibly can. Then create a web site for yourself and a great demo—and let everybody know what you can do. Finally, join the Game Audio Network Guild (GANG), go to the Game Developers Conference (GDC), and network as much as you can! It takes luck and timing—and it won't be easy. But, if you're passionate about games and have patience and persistence, then you will succeed!

Tom Graczkowski (Composer/Graphic Designer, TDimension Studios)

Know the difference between good and bad audio. This sounds easy, but I still hear quite a bit of audio that doesn't do anything to help progress the story or underscore emotion in a successful manner. Listen to movies and games as much as you can to see what works!

Tim Larkin (Composer/Sound Designer/Audio Director, Soundminds/Cyan Worlds)

Study music and the history of music composition—especially as it applies to the theatre, film, and even opera—to see how audio can elevate an experience to new heights beyond the visual.

Bill Louden (Founder, GEnie; Professor, Austin Community College)

Get an education and gain a solid musical foundation, thereby increasing your confidence. When first starting out, sometimes it may seem that confidence is all you have. Realize that you're most likely not going to be making a living off it for years and get a day job while working with up-and-coming developers.

Matt Sayre (Owner, The Game Composer)

Keith Arem, Richard Jacques & Roddy Toomim on Game Audio Education :::::

Keith Arem
(President & Creative Director,
PCB Productions)

Known for his composition and production work with Capitol recording artist Contagion and LA Underground industrialist Biohazard PCB, Keith has been a leading director, producer, writer, and engineer for over 15 years. Arem's background in game and interactive production includes serving as Director of Audio for Virgin Interactive Entertainment and Electronic Arts Pacific (1994-1999). Keith has produced and recorded over 500 commercial title releases in the game, film, animation, and music industries—including franchises for *Call of Duty*, *The Lord of the Rings*, *Tony Hawk's Pro Skater*, *Spiderman*, *Tom Clancy's Splinter Cell* and *Ghost Recon*, *Far Cry Instincts*, *Prince of Persia*, *X-Men*, *Star Wars*, *Ridge Racer*, *Iron Man*, *EverQuest*, *Army of Two*, *.hack,* and *Ascend*.

Specializing in one field will help you relate and adapt to other skills. For example, vocal recording helped me learn about dialogue engineering, and music composition made me a better sound designer. Identifying and learning specific fields of development is the biggest step in learning how to become an audio professional. Learning the basics of each field helps relate to other aspects of development. Sound design, editing, music composition, dialogue production, and mixing all have similar production processes—even though the end result may be different.

Richard Jacques
(Composer, Richard Jacques Studios)

Classically trained with an extensive music repertoire in orchestral, electronic, jazz, and many other contemporary music genres, Richard is a multiple award-winning game, film, and television composer—internationally recognized as one of the A-list composers in the game industry and described by *PLAY Magazine* as "one of the truly distinctive game music composers in the industry today." Richard has received numerous awards and accolades for his music—including Best Original Music awards from GameSpot and GameSpy and the Game Audio Network Guild Recognition Award. Richard recently scored cinematics and additional in-game music for *Mass Effect* (BioWare/Microsoft) and the original scores for *The Club* (Bizarre Creations/Sega), *Conflict: Denied Ops* (Pivotal Games/Eidos), and *Eight Days* (Sony Computer Entertainment Europe). His highly acclaimed live orchestral score for Sega Europe's cinematic action/adventure title *Headhunter* was the first game soundtrack to utilize the world famous Abbey Road Studios' Studio One and record with the London Session Orchestra. His other scoring credits include *Pursuit Force* (Sony), *Battlestations: Midway* (Eidos), *Starship Troopers* (Empire), *Headhunter: Redemption* (Sega), *Outrun 2* (Sega), *Jet Set Radio/Jet Set Radio Future* (Sega), *Metropolis Street Racer* (Sega), and *Sonic R* (Sega).

It would be unwise to say that it is easy to become an audio professional in the game industry today—especially compared to 10 years ago. The audio sectors of the game industry are indeed very competitive, and I would guess that the number of people wanting to join the industry outnumber the available positions by 100 to 1. However, I give some practical advice: Make sure you have studied at a good college or university in a recognized program relevant to your individual discipline. In my field of interactive composition, I have many people contact me who expect to score the next AAA action-adventure game just because they have some orchestral sound libraries and a computer. The reality is that this will not get you a position scoring the next AAA game! To really set yourself apart from the others, you need to study music at a university degree level—with at least two instrumental disciplines and experience of performance. Knowing the basics is incredibly crucial—so learning about music history, theory, composition, orchestration, business, music technology, performance, world music, etc., are all incredibly relevant and give you the right grounding for becoming a composer working in the game industry. (Practical experience is also invaluable. It is relatively easy to become part of a fan-based mod team or to score some smaller web-based projects or Xbox live arcade titles with smaller developers. Even though the budgets would be fairly small, the experience gained through doing this would be vital for progressing further.)

Roddy is known for one of the first and most professional homebrew releases on the Sega Dreamcast: *Feet of Fury*. His company, Cryptic Allusion, created all of the assets for the game from scratch—without middleware. Roddy is primarily responsible for creating all music, sound effects, and music contracts for the company.

I teach kids and sometimes adults about game audio on a semi-regular basis. If you're interested in game audio, there is just one thing you must remember: Never stop learning—and never stop practicing your art. Learn by doing! There are other ideals that will be helpful along your path to outstanding game audio, but this one encompasses them all. One of the best ways to learn is to ask someone more experienced than yourself. Keep in mind that you're never wrong as long as you're using your ears, or someone else's, to judge if your project sounds right or wrong.

Roddy Toomim
(Co-Owner &
Audio Director,
Cryptic Allusion, LLC)

Know the Technology

Get some programming in addition to other skills. It's the marriage of the creative and the technical that is the crux of making good game audio, and both skills will help you stand out in the crowd.

Simon Amarasingham (CEO, dSonic Inc)

Take care to learn your multitrack tools well—such as Nuendo or Pro Tools—and create a solid demo. Practice with 5.1 as early as you can. As consoles and tools change, there are very few games that are made the same way. However, the audio principles we use are often the same—so look into experimenting with game audio engine demos such as FMOD and Wwise to give you an understanding of the technical aspects.

Rodney Gates (Lead Sound Designer, High Moon Studios)

If you are an aspiring composer/sound designer, then take the time to also learn some programming or at least some middleware apps. This will bring you closer to understanding the enormous amount of work that goes into a game.

Ben Long (Composer, Noise Buffet)

Create Your Own Gig

One thing that helped me get started was working with modding teams. Modders create expansions and completely new games out of the existing engines and framework. They need music and sound effects! Also, consider working with Flash and Shockwave online game developers. Build a list of credits and just continue learning your craft. There are tremendous resources out there—online and this book included. Use them!

Adam DiTroia (Composer/Sound Designer, DiTroia Audio Creations)

Work! Even if you don't have a gig lined up, download XNA and replace all the sounds in the example game. Find a mod crew to work with. Redo movie trailers from the web. Just keep working. (The busier you are, the more desirable you are!)

Matt Piersall (New School Beast Handler [a.k.a. Audio Director], OkraTron5000)

Nathan Madsen & Tim Rideout on Effective Networking & Relationship Building :::::

Nathan Madsen is an active composer/sound designer with over 130 credits on the Sony PSP, Nintendo DS, PC, and web-based games. He has also worked extensively in the anime industry on such notable titles as *Dragon Ball, Dragon Ball Z, Full Metal Alchemist,* and *Witchblade*. Nathan has been a studio musician, college professor, and music teacher for public and private schools.

Nathan Madsen
(Lead Composer/
Sound Designer,
NetDevil)

The best thing students can do while in school is to become the best musicians and/or audio technicians possible. Once you've achieved a high level of skill, begin to network; build your experience by creating audio for hobbyist/amateur hobbyist groups that are making small games. Try your best not to work for free; not only does it hurt the industry as a whole, but it cheats your talent, craft, and efforts. Attend conferences such as GDC to meet and learn from professionals; they remember what they went through to get where they are, and they're more than willing to pass along a few tips. Network, network, network! Create personalized business cards to hand out, and always keep an updated demo reel on a personal web site; you are more likely to land a job when prospective clients can read your bio, see your picture, and listen to your music all at once. These kinds of jobs pop up quickly and are filled even faster; you need to always be prepared to present your best and most recent work.

Tim Rideout is a classically schooled musician—trained in the Jedi arts of jazz—with a serious jones for electronica. Equal parts urban chic, small town freak, and knob-twiddlin' geek, the Montreal resident has worked on countless television shows, films, theatre productions, and games—and he has three solo CD releases to his credit. From his private studio in Montreal, Tim combines live instrumental performance with electronic production techniques to create rich musical hybrids that speak to instrumentalists and DJs alike.

Tim Rideout
(Executive Hit Writer &
Groupie Herder,
Tim Rideout dot com)

My best advice is to get out into the mix. And I'm not talking about the audio mix; I'm referring to the *people* mix. The business is always about the people. And so is the music, and getting the gigs to make the music. It's about who you know and who knows you. Maintain a presence. Go to events. Do pro bono. Get involved. Work hard, but work smart. Get out there and be nice to people. Be yourself. Have fun. Do research. Play, play, play. And rock out.

Billy Martin & Watson Wu on Tips for Aspiring Students :::::

Billy Martin
(Composer, Lunch With
Picasso Music)

Billy has composed music for a wide a range of companies including Sony Online, EA, Ubisoft, and Disney Interactive. His recent scores include *Free Realms, Chicken Little*, and *Skate* (additional music). Billy is a five-time Game Audio Network Guild (GANG) Award nominee—including Best Edutainment/ Children Audio for his score to the PC game *Disney•Pixar Learning 2nd & 3rd Grade with Buzz Lightyear.* For television, Billy wrote the theme for the long-running celebrity interview program *Entertainers* featuring Byron Allen. He has contributed songs to feature films including *Spiderman 2* and *Selena*—and television series such as *Desperate Housewives* and *Will & Grace* have featured his lyrics and music.

This is a list of tips I give to students interested in getting into the business:

1. *Create a demo of your best music.* People will want to hear what you can do. Be prepared to distribute CDs, send MP3s, or post files on your web site. If you haven't been hired to write anything yet, just write some tracks that demonstrate what you can do.

2. *Have a professional looking web site.* This is the first place people will look to check you out. A myspace page is fine, too—but it tends to look a lot less formal. Put together a web site that makes you look like someone your clients will trust enough to hire. Take a look at the sites of Tom Salta, Mark Griskey, and Jack Wall for some examples.

3. *Join the Game Audio Network Guild (GANG).* If you're interested in game audio, GANG is the place to be. The member message boards are full of great information—including messages about gigs at game companies.

4. *Join the Society of Composers & Lyricists (SCL).* A non-profit organization for professional film/television/game composers, songwriters, and lyricists, SCL has a long and distinguished history in the fine art of scoring for motion pictures and television. The Advisory Board includes legends such as Howard Shore, James Newton Howard, Thomas Newman, and Hans Zimmer. SCL sponsors many events and film screenings that are great networking opportunities.

5. *Do **not** call established composers to try and get work.* Composers are not clients; they are your competition. If you were opening a dry cleaning business, you wouldn't go around to other dry cleaners and ask if they had any extra work for you. The same goes for composing. The exception would be if you live near a composer and are willing to work for little or nothing as an intern. You can learn a lot about the business that way.

6. *Attend the Game Developers Conference (GDC).* This annual event is the best place to meet everyone involved in game production and to learn about what's happening in game audio.

7. *Get your first gig.* Sending out "cold call" emails and packages isn't going to get you a job. The business is small, and networking is everything. Your first job will almost certainly come through someone you know or have met in person. Start with friends and relatives. You probably know somebody who knows somebody who works at a game company. Then meet as many people as you can at the events you go to. Things will grow from there.

8. *Do you need an agent? Actually, no.* An established agent won't even consider taking you on as a client unless you already have solid credits and are getting your own gigs. At that point, an agent can help you get more and better-paying gigs.

During high school and university days, Watson studied music education along with classical composition, music technology, conducting, and music business. He also performed and managed live mixing of rock and club music. With the experience, passion, and drive to increase the quality of audio, Watson has worked hard to complete multiple titles. If a project requires near impossible field recordings of animals, weapons, or vehicles—or tons of music—he has always completed the necessary tasks.

Watson Wu
(President, Producer
& Sound Designer,
WOOTONES, LLC)

You should tell everyone you know what you do or what you intend to do. I personally found work by meeting a nice grandmother whose grandson is a game producer. How you treat everyone will usually be repaid back to you. Automatically give every hand you shake two of your business cards—one for them to keep and the other for them to give away. After acquiring a business card, write something about that person on the back so that you can remember who they are. Avoid working for free or for pennies unless it is a promising internship at a great game company. Never stop learning new software, and enjoy playing every game you can.

I have a great memory for what games are developed by which companies. At trade shows, I often compliment and ask questions about what and how certain parts of the game are developed. This is a great way to make conversation. Be sure to network at events such as the Game Developers Conference (GDC). Since all game studios are distinct with regard to the software they use, learning all the available tools is highly recommended. Read and/or listen to business and negotiation books. Flashy business cards, a catchy name, a great web site, and studio gear are all necessary before students begin the networking process. I have recommended and seen many beginners achieve full-time audio positions through internships. These individuals worked hard, proved their worth, and were hired.

Game Audio Resources

The creation and implementation of game audio is ambitious, highly complex, and fraught with many creative and technical challenges. For any one person to attempt navigation through this difficult landscape alone borders on madness. It is impossible for any single person to know everything about the wide variety of game audio issues—and the good news is that they don't have to!

Those who create game audio understand that working in a bubble does nothing for the good of the industry or the livelihood they value so greatly. Technology and ideas are moving at an incredible pace, and it is absolutely essential that a free flow of information is maintained. It is in this particular spirit that many organizations and resources have been created not only to encourage the development of ideas and improvements, but to exchange information among those working in this industry. They've also become valuable communities where networking, assistance, and even friendships are prevalent.

Game Audio Network Guild

The Game Audio Network Guild (GANG) [www.audiogang.org] is a non-profit organization that provides game audio industry information, instruction, resources, guidance, and enlightenment to members, content providers, and listeners throughout the world. It empowers its members by establishing resources for education, business, technical issues, community, publicity, and recognition—and it also supports career development for aspiring game audio professionals, publishers, developers, and stu-

Courtesy of Game Audio Network Guild

dents. GANG is a resource for composers, sound designers, programmers, musicians, actors, engineers, producers, designers, directors, and others who have a genuine interest in interactive audio. By banding together and providing one voice, members can better articulate, discuss, and confront issues inside the interactive entertainment community. One of the goals of GANG is to encourage and promote the creation of better audio, which advances interactive industries by helping produce more competitive and entertaining products.

Interactive Audio SIG

The Interactive Audio Special Interest Group (IASIG) [www.iasig.org] exists to allow developers of audio software, hardware, and content to freely exchange ideas about improving the performance of interactive applications by influencing hardware, software, and tool design. The IASIG provides resources in the form of standards creation and maintenance, research reports, and recommended practices. Anyone with a commercial interest in audio for interactive entertainment is encouraged to join.

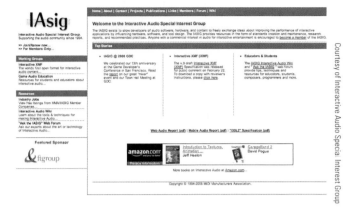

Audio Engineering Society

The Game Audio Technical Committee [www.aes.org/technical/ag] is a sub-area of the Audio Engineering Society (AES) that focuses on game audio needs. The committee's purpose is to proactively define recommended game audio practices, capabilities, services, and standards. Its mission is to cooperatively influence hardware and software design, leverage the combined skills of the diverse audio community, and improve the performance of audio across all game platforms and applications.

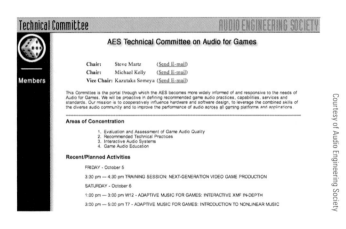

Project Bar-B-Q

The Project Bar-B-Q [www.projectbarbq.com] "think tank" conference is held annually on a Texas ranch resort. Its goal is to influence music hardware and software over the next five years. To this end, attendees form workgroups, each consisting of hardware and software developers, audio engineers, composers, and tech executives. Each group tackles a significant industry problem and spends two days of facilitated brainstorming to formulate its best shot at a solution. The result is the annual "BBQ report."

George "The Fat Man" Sanger on Following Your Passion :::::

George Sanger
"The Fat Man"
(Composer & Author)

The Fat Man has been creating music and other audio for games since 1983. He is internationally recognized for having contributed to the atmosphere of over 130 games—including such sound barrier breaking greats as *Loom, Wing Commander I* and *II, The 7th Guest I/II, NASCAR Racing, Putt-Putt Saves the Zoo,* and *ATF.* He wrote the first general MIDI soundtrack for a game, the first direct-to-MIDI live recording of musicians, the first Redbook soundtrack included with a game as a separate disc, the first music for a game that was considered a "work of art," and the first soundtrack that was considered a selling point for the game. On a 380-acre ranch on the Guadalupe River, the Fat Man hosts the annual Texas Interactive Music Conference & BBQ (Project BBQ)—the game audio industry's most prestigious and influential conference. His GamePlayMusic project is aimed at redefining the business and creative models of music for games, to benefit users, developers, and musicians alike.

If you are up for a real challenge, I think it would be equally smart for you to be a game audio professional or to be a mime. The number of people who want to do game audio is much higher than the number of people who want to be mimes. On the other hand, the number of jobs available for each is about equal. One should bear that in mind. You are not necessarily bringing something to the world that the world needs. There are a lot of things you can do that are helpful to people. I think the balance is finding something to do that results in: "Oh, that is so cool! You were able to solve my problem by doing this thing." Any career is great with that. That's the part for others.

The part for yourself is some kind of a job that makes you belly laugh and laugh sodas out your nose—and you need to work with friends who like who you are when you are around them. When you have those elements, then do that for a living. If you can do that with game audio, then totally go for it. And if you can do it with something else, like bricklaying—well, just think about the end of *Office Space*: Peter is outdoors, he's working in the sun with his neighbor Lawrence, he's breathing in the fresh air, and he's thinking he's probably not going to go back and work at Intertrobe or wherever it was. It's like he won. That's where he wins the movie. You win when you aren't stuck to the idea that you had in the first place.

The Joys of Networking

When meeting working professionals, keep in mind that, by definition, they could use some help with their current project. It's okay to tell them about yourself and your accomplishments—but approaching the conversation from a "What is your team up to, and how can I help?" standpoint, you stand a better chance of being put to work and beginning your career in game audio.

Clint Bajakian (Senior Music Manager, Sony Computer Entertainment America)

More than being talented or even having passion, persistence, and perseverance, you should strive to establish great relationships in the business. It really is a small world, and developers want to work with people they (a) know and (b) like.

Mike Brassell (Composer, Brassell Entertainment, Inc.)

Consider networking as a way to make friends—not as a way to find jobs. I am always put off by the number of people who approach me by handing me a demo and reeling off reasons why they are awesome without any regard to whether I am interested or not. This just tells me that you are desperate for a job. Instead, take some time to genuinely get to know people and develop a relationship. Find out how you can help others instead of how they can help you. In the end, you'll find this much more rewarding.

Chris Rickwood (Composer, Rickwood Music for Media)

Get out and meet people doing what you think you want to do. The importance of being in the mix can't be stressed enough. Temper formal education with a drive to actually be around what you want to do, and learn about it first-hand.

Jed Smith (Lead Producer, betafish music)

Music4Games (www.Music4Games.net) is an excellent news resource for all things game audio. In addition to current newsworthy events, the site includes reviews of game music, soundtracks, and audio creation tools, composer and sound designer interviews, and a forum for game audio related conversations.

Xbox Developer Programs (www.xbox.com/en-US/dev/contentproviders.htm) is a series of content creator programs sponsored and supported directly by Microsoft. Candidates are screened, and those who are accepted are given access to development tools and other Xbox-related content.

Game Audio Forum (www.gameaudioforum.com) is a community of game audio professionals at every level—from veterans to those with aspirations in the industry. A variety of topics are discussed, including demo critiques for those so inclined.

Professional Sound Designers Forum (psd.freeforums.org) is similar in format to the Game Audio Forum, but with a focus on film, television, and game sound design techniques, advice, and discussions. Many well respected sound designers frequent this community and offer their valuable experience.

Game Audio Pro Tech Group (groups.yahoo.com/group/gameaudiopro) and *Sound Design Forum* (groups.yahoo.com/group/sound_design) are popular Yahoo groups full of robust conversation, job opportunities, advice, and game audio-related topics. The forums are free to join and contain RSS feeds.

Northern Sound Source (www.northernsounds.com) offers a wide variety of music-related forums as well as a separate game audio section. This resource delves into the nuts and bolts of music creation software and offers user tips.

Gamasutra (www.gamasutra.com) is a highly popular game development web resource that details all aspects of game creation. Topics such as programming, art, and game audio are fully covered through articles, interviews, and product reviews. Free registration is available for those working in the game industry, and it allows access to their archives, job and project listings, and many other features.

Game Developer Magazine (www.gdmag.com), the sister print publication of Gamasutra, is the leading industry magazine for game developers. This monthly publication offers game creation tool reviews, industry news, columns, and many other features.

Digital Playroom (www.dplay.com) focuses on professional audio for broadcast, film, and interactive media. The site is maintained by Clio and Emmy winning sound designer Jay Rose. (See www.dplay.com/de/0104edit for an excellent dialogue editing resource.)

Additional resources associated with all aspects of game development are listed in the section at the end of this book.

chapter 9   Future of Game Audio Development: the best is yet to come

Developing games is considered a dream job for many—offering a unique way to truly live one's passion. What better way to make a living than playing games?! It's also common knowledge the real "rock stars" of game development—the ones who steal most of the spotlight in this industry—are those who create the audio. However, despite the perceived glamour and popularity of this particular profession, creating games is a team effort in every sense of the word—where the success of a game can only be realized if everyone pulls together.

::

This is an incredible time to be involved in games. Advanced technologies are being introduced at a rapid pace, new ideas and improvements are implemented with every game, and the industry is taking this medium to the next level—toward a more amazing experience. Game audio was once limited entirely by technology—but the only true limiting factor today is the imaginations of those who create and implement it. For once, storage space or processor speed isn't the first consideration—and the landscape is wide open. The most difficult aspect of creativity, especially in the highly technical world of video games, involves the mechanics required to integrate audio in the most useful and seamless fashion. As the complexity continues to increase, so will the talents and abilities of those who create the music and sound—further differentiating this profession into an entirely new specialty of audio developers. With continued free flow of information and available knowledge, the years to come will be incredibly exciting for both developers and players.

:::CHAPTER REVIEW:::

1. What are your thoughts on the future of game audio development? Choose sound effects, music, or voiceovers and discuss how you feel this area of game audio will evolve and change over the next 5–10 years. Do you agree or disagree with the predictions mentioned in this chapter?

2. Come up with your own personal strategic plan for becoming a game audio professional. How will you attain your position of choice in terms of skill building, education, networking, research, internships, outside projects, and contributions within the game audio community?

3. Participate in at least one of the online audio forums discussed in this chapter by posting at least 3 responses. Discuss your experience with the forum in terms of networking, job opportunities, projects, audio techniques, and industry news.

Resources

There's a wealth of information on game development and related topics discussed in this book. Here is just a sample list of books, news sites, organizations, and events you should definitely explore!

Communities & Directories

APM Music   www.apmmusic.com

Apple Developer Connection   developer.apple.com

ArtBarf.com   www.artbarf.com

Betawatcher.com   www.betawatcher.com

CG Society   www.cgtalk.com

CG Textures   www.cgtextures.com

EntertainmentCareers.net   www.entertainmentcareers.net

Gamasutra   www.gamasutra.com

Game Audio Forum   www.gameaudioforum.com

Game Audio Pro Tech Group   groups.yahoo.com/group/gameaudiopro

GameDev.net   www.gamedev.nct

Game Development Search Engine   www.gdse.com

GameFAQs   www.gamefaqs.com

Game Music.com   www.gamemusic.com

Game Music Revolution (GMR)   www.gmronline.com

Games Tester   www.gamestester.com

GarageGames   www.garagegames.com

International Dialects of English Archive (IDEA)   web.ku.edu/idea/

Machinima.com   www.machinima.com

Mayang's Free Texture Library   www.mayang.com/textures

Moby Games   www.mobygames.com

Northern Sounds   www.northernsounds.com

Overclocked Remix   www.overclocked.org

Professional Sound Designers Forum   psd.freeforums.org

PS3   www.ps3.net

Sound Design Forum   groups.yahoo.com/group/sound_design

3D Buzz   www.3dbuzz.com

3D Total   www.3dtotal.com

VGMix   www.vgmix.com

Video Game Music Database (VGMdb)   www.vgmdb.net

Voicebank.net   www.voicebank.net

Wii-Play   www.wii-play.com

Xbox.com   www.xbox.com

XBOX 360 Homebrew   www.xbox360homebrew.com

News, Reviews & Research

Blues News   www.bluesnews.com

Computer Games Magazine   www.cgonline.com

Digital Playroom   www.dplay.com

Game Daily Newsletter   www.gamedaily.com

Game Developer Magazine   www.gdmag.com

Gamers Hell   www.gamershell.com

Game Industry News   www.gameindustry.com

Game-Machines.com   www.game-machines.com

Game Rankings   www.gamerankings.com

GamesIndustry.biz   www.gamesindustry.biz

GameSlice Weekly   www.gameslice.com

GameSpot   www.gamespot.com

GameSpy   www.gamespy.com

Games Radar (PC Gamer)   www.gamesradar.com/pc

GIGnews.com   www.gignews.com

Guide to Sound Effects   www.epicsound.com/sfx/

Internet Gaming Network (IGN)   www.ign.com

Mayang's Free Texture Library   www.mayang.com/textures

Metacritic   www.metacritic.com

MMOGChart.com   www.mmogchart.com

Music4Games.net   www.music4games.net

Next Generation   www.next-gen.biz

1UP   www.1up.com

Planet Unreal   planetunreal.gamespy.com

PolyCount   www.polycount.com

Recording History: The History of Recording Technology   www.recording-history.org

Showfax   www.showfax.com

Star Tech Journal   www.startechjournal.com

Tongue Twisters   www.geocities.com/Athens/8136/tonguetwisters.html

UnderGroundOnline (UGO)   www.ugo.com

Unreal Technology   www.unrealtechnology.com

Unreal Wiki   wiki.beyondunreal.com

Voiceover Demos   www.compostproductions.com/demos.html

Xbox Developer Programs   www.xbox.com/en-US/dev/contentproviders.htm

Wired Magazine   www.wired.com

Organizations

Academy of Interactive Arts & Sciences (AIAS)   www.interactive.org

Academy of Machinima Arts & Sciences   www.machinima.org

Association of Computing Machinery (ACM)   www.acm.org

Audio Engineering Society (AES)   www.aes.org

Business Software Alliance (BSA)   www.bsa.org

Digital Games Research Association (DiGRA)   www.digra.org

Entertainment Software Association (ESA)   www.theesa.com

Entertainment Software Ratings Board (ESRB)   www.esrb.org

Game Audio Network Guild (GANG)   www.audiogang.org

Game Audio Technical Committee   www.aes.org/technical/ag

Interactive Audio Special Interest Group (IASIG)   www.iasig.org

International Computer Games Association (ICGA)   www.cs.unimaas.nl/icga

International Game Developers Association (IGDA)   www.igda.org

SIGGRAPH   www.siggraph.org

Events

Consumer Electronics Show (CES)
January   Las Vegas, NV
www.cesweb.org

Game Developers Conference (GDC)
February   San Francisco, CA
www.gdconf.com

D.I.C.E. Summit (AIAS)
March   Las Vegas, NV
www.dicesummit.org

SIGGRAPH (ACM)
Summer   Los Angeles, CA; San Diego, CA;
Boston, MA (location varies)
www.siggraph.org

E3 Business & Media Summit
July   Santa Monica, CA
www.e3expo.com

Tokyo Game Show (TGS)
Fall   Japan
tgs.cesa.or.jp/english/

Austin Game Developers Conference
September   Austin, TX
www.gameconference.com

IndieGamesCon (IGC)
October   Eugene, OR
www.indiegamescon.com

E for All Expo
October   Los Angeles, CA
www.eforallexpo.com

Project Bar-B-Q
October   Lake Buchanan, TX
www.projectbarbq.com

Colleges & Universities

Here is a list of schools that have strong game degree or certificate programs:

Academy of Art University   www.academyart.edu

Arizona State University   www.asu.edu

Art Center College of Design   www.artcenter.edu

Art Institute of Pittsburgh - Online Division   www.aionline.edu

The Art Institutes   www.artinstitutes.edu

Carnegie Mellon University/Entertainment Technology Center   www.cmu.edu

DeVry University   www.devry.edu

DigiPen Institute of Technology   www.digipen.edu

Ex'pression College for Digital Arts   www.expression.edu

Full Sail Real World Education   www.fullsail.edu

Guildhall at SMU   guildhall.smu.edu

Indiana University - MIME Program   www.mime.indiana.edu

Iowa State University   www.iastate.edu

ITT Technical Institute   www.itt-tech.edu

Massachusetts Institute of Technology (MIT)   media.mit.edu

Rensselaer Polytechnic Institute   www.rpi.edu

Ringling College of Art & Design   www.ringling.edu

SAE Institute   www.sae.edu

Santa Monica College Academy of Entertainment & Technology   academy.smc.edu

Savannah College of Art & Design   www.scad.edu

Tomball College   www.tomballcollege.com

University of California, Los Angeles (UCLA) Extension   www.uclaextension.edu

University of Central Florida - Florida Interactive Entertainment Academy   fiea.ucf.edu

University of Southern California (USC) - Information Technology Program   itp.usc.edu

University of Southern California (USC) School of Cinematic Arts   interactive.usc.edu

Vancouver Film School   www.vfs.com

Westwood College   www.westwood.edu

Adams, E. (2003). *Break into the game industry.* McGraw-Hill Osborne Media.

Adams, E. & Rollings, A. (2006). *Fundamentals of game design.* Prentice Hall.

Ahearn, L. & Crooks II, C.E. (2002). *Awesome game creation: No programming required. (2nd ed).* Charles River Media.

Ahlquist, J.B., Jr. & Novak, J. (2007). *Game development essentials: Game artificial intelligence.* Cengage Delmar.

Aldrich, C. (2003). *Simulations and the future of learning.* Pfeiffer.

Aldrich, C. (2005). *Learning by doing.* Jossey-Bass.

Allison, S.E. et al. (March 2006). "The development of the self in the era of the Internet & role-playing fantasy games. *The American Journal of Psychiatry.*

Atkin, M. & Abercrombie, J. (2005). "Using a goal/action architecture to integrate modularity and long-term memory into AI behaviors." *Game Developers Conference.*

Axelrod, R. (1985). *The evolution of cooperation.* Basic Books.

Bartle, R.A. (1996). "Hearts, clubs, diamonds, spades: Players who suit MUDs." *MUSE Multi-User Entertainment Ltd* (www.mud.co.uk/richard/hcds.htm).

Bates, B. (2002). *Game design: The art & business of creating games.* Premier Press.

Beck, J.C. & Wade, M. (2004). *Got game: How the gamer generation is reshaping business forever.* Harvard Business School Press.

Bethke, E. (2003). *Game development and production.* Wordware.

Birn, J. (2006). *Digital lighting and rendering (2nd ed.).* New Riders Press.

Boer, J. (2002). *Game audio programming.* Charles River Media.

Brandon, A. (2004). *Audio for games: Planning, process, and production.* New Riders.

Brin, D. (1998). *The transparent society.* Addison-Wesley.

Broderick, D. (2001). *The spike: How our lives are being transformed by rapidly advancing technologies.* Forge.

Brooks, D. (2001). *Bobos in paradise: The new upper class and how they got there.* Simon & Schuster.

Busby, A., Parrish, Z. & Van Eenwyk, J. (2004). *Mastering Unreal technology: The art of level design.* Sams.

Business Software Alliance. (May 2005). "Second annual BSA and IDC global software piracy study." *Business Software Alliance* (www.bsa.org/globalstudy).

Byrne, E. (2004). *Game level design.* Charles River Media.

Campbell, J. (1972). *The hero with a thousand faces.* Princeton University Press.

Campbell, J. & Moyers, B. (1991). *The power of myth.* Anchor.

Castells, M. (2001). *The Internet galaxy: Reflections on the Internet, business, and society.* Oxford University Press.

Castillo, T. & Novak, J. (2008). *Game development essentials: Game level design.* Cengage Delmar.

Castronova, E. (2005). *Synthetic worlds: The business and culture of online games.* University of Chicago Press.

Chase, R.B., Aquilano, N.J. & Jacobs, R. (2001). *Operations management for competitive advantage (9th ed).* McGraw-Hill/Irwin

Cheeseman, H.R. (2004). *Business law (5th ed).* Pearson Education, Inc.

Chiarella, T. (1998). *Writing dialogue.* Story Press.

Childs, G.W. (2006). *Creating music and sound for games.* Course Technology PTR.

Christen, P. (November 2006). "Serious expectations" *Game Developer Magazine.*

Clayton, A.C. (2003). *Introduction to level design for PC games.* Charles River Media.

Co, P. (2006). *Level design for games: Creating compelling game experiences.* New Riders Games.

Cooper, A., & Reimann, R. (2003). *About face 2.0: The essentials of interaction design.* Wiley.

Cornman, L.B. et al. (December 1998). A fuzzy logic method for improved moment estimation from Doppler spectra. *Journal of Atmospheric & Oceanic Technology.*

Cox, E. & Goetz, M. (March 1991). Fuzzy logic clarified. *Computerworld.*

Crawford, C. (2003). *Chris Crawford on game design.* New Riders.

Crowley, M. (2004). "'A' is for average." *Reader's Digest.*

Csikszentmihalyi, M. (1991). *Flow: The psychology of optimal experience.* Perennial.

DeMaria, R. & Wilson, J.L. (2003). *High score!: The illustrated history of electronic games.* McGraw-Hill.

Demers, O. (2001). *Digital texturing and painting.* New Riders Press.

Digital Media Wire. *Project Millennials Sourcebook (2nd Ed.).* (2008). Pass Along / Digital Media Wire.

Duffy, J. (August 2007). "The Bean Counters." *Game Developer Magazine.*

Dunniway, T. & Novak, J. (2008). *Game development essentials: Gameplay mechanics.* Cengage Delmar.

Egri, L. (1946). *The art of dramatic writing: Its basis in the creative interpretation of human motives.* Simon and Schuster.

Erikson, E.H. (1994). *Identity and the life cycle.* W.W. Norton & Company.

Erikson, E.H. (1995). *Childhood and society.* Vintage.

Escober, C. & Galindo, J. (2004). Fuzzy control in agriculture: Simulation software. *Industrial Simulation Conference 2004.*

Evans, A. (2001). *This virtual life: Escapism and simulation in our media world.* Fusion Press.

Fay, T. (2003). *DirectX 9 audio exposed: Interactive audio development,* Wordware Publishing.

Feare, T. (July 2000). "Simulation: Tactical tool for system builders." *Modern Materials Handling.*

Friedl, M. (2002). *Online game interactivity theory.* Charles River Media.

Fruin, N. & Harringan, P. (Eds.) (2004). *First person: New media as story, performance and game.* MIT Press.

Fullerton, T., Swain, C. & Hoffman, S. (2004). *Game design workshop: Designing, prototyping & playtesting games.* CMP Books.

Galitz, W.O. (2002). *The essential guide to user interface design: An introduction to GUI design principles and techniques.* (2nd ed.). Wiley.

Gamma, E., Helm, R., Johnson, R. & Vlissides, J. (1995). *Design patterns: Elements of reusable object-oriented software.* Addison-Wesley.

Gardner, J. (1991). *The art of fiction: Notes on craft for young writers.* Vintage Books.

Gee, J.P. (2003). *What video games have to teach us about learning and literacy.* Palgrave Macmillan.

Gershenfeld, A., Loparco, M. & Barajas, C. (2003). *Game plan: The insiders guide to breaking in and succeeding in the computer and video game business.* Griffin Trade Paperback.

Giarratano, J.C. & Riley, G.D. (1998). *Expert systems: Principles & programming (4th ed).* Course Technology.

Gibson, D., Aldrich, C. & Prensky, M. (Eds.) (2006). *Games and simulations in online learning.* IGI Global.

Gladwell, M. (2000). *The tipping point: How little things can make a big difference.* New York, NY: Little Brown & Company.

Gladwell, M. (2007). *Blink: The power of thinking without thinking.* Back Bay Books.

Gleick, J. (1987). *Chaos: Making a new science.* Viking.

Gleick, J. (1999). *Faster: The acceleration of just about everything.* Vintage Books.

Gleick, J. (2003). *What just happened: A chronicle from the information frontier.* Vintage.

Godin, S. (2003). *Purple cow: Transform your business by being remarkable.* Portfolio.

Godin, S. (2005). *The big moo: Stop trying to be perfect and start being remarkable.* Portfolio.

Goldratt, E.M. & Cox, J. (2004). *The goal: A process of ongoing improvement (3rd ed).* North River Press.

Gordon, T. (2000). *P.E.T.: Parent effectiveness training.* Three Rivers Press.

Hall, R. & Novak, J. (2008). *Game development essentials: Online game development.* Cengage Delmar.

Hamilton, E. (1940). *Mythology: Timeless tales of gods and heroes.* Mentor.

Hart, S.N. (1996-2000). "A Brief History of Home Video Games." *geekcomix* (www.geekcomix.com/vgh/main.shtml).

Heim, M. (1993). *The metaphysics of virtual reality.* Oxford University Press.

Hight, J. & Novak, J. (2007). *Game development essentials: Game project management.* Cengage Delmar.

Hornyak, T.N. (2006). *Loving the machine: The art and science of Japanese robots.* Kodansha International.

Hsu, F. (2004). *Behind Deep Blue: Building the computer that defeated the world chess champion.* Princeton University Press.

Hunt, C.W. (October 1998). "Uncertainty factor drives new approach to building simulations." *Signal.*

Jensen, E. (2006). *Enriching the brain: How to maximize every learner's potential.* John Wiley & Sons.

Isla, D. (2005). "Handling complexity in the *Halo 2* AI." Game Developers Conference.

Johnson, S. (1997). *Interface culture: How new technology transforms the way we create & communicate.* Basic Books.

Johnson, S. (2006). *Everything bad is good for you.* Riverhead.

Jung, C.G. (1969). *Man and his symbols.* Dell Publishing.

Kent, S.L. (2001). *The ultimate history of video games.* Prima.

King, S. (2000). *On writing.* Scribner.

Knoke, W. (1997). *Bold new world: The essential road map to the twenty-first century.* Kodansha International.

Koster, R. (2005). *Theory of fun for game design.* Paraglyph Press.

Krawczyk, M. & Novak, J. (2006). *Game development essentials: Game story & character development.* Cengage Delmar.

Kurzweil, R. (2000). *The age of spiritual machines: When computers exceed human intelligence.* Penguin.

Laramee, F.D. (Ed.) (2002). *Game design perspectives.* Charles River Media.

Laramee, F.D. (Ed.) (2005). *Secrets of the game business. (3rd ed).* Charles River Media.

Levy, P. (2001). *Cyberculture.* University of Minnesota Press.

Lewis, M. (2001). *Next: The future just happened.* W.W.Norton & Company.

Mackay, C. (1841). *Extraordinary popular delusions & the madness of crowds.* Three Rivers Press.

Marks, A. (2008). *The complete guide to game audio.* Elsevier/Focal Press.

McConnell, S. (1996). *Rapid development.* Microsoft Press.

McCorduck, P. (2004). *Machines who think: A personal inquiry into the history and prospects of artificial intelligence (2nd ed).* AK Peters.

McKenna, T. (December 2003). "This means war." *Journal of Electronic Defense.*

Meigs, T. (2003). *Ultimate game design: Building game worlds.* McGraw-Hill Osborne Media.

Mencher, M. (2002). *Get in the game: Careers in the game industry.* New Riders.

Meyers, S. (2005). *Effective C++: 55 specific ways to improve your programs and designs (3rd ed).* Addison-Wesley.

Michael, D. (2003). *The indie game development survival guide.* Charles River Media.

Montfort, N. (2003). *Twisty little passages: An approach to interactive fiction.* MIT Press.

Moravec, H. (2000). *Robot.* Oxford University Press.

Morris, D. (September/October 2004). Virtual weather. *Weatherwise.*

Morris, D. & Hartas, L. (2003). *Game art: The graphic art of computer games.* Watson-Guptill Publications.

Muehl, W. & Novak, J. (2007). *Game development essentials: Game simulation development.* Cengage Delmar.

Mulligan, J. & Patrovsky, B. (2003). *Developing online games: An insider's guide.* New Riders.

Mummolo, J. (July 2006). "Helping children play." *Newsweek.*

Murray, J. (2001). *Hamlet on the holodeck: The future of narrative in cyberspace.* MIT Press.

Negroponte, N. (1996). *Being digital.* Vintage Books.

Nielsen, J. (1999). *Designing web usability: The practice of simplicity.* New Riders.

Novak. J. (2007). *Game development essentials: An introduction. (2ⁿᵈ ed.).* Cengage Delmar.

Novak, J. & Levy, L. (2007). *Play the game: The parents guide to video games.* Cengage Course Technology PTR.

Novak, J. (2003). "MMOGs as online distance learning applications." University of Southern California.

O'Donnell, M. & Marks, A. (2002). "The use and effectiveness of audio in *Halo:* Game music evolved." *Music4Games* (www.music4games.net/Features_Display.aspx?id=24)

Omernick, M. (2004). *Creating the art of the game.* New Riders Games.

Oram, A. (Ed.) (2001). *Peer-to-peer.* O'Reilly & Associates.

Patow, C.A. (December 2005). "Medical simulation makes medical education better & safer." *Health Management Technology.*

Peck, M. (January 2005). "Air Force's latest video game targets potential recruits." *National Defense.*

Piaget, J. (2000). *The psychology of the child.* Basic Books.

Piaget, J. (2007). *The child's conception of the world.* Jason Aronson.

Pohflepp, S. (January 2007). "Before and after Darwin." *We Make Money Not Art* (www.we-make-money-not -art.com/archives/009261.php).

Poole, S. (2004). *Trigger happy: Videogames and the entertainment revolution.* Arcade Publishing.

Prensky, M. (2006). *Don't bother me, Mom: I'm learning!* Paragon House.

Ramirez, J. (July 2006). "The new ad game." *Newsweek.*

Rheingold, H. (1991). *Virtual reality.* Touchstone.

Rheingold, H. (2000). *Tools for thought: The history and future of mind-expanding technology.* MIT Press.

Robbins, S.P. (2001). *Organizational behavior (9ᵗʰ ed).* Prentice-Hall, Inc.

Rogers, E.M. (1995). *Diffusion of innovations.* Free Press.

Rollings, A. & Morris, D. (2003). *Game architecture & design: A new edition.* New Riders.

Rollings, A. & Adams, E. (2003). *Andrew Rollings & Ernest Adams on game design.* New Riders.

Rouse, R. (2001) *Game design: Theory & practice (2ⁿᵈ ed).* Wordware Publishing.

Salen, K. & Zimmerman, E. (2003). *Rules of play.* MIT Press.

Sanchanta, M. (2006 January). "Japanese game aids U.S. war on obesity: Gym class in West Virginia to use an interactive dance console." *Financial Times.*

Sanger, G.A. [a.k.a. "The Fat Man"]. (2003). *The Fat Man on game audio.* New Riders.

Saunders, K. & Novak, J. (2007). *Game development essentials: Game interface design.* Cengage Delmar.

Schildt, H. (2006). *Java: A beginner's guide (4ᵗʰ ed).* McGraw-Hill Osborne Media.

Schomaker, W. (September 2001). "Cosmic models match reality." *Astronomy.*

Sellers, J. (2001). *Arcade fever.* Running Press.

Shaffer, D.W. (2006). *How computer games help children learn.* Palgrave Macmillan.

Standage, T. (1999). *The Victorian Internet.* New York: Berkley Publishing Group.

Strauss, W. & Howe, N. (1992). *Generations.* Perennial.

Strauss, W. & Howe, N. (1993). *13th gen: Abort, retry, ignore, fail?* Vintage Books.

Strauss, W. & Howe, N. (1998). *The fourth turning.* Broadway Books.

Strauss, W. & Howe, N. (2000). *Millennials rising: The next great generation.* Vintage Books.

Strauss, W., Howe, N. & Markiewicz, P. (2006). *Millennials & the pop culture.* LifeCourse Associates.

Stroustrup, B. (2000). *The C++ programming language (3rd ed).* Addison-Wesley.

Szinger, J. (1993-2006). "On Composing Interactive Music." *Zing Man Productions* (www.zingman.com/spew/CompIntMusic.html).

Trotter, A. (November 2005). "Despite allure, using digital games for learning seen as no easy task." *Education Week.*

Tufte, E.R. (1983). *The visual display of quantitative information.* Graphics Press.

Tufte, E.R. (1990). *Envisioning information.* Graphics Press.

Tufte, E.R. (1997). *Visual explanations.* Graphics Press.

Tufte, E.R. (2006). *Beautiful evidence.* Graphics Press.

Turkle, S. (1997). *Life on the screen: Identity in the age of the Internet.* Touchstone.

Van Duyne, D.K. et al. (2003). *The design of sites.* Addison-Wesley.

Vogler, C. (1998). *The writer's journey: Mythic structure for writers. (2nd ed).* Michael Wiese Productions.

Welch, J. & Welch, S. (2005). *Winning.* HarperCollins Publishers.

Weizenbaum, J. (1984). *Computer power and human reason.* Penguin Books.

Wilcox, J. (2007). *Voiceovers: Techniques & Tactics for Success.* Allworth Press.

Williams, J.D. (1954). *The compleat strategyst: Being a primer on the theory of the games of strategy.* McGraw-Hill.

Wolf, J.P. & Perron, B. (Eds.). (2003). *Video game theory reader.* Routledge.

Wong, G. (November 2006). "Educators explore 'Second Life' online." *CNN.com* (www.cnn.com/2006/TECH/11/13/second.life.university/index.html).

Wysocki, R.K. (2006). *Effective project management (4th ed).* John Wiley & Sons.

Index

Extended Copyright & Trademark Notices

IMPORTANT! READ CAREFULLY: This End User License Agreement ("Agreement") sets forth the conditions by which Cengage Learning will make electronic access to the Cengage Learning-owned licensed content and associated media, software, documentation, printed materials, and electronic documentation contained in this package and/or made available to you via this product (the "Licensed Content"), available to you (the "End User"). BY CLICKING THE "I ACCEPT" BUTTON AND/OR OPENING THIS PACKAGE, YOU ACKNOWLEDGE THAT YOU HAVE READ ALL OF THE TERMS AND CONDITIONS, AND THAT YOU AGREE TO BE BOUND BY ITS TERMS, CONDITIONS, AND ALL APPLICABLE LAWS AND REGULATIONS GOVERNING THE USE OF THE LICENSED CONTENT.

1.0 SCOPE OF LICENSE

1.1 <u>Licensed Content.</u> The Licensed Content may contain portions of modifiable content ("Modifiable Content") and content which may not be modified or otherwise altered by the End User ("Non-Modifiable Content"). For purposes of this Agreement, Modifiable Content and Non-Modifiable Content may be collectively referred to herein as the "Licensed Content." All Licensed Content shall be considered Non-Modifiable Content, unless such Licensed Content is presented to the End User in a modifiable format and it is clearly indicated that modification of the Licensed Content is permitted.

1.2 Subject to the End User's compliance with the terms and conditions of this Agreement, Cengage Learning hereby grants the End User, a nontransferable, nonexclusive, limited right to access and view a single copy of the Licensed Content on a single personal computer system for noncommercial, internal, personal use only. The End User shall not (i) reproduce, copy, modify (except in the case of Modifiable Content), distribute, display, transfer, sublicense, prepare derivative work(s) based on, sell, exchange, barter or transfer, rent, lease, loan, resell, or in any other manner exploit the Licensed Content; (ii) remove, obscure, or alter any notice of Cengage Learning's intellectual property rights present on or in the Licensed Content, including, but not limited to, copyright, trademark, and/or patent notices; or (iii) disassemble, decompile, translate, reverse engineer, or otherwise reduce the Licensed Content.

2.0 TERMINATION

2.1 Cengage Learning may at any time (without prejudice to its other rights or remedies) immediately terminate this Agreement and/or suspend access to some or all of the Licensed Content, in the event that the End User does not comply with any of the terms and conditions of this Agreement. In the event of such termination by Cengage Learning, the End User shall immediately return any and all copies of the Licensed Content to Cengage Learning.

3.0 PROPRIETARY RIGHTS

3.1 The End User acknowledges that Cengage Learning owns all rights, title and interest, including, but not limited to all copyright rights therein, in and to the Licensed Content, and that the End User shall not take any action inconsistent with such ownership. The Licensed Content is protected by U.S., Canadian and other applicable copyright laws and by international treaties, including the Berne Convention and the Universal Copyright Convention. Nothing contained in this Agreement shall be construed as granting the End User any ownership rights in or to the Licensed Content.

3.2 Cengage Learning reserves the right at any time to withdraw from the Licensed Content any item or part of an item for which it no longer retains the right to publish, or which it has reasonable grounds to believe infringes copyright or is defamatory, unlawful, or otherwise objectionable.

4.0 PROTECTION AND SECURITY

4.1 The End User shall use its best efforts and take all reasonable steps to safeguard its copy of the Licensed Content to ensure that no unauthorized reproduction, publication, disclosure, modification, or distribution of the Licensed Content, in whole or in part, is made. To the extent that the End User becomes aware of any such unauthorized use of the Licensed Content, the End User shall immediately notify Cengage Learning. Notification of such violations may be made by sending an e-mail to:

infringement@cengage.com

5.0 MISUSE OF THE LICENSED PRODUCT

5.1 In the event that the End User uses the Licensed Content in violation of this Agreement, Cengage Learning shall have the option of electing liquidated damages, which shall include all profits generated by the End User's use of the Licensed Content plus interest computed at the maximum rate permitted by law and all legal fees and other expenses incurred by Cengage Learning in enforcing its rights, plus penalties.

6.0 FEDERAL GOVERNMENT CLIENTS

6.1 Except as expressly authorized by Cengage Learning, Federal Government clients obtain only the rights specified in this Agreement and no other rights. The Government acknowledges that (i) all software and related documentation incorporated in the Licensed Content is existing commercial computer software within the meaning of FAR 27.405(b)(2); and (2) all other data delivered in whatever form, is limited rights data within the meaning of FAR 27.401. The restrictions in this section are acceptable as consistent with the Government's need for software and other data under this Agreement.

7.0 DISCLAIMER OF WARRANTIES AND LIABILITIES

7.1 Although Cengage Learning believes the Licensed Content to be reliable, Cengage Learning does not guarantee or warrant (i) any information or materials contained in or produced by the Licensed Content, (ii) the accuracy, completeness or reliability of the Licensed Content, or (iii) that the Licensed Content is free from errors or other material defects. THE LICENSED PRODUCT IS PROVIDED "AS IS," WITHOUT ANY WARRANTY OF ANY KIND AND CENGAGE LEARNING DISCLAIMS ANY AND ALL WARRANTIES, EXPRESSED OR IMPLIED, INCLUDING, WITHOUT LIMITATION, WARRANTIES OF MERCHANTABILITY OR FITNESS FOR A PARTICULAR PURPOSE. IN NO EVENT SHALL CENGAGE LEARNING BE LIABLE FOR: INDIRECT, SPECIAL, PUNITIVE OR CONSEQUENTIAL DAMAGES INCLUDING FOR LOST PROFITS, LOST DATA, OR OTHERWISE. IN NO EVENT SHALL CENGAGE LEARNING'S AGGREGATE LIABILITY HEREUNDER, WHETHER ARISING IN CONTRACT, TORT, STRICT LIABILITY OR OTHERWISE, EXCEED THE AMOUNT OF FEES PAID BY THE END USER HEREUNDER FOR THE LICENSE OF THE LICENSED CONTENT.

8.0 GENERAL

8.1 <u>Entire Agreement.</u> This Agreement shall constitute the entire Agreement between the Parties and supercedes all prior Agreements and understandings oral or written relating to the subject matter hereof.

8.2 <u>Enhancements/Modifications of Licensed Content.</u> From time to time, and in Cengage Learning's sole discretion, Cengage Learning may advise the End User of updates, upgrades, enhancements and/or improvements to the Licensed Content, and may permit the End User to access and use, subject to the terms and conditions of this Agreement, such modifications, upon payment of prices as may be established by Cengage Learning.

8.3 <u>No Export.</u> The End User shall use the Licensed Content solely in the United States and shall not transfer or export, directly or indirectly, the Licensed Content outside the United States.

8.4 <u>Severability.</u> If any provision of this Agreement is invalid, illegal, or unenforceable under any applicable statute or rule of law, the provision shall be deemed omitted to the extent that it is invalid, illegal, or unenforceable. In such a case, the remainder of the Agreement shall be construed in a manner as to give greatest effect to the original intention of the parties hereto.

8.5 <u>Waiver.</u> The waiver of any right or failure of either party to exercise in any respect any right provided in this Agreement in any instance shall not be deemed to be a waiver of such right in the future or a waiver of any other right under this Agreement.

8.6 <u>Choice of Law/Venue.</u> This Agreement shall be interpreted, construed, and governed by and in accordance with the laws of the State of New York, applicable to contracts executed and to be wholly preformed therein, without regard to its principles governing conflicts of law. Each party agrees that any proceeding arising out of or relating to this Agreement or the breach or threatened breach of this Agreement may be commenced and prosecuted in a court in the State and County of New York. Each party consents and submits to the nonexclusive personal jurisdiction of any court in the State and County of New York in respect of any such proceeding.

8.7 <u>Acknowledgment.</u> By opening this package and/or by accessing the Licensed Content on this Web site, THE END USER ACKNOWLEDGES THAT IT HAS READ THIS AGREEMENT, UNDERSTANDS IT, AND AGREES TO BE BOUND BY ITS TERMS AND CONDITIONS. IF YOU DO NOT ACCEPT THESE TERMS AND CONDITIONS, YOU MUST NOT ACCESS THE LICENSED CONTENT AND RETURN THE LICENSED PRODUCT TO CENGAGE LEARNING (WITHIN 30 CALENDAR DAYS OF THE END USER'S PURCHASE) WITH PROOF OF PAYMENT ACCEPTABLE TO CENGAGE LEARNING, FOR A CREDIT OR A REFUND. Should the End User have any questions/comments regarding this Agreement, please contact Cengage Learning at:

Delmar.help@cengage.com